4B Newton Mearns

DONALD MACLEO

CW00369166

GLASGOW

ESTATE PUBLICATIONS
Bridewell House,
Tenterden, Kent.
TN30 6EP
Tel: 01580 764225

© Estate Publications 369 D   ISBN 1 84192 024 X   © Crown Copyright 398713

ESTATE PUBLICATIONS

GLASGOW

**PAISLEY · BARRHEAD · BEARSDEN
BISHOPBRIGGS · CLYDEBANK · MILNGAVIE
NEILSTON · RUTHERGLEN**

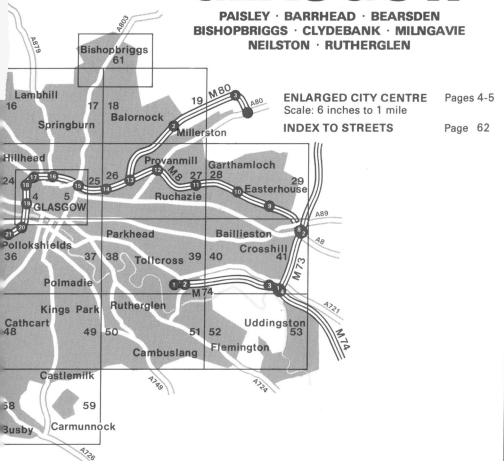

ENLARGED CITY CENTRE   Pages 4-5
Scale: 6 inches to 1 mile

INDEX TO STREETS   Page 62

Every effort has been made to verify the
accuracy of information in this book
but the publishers cannot accept
responsibility for expense or loss caused
by any error or omission. Information
that will be of assistance to the user of
the maps will be welcomed.

The representation of a road, track or
footpath on the maps in this atlas is no
evidence of the existence of a right of way.

One-way Street	→
Car Park	Ᵽ
Post Office	●
Public Convenience	©
Pedestrianized	▨
Place of Worship	✦
Underground Station	Ⓤ

Scale of Street Plans: 4 inches to 1 mile

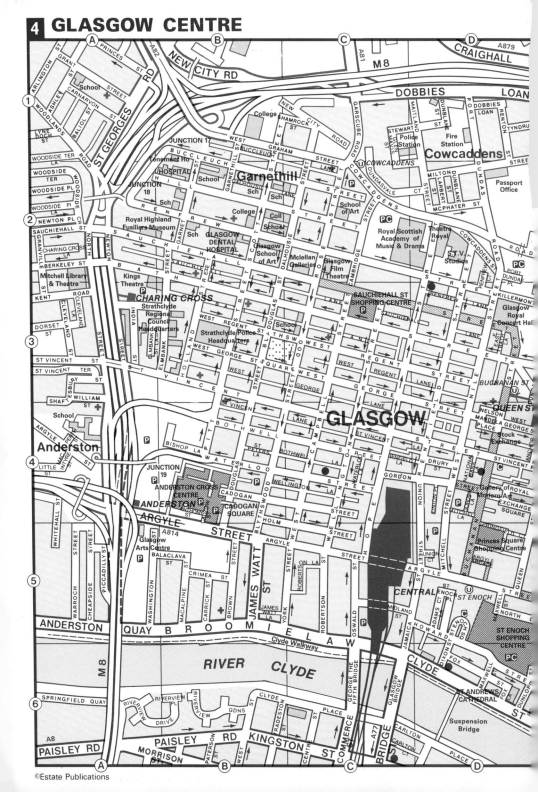

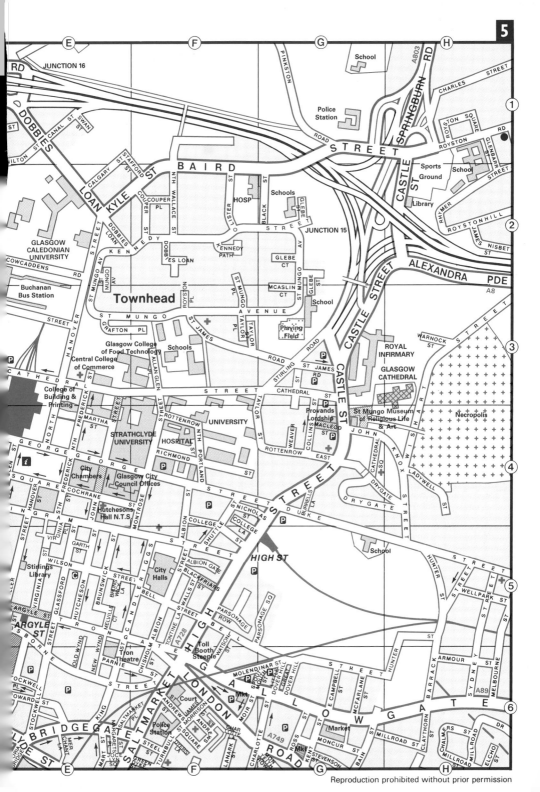

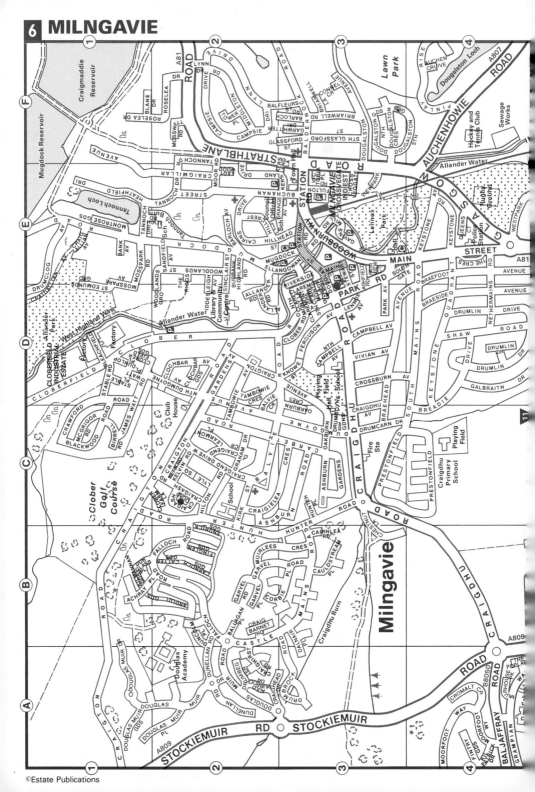

6 MILNGAVIE

Craigmaddie Reservoir

Mugdock Reservoir

Lawn Park

A807 ROAD

AUCHENHOWIE

Hockey and Tennis Club

Sewage Works

Allander Water

Rugby Ground

Police Station

Tannoch Loch

Dougalston Loch

STRATHBLANE

STATION

MILNGAVIE CROSSVEGATE

Lennox Park

MAIN STREET

A81

AVENUE

AVENUE

West Highland Way

Allander Water

Library & Arts Community Centre

CLOBERFIELD INDUSTRIAL ESTATE

Allander Park

DRUMLIN DRIVE

DRUMLIN DR

Clober Golf Course

Club House

Playing Field

Dun's School

Fire Sta

Craigdhu Primary School

Prestonfield

Playing Field

CRAIGDHU ROAD

School

Milngavie

Douglas Academy

CASTLE ROAD

Craigdhu Burn

A809 ROAD

CRAIGDHU ROAD

BALJAFFRAY

STOCKIEMUIR RD STOCKIEMUIR

A809

B8050

©Estate Publications

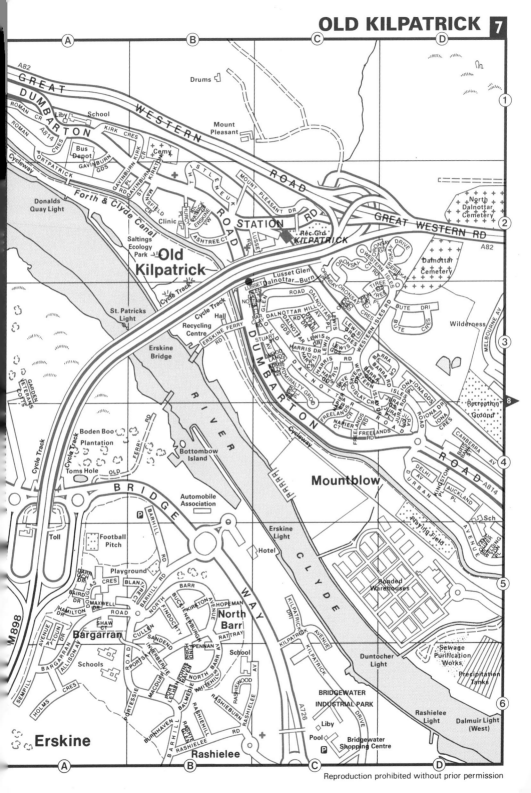

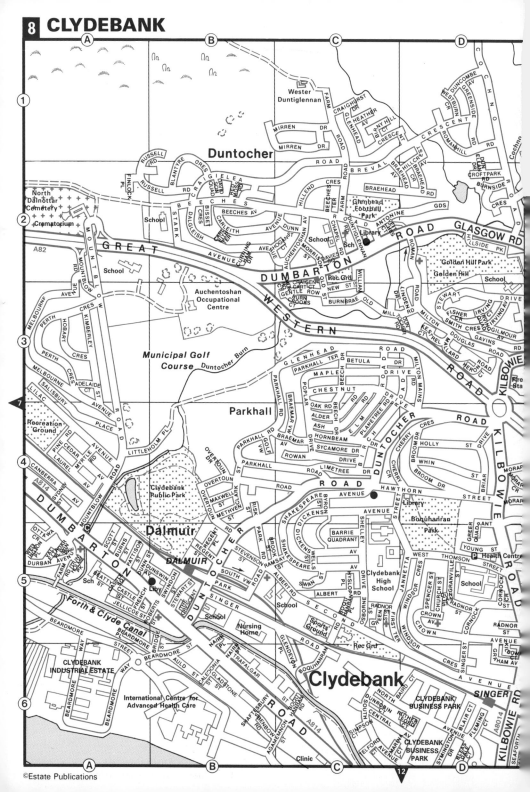

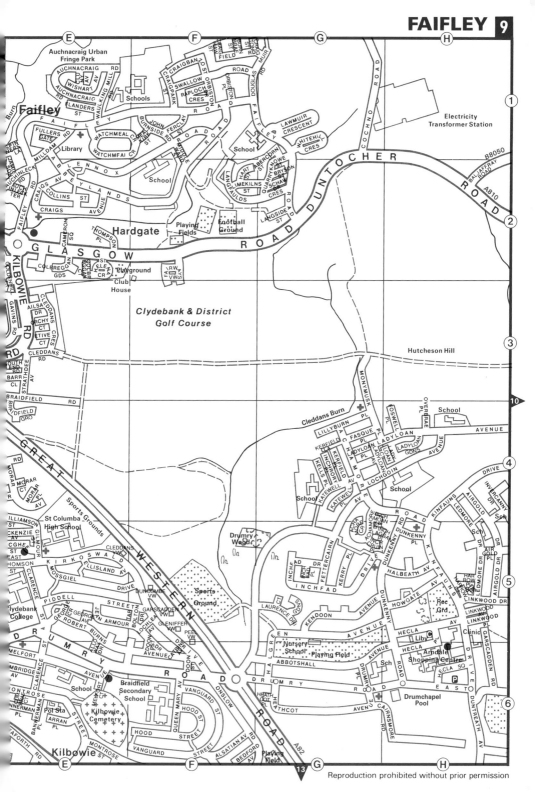

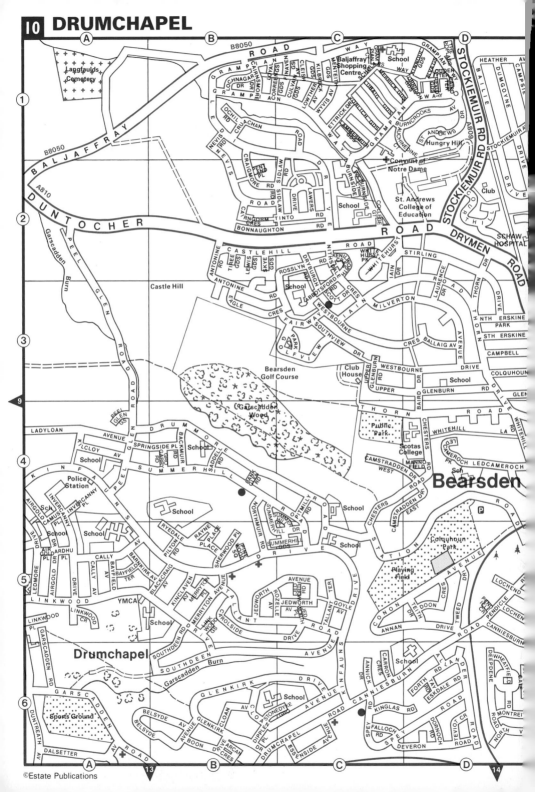

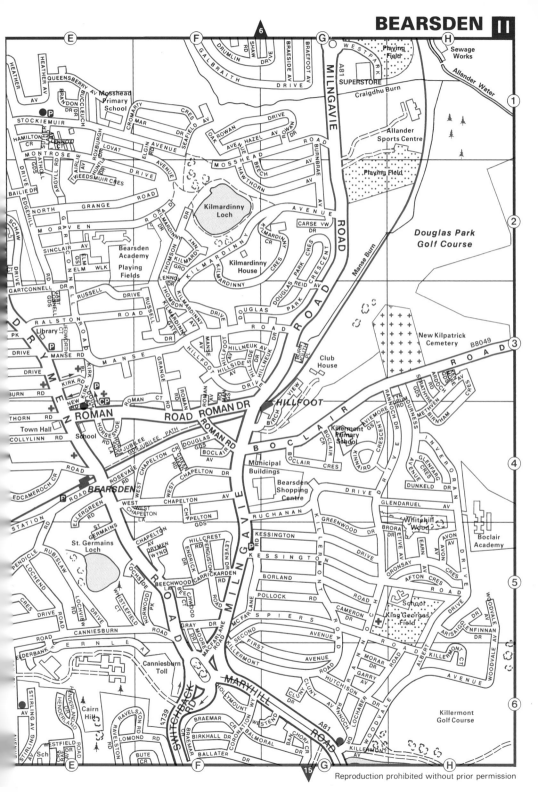

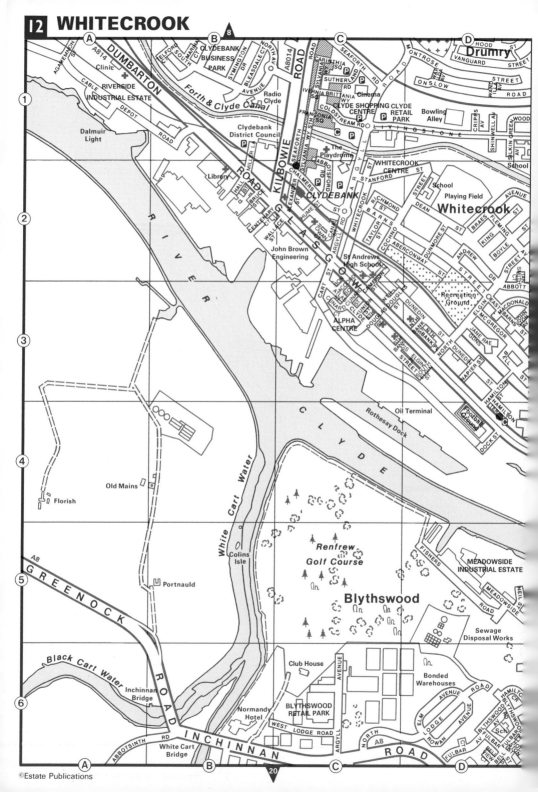

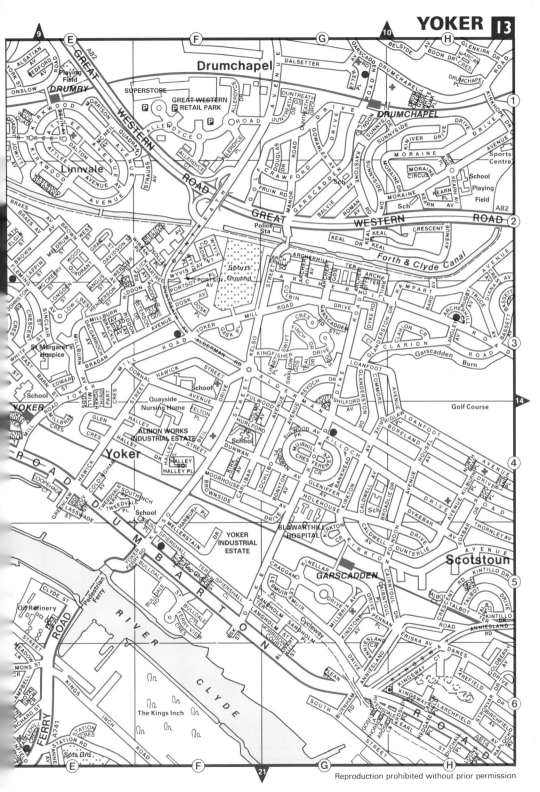

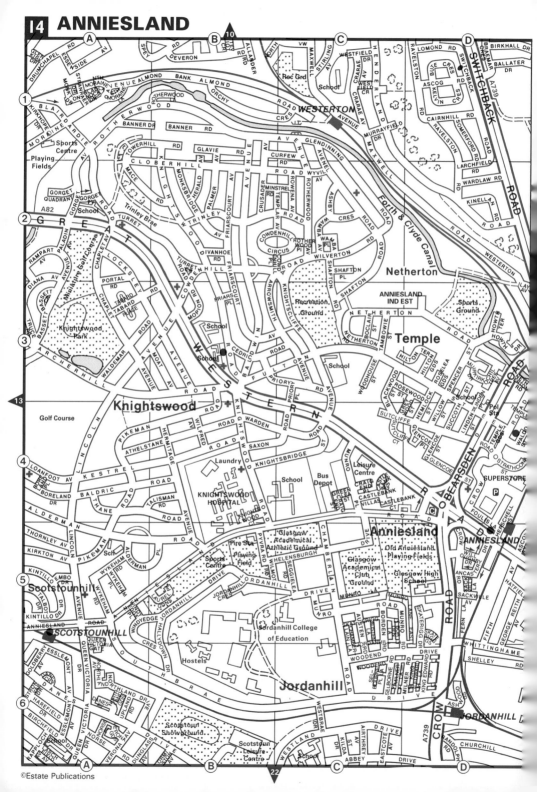

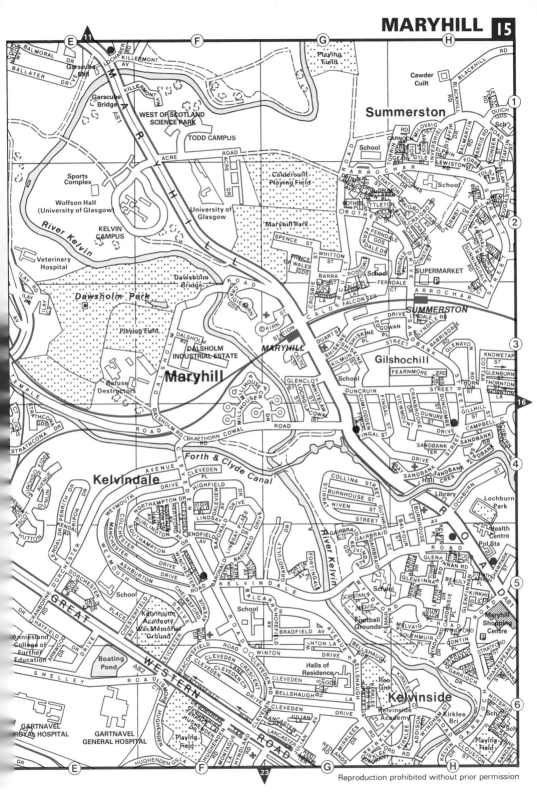

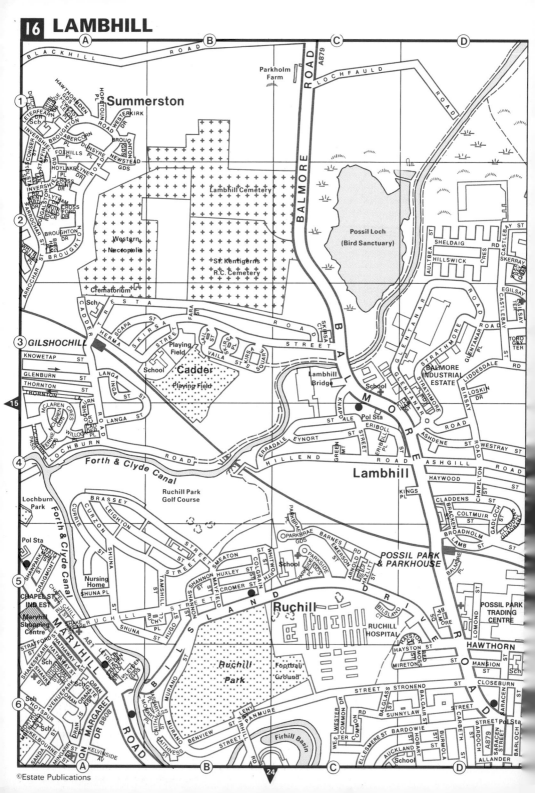

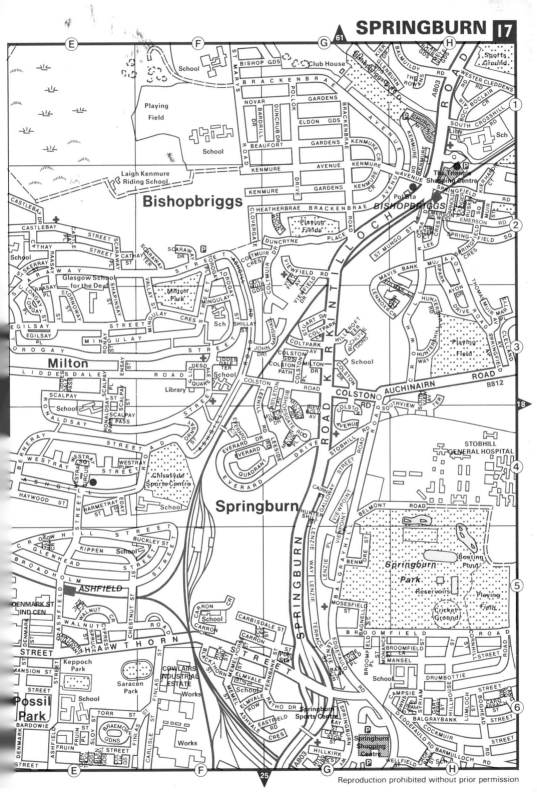

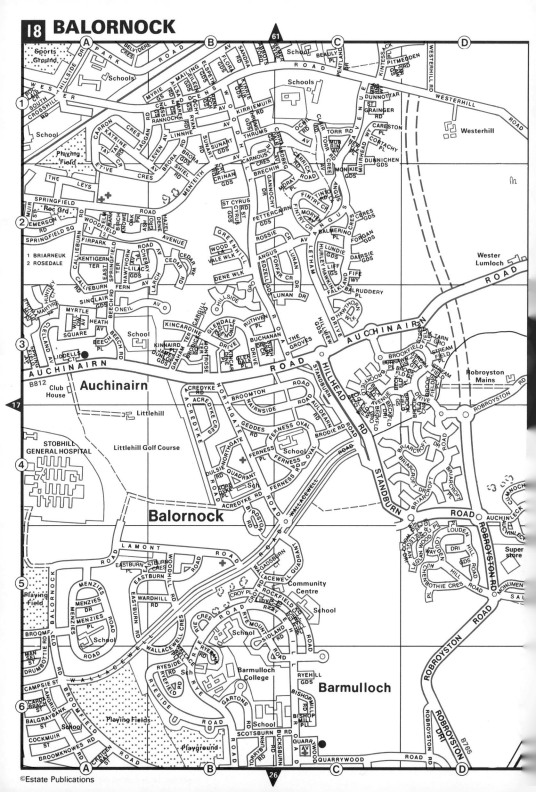

18 BALORNOCK

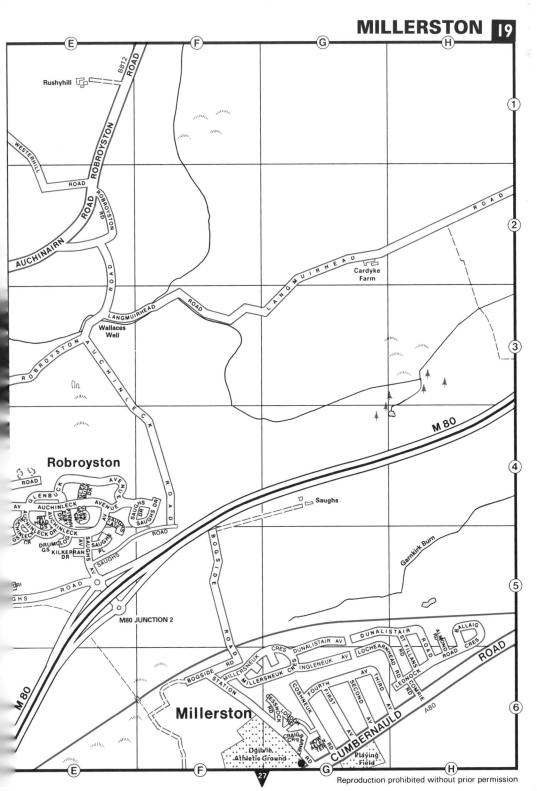

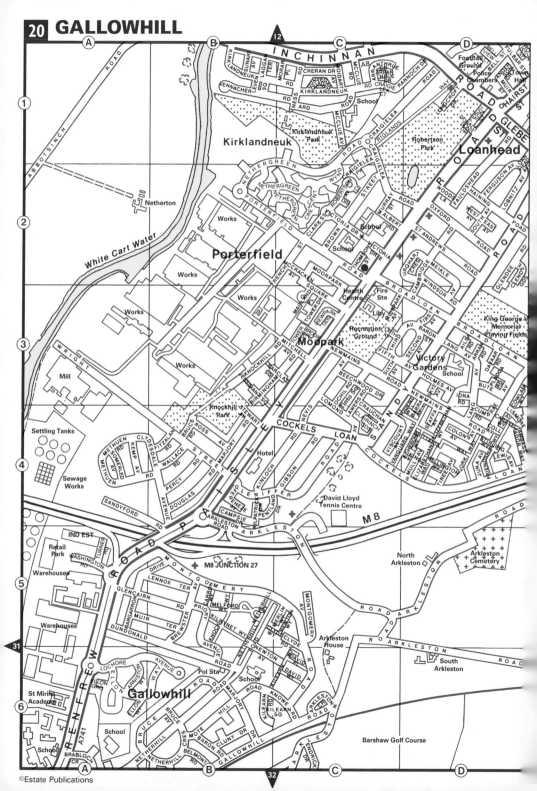

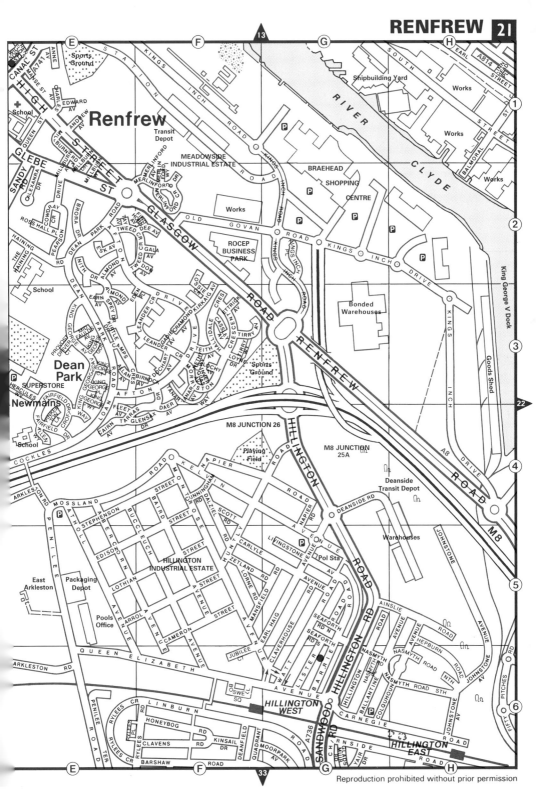

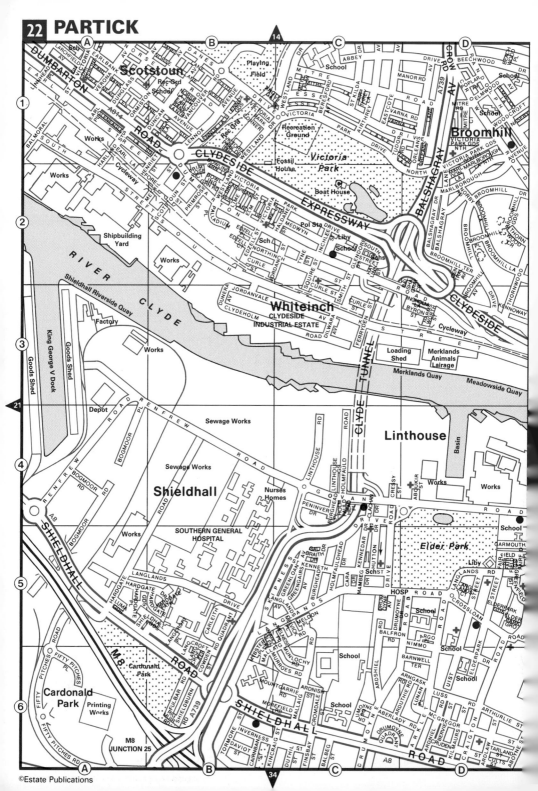

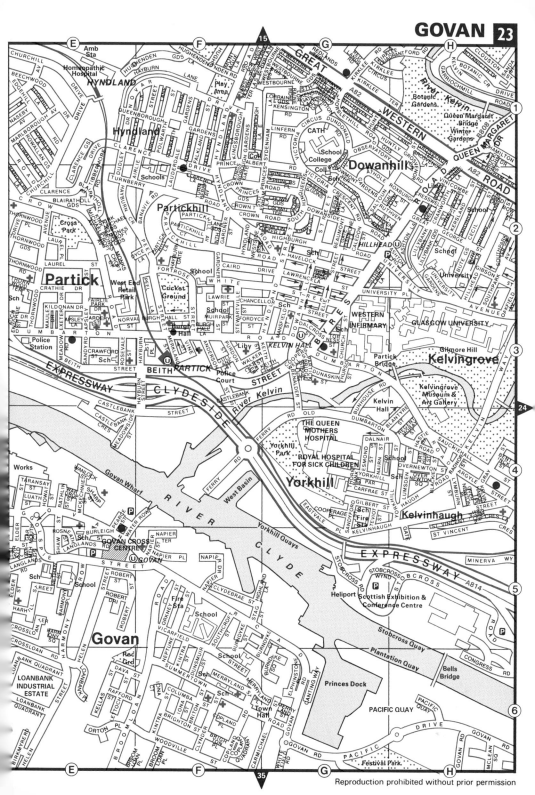

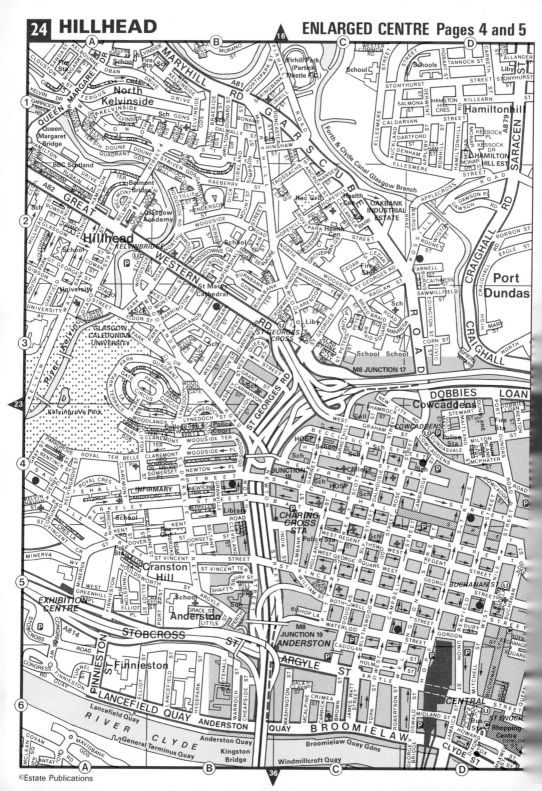

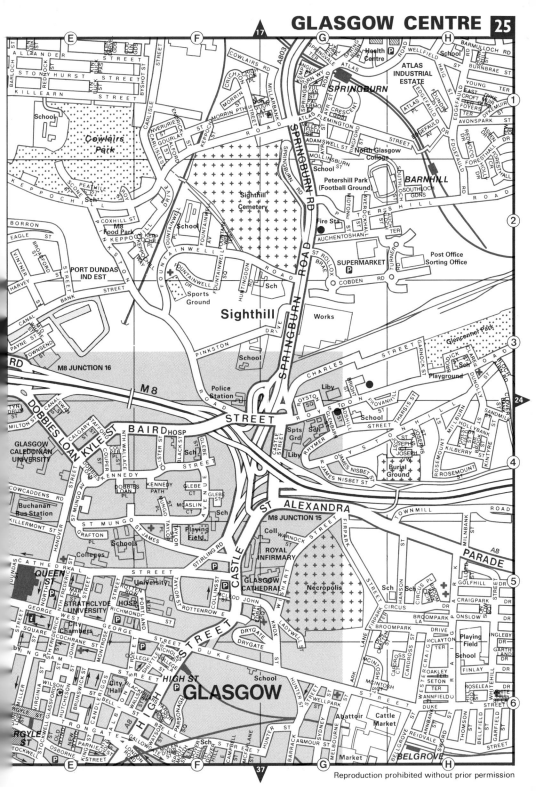

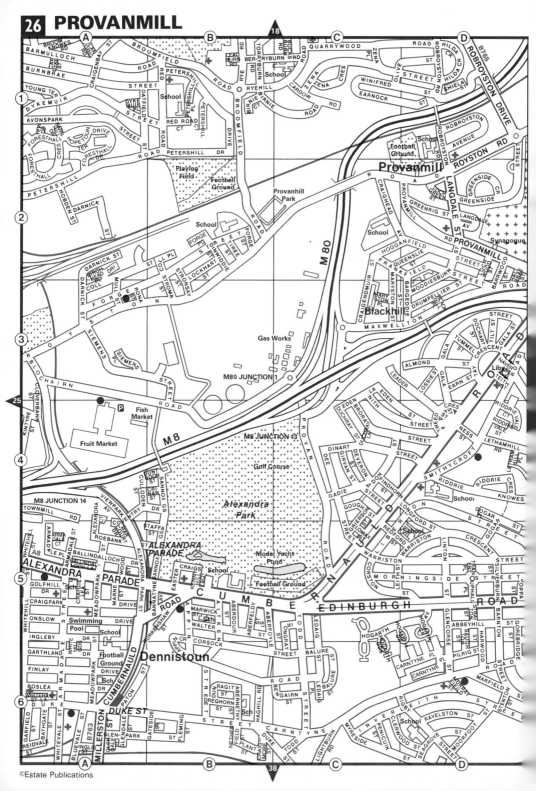

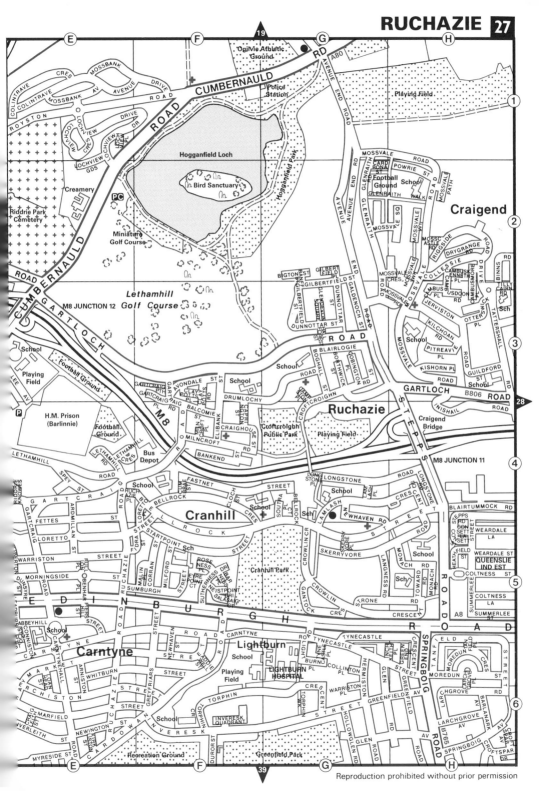

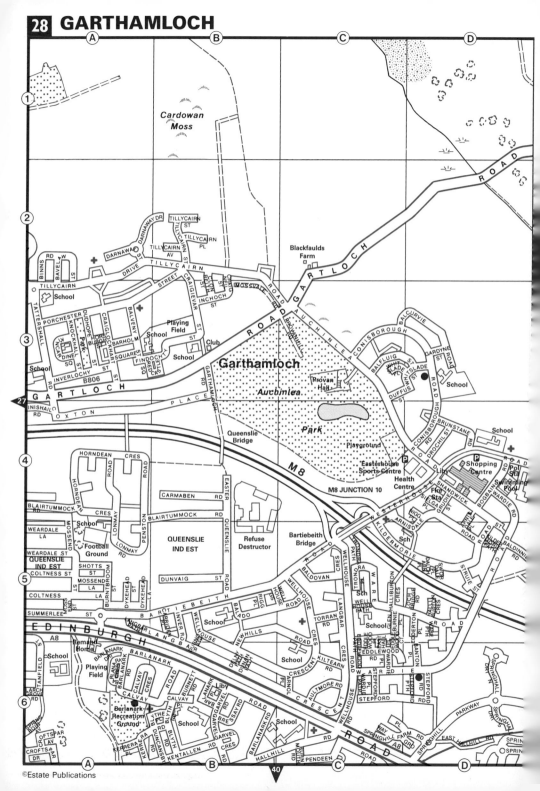

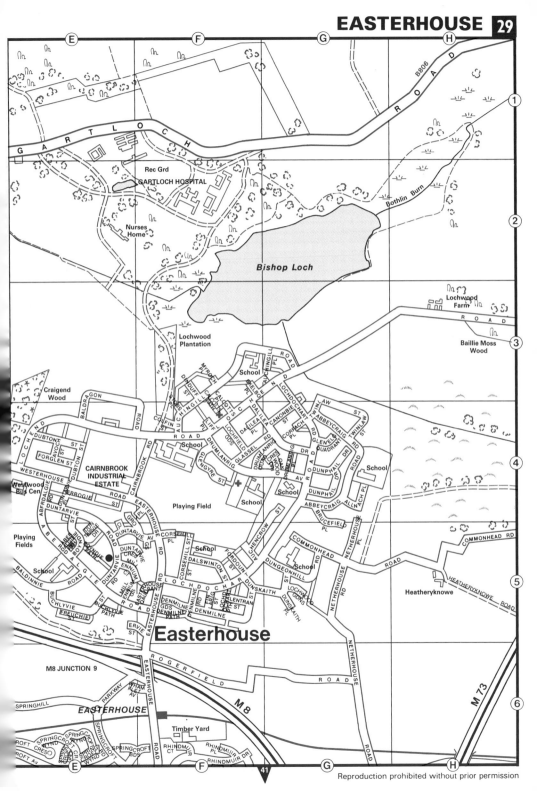

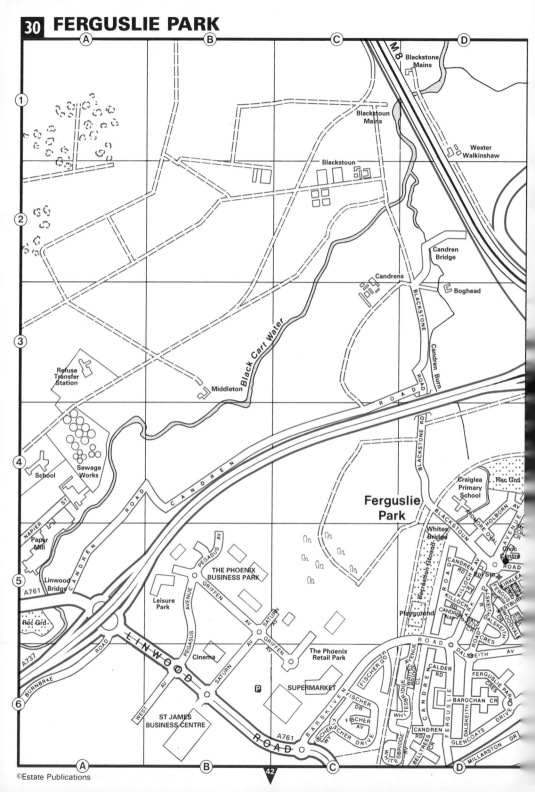

©Estate Publications

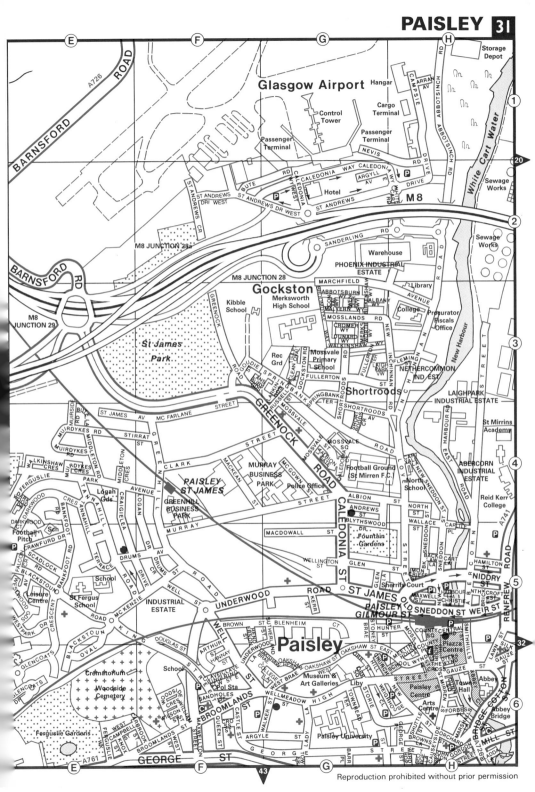

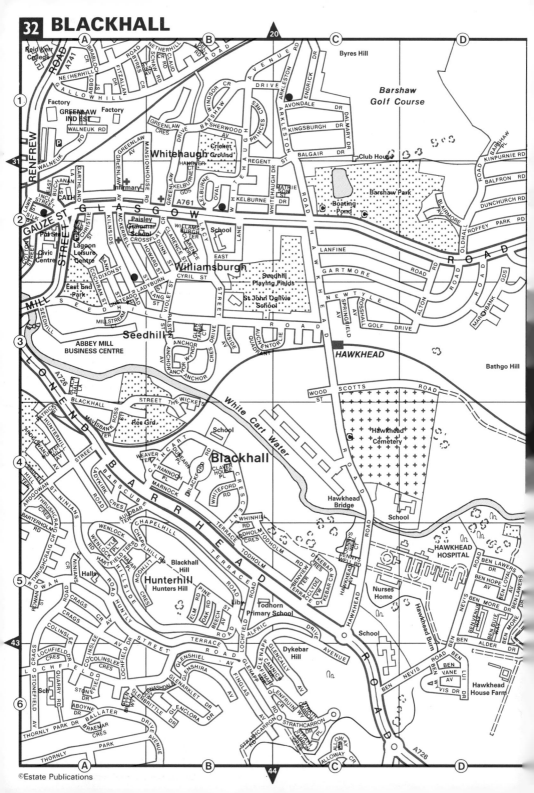

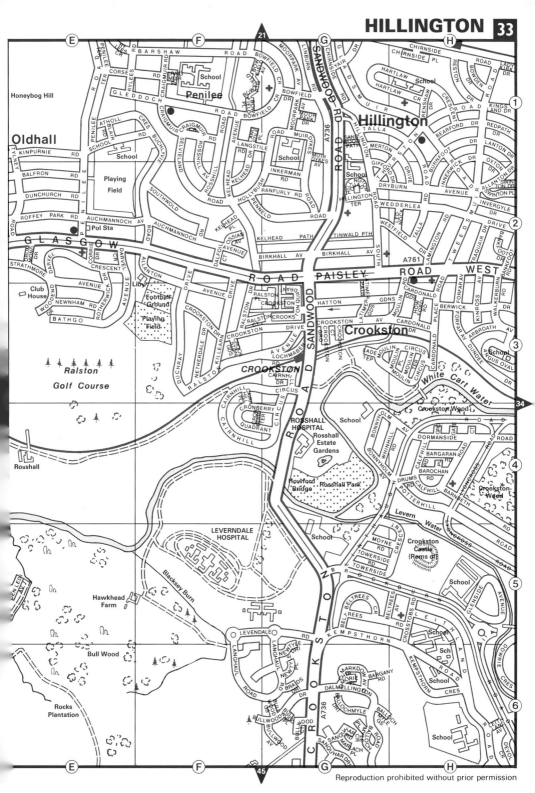

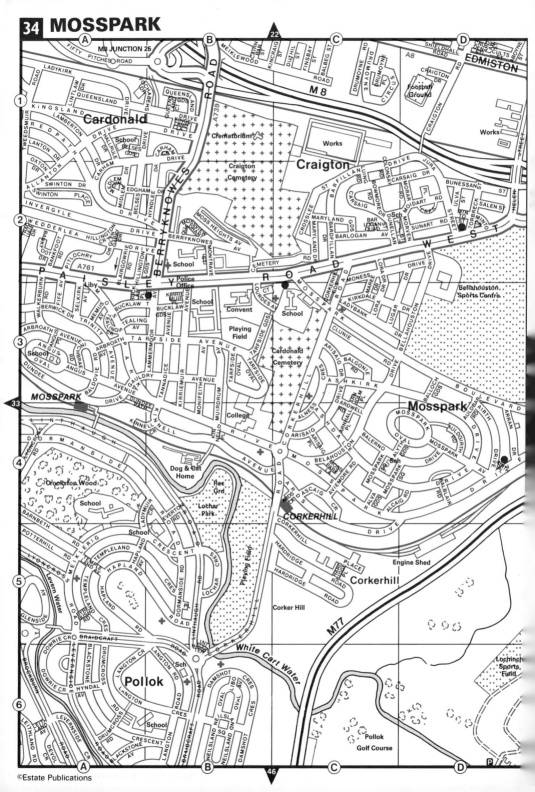

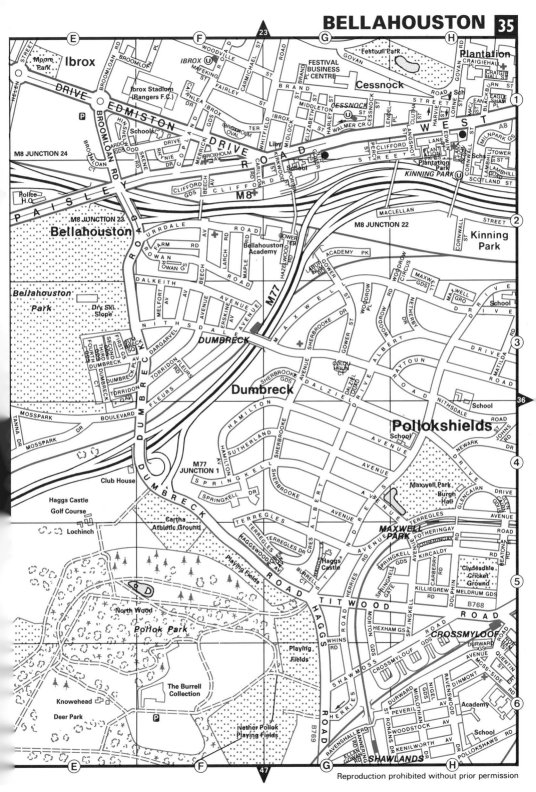

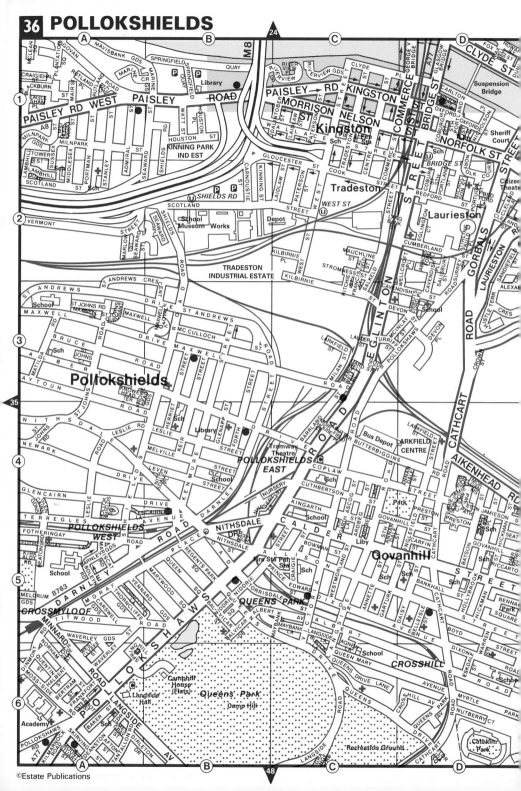

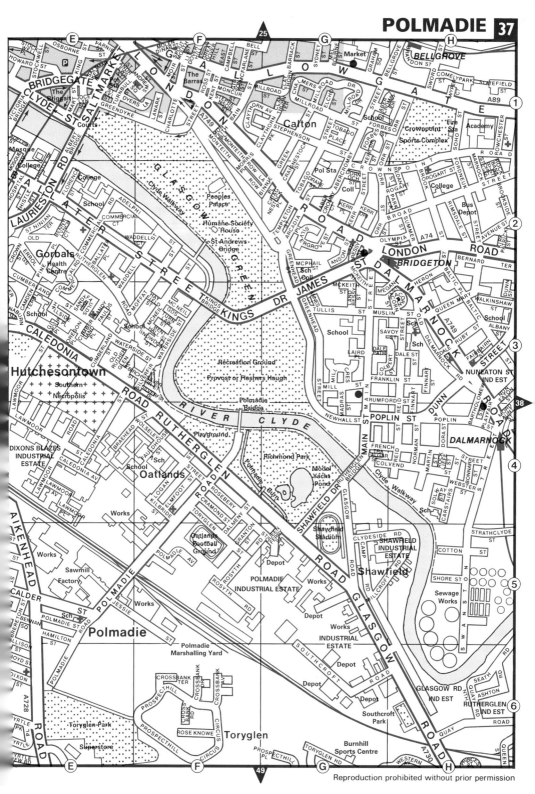

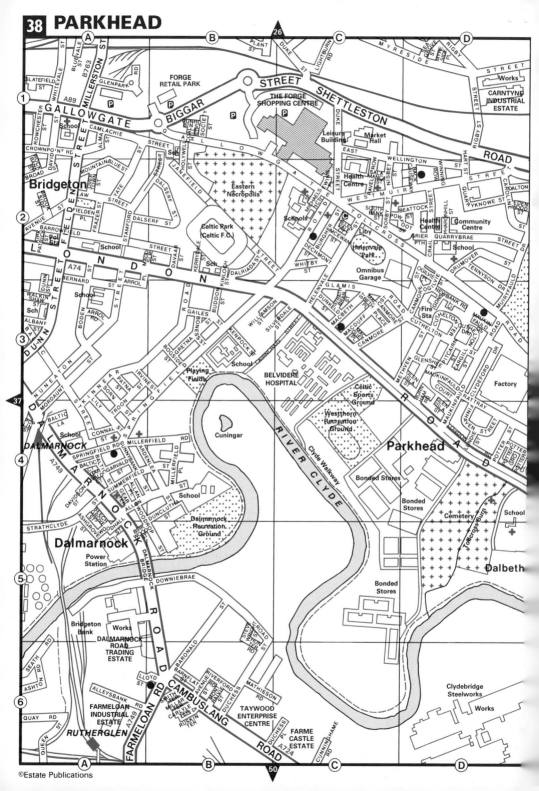

38 PARKHEAD

©Estate Publications

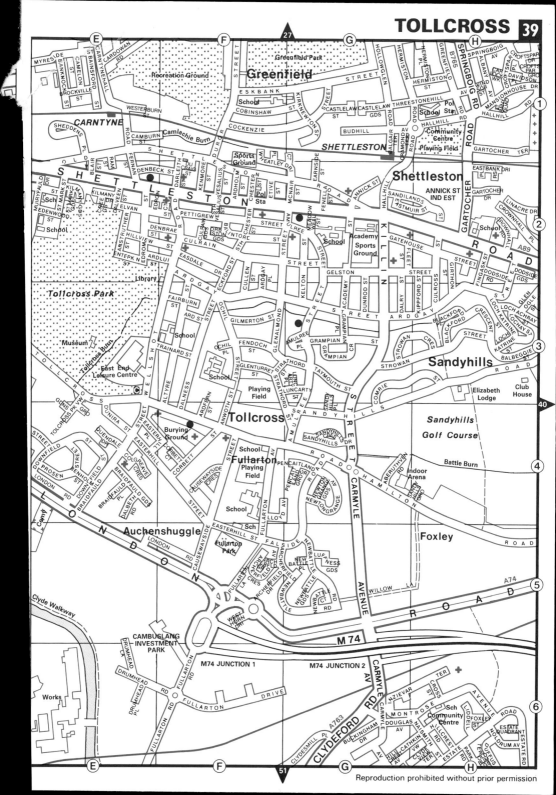

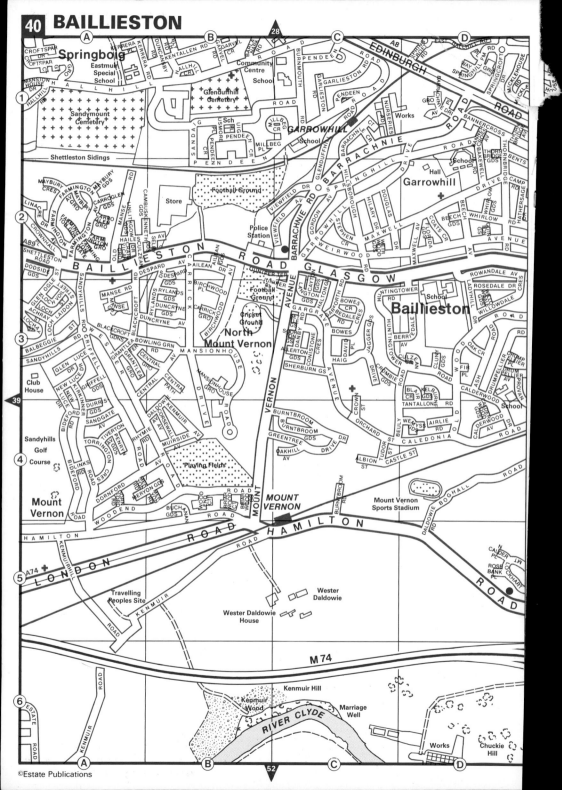

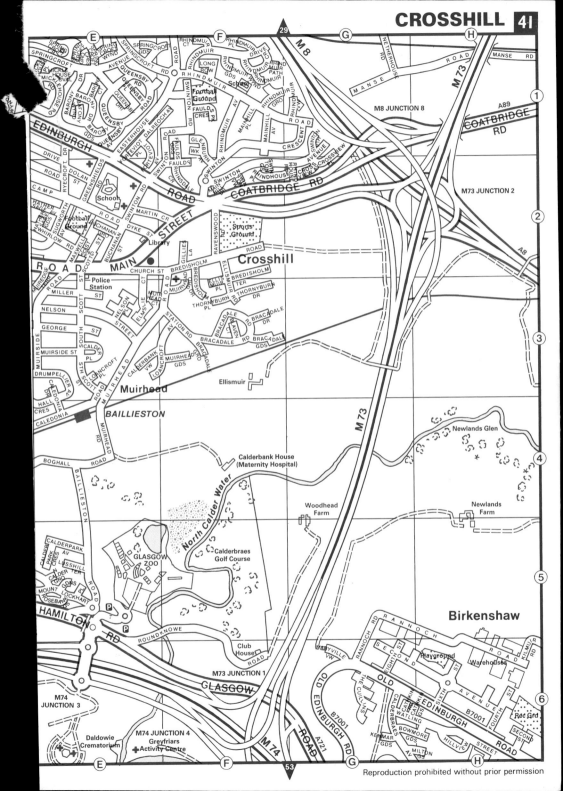

CROSSHILL **41**

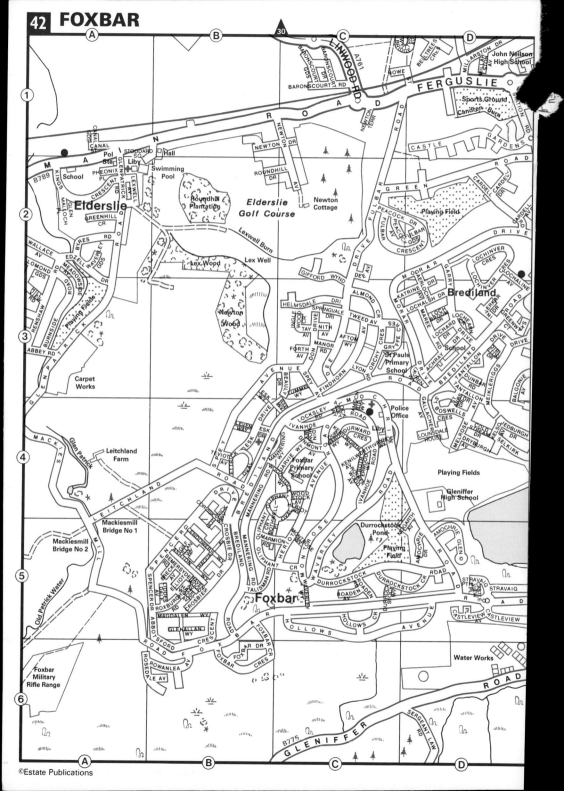

A B 30 C D

1

LINWOOD RD A76I
BARONSCOURT GDS
BARONSCOURT RD
ROWE
BELLTREES CRES
MILLARSTON DR
John Neilson High School
FERGUSLIE
Sports Ground
Candren Burn

ROAD
CANAL ST
STODDARD SQ
Pol Sta
Liby
Hall
NEWTON DR
ROUNDHILL DR
ROUNDHILL AV
NEWTON TERR
CASTLE
GARDENS
CARDELL
CARDELL
ROAD

B789
KINGS RD
GLEN MALLOCH
School
PHEONIX PL
GLENPATRICK RD
LEXWELL AV
Swimming Pool
Roundhill Plantation
Elderslie Golf Course
Newton Cottage
FULBAR GREEN
Playing Field
DRIVE

2

Eldersile
GREENHILL CR
BARES RD
WAVERLEY GDS
EDZELL DR
Lexwell Burn
Lex Wood
Lex Well
GIFFORD WYND
DEE AV
PEACOCK DR
FULBAR CRESCENT
FULBAR AV
MOOR AR
MAERLOCH
LOCHALSH DR
GARRY
MARLE
KATRINE
Brediland
LOCHINVER CRES
LOCHINVER DR
GREENER
CLOCHMALINE

WALLACE AV
LOMOND GDS
VILL RD
RENSHAW
Playing Fields
BURNSIDE
GLEN PATRICK
MEADOWSIDE DR
Newton Wood
HELMSDALE DRI
INGLE WOOD CR
TAY AV
SPRINGVALE DRI
NITH AV
TWEED AV
ALMOND AV
AFTON WY
CRES
DRIVE
LOCHARD DR
LOCHER CR
ACHRAY DR
BREDILAND
TANTALLON
TANTALLON
DUNBAR
School
MEIKLERIGGS
BALGONIE AV

3

ABBEY RD
Carpet Works
FORTH AV
MANOR AV
LYON WY
ORCHY CRES
St Pauls Primary School
ROAD
ST BOSWELLS
GALLACHER
LOUNSDALE HOUSE
MELROSE
DRYBURGH
JEDBURGH
SELKIRK

MACKIES
Glen Patrick
Leitchland Farm
LEITCHLAND
AVENUE
BEAUTY DRIVE
SPEY
FINDHORN
LUMME WY
ROAD
Police Office
Liby
DRIVE
EDEN
SEVEN WY
ESK
TEVIOT
ESK RD
IVANHOE
Foxbar Primary School
LOCKSLEY RD
MANNERING
WYNMONT
CRES
WOODSIDE
DURWARD CRES
IVANHOE WY
KENILWORTH
NORTH IVANHOE WY
Playing Fields
Gleniffer High School

4

MACKIES
Mackiesmill Bridge No 1
MILL
SPENCER DR
GLENDOWER
CROSBIE DR
BREDILAND
MANNERING RD
MARJVE WY
OLIPHANT
WOODSTOCK RD
Durrockstock Pond
WAVERLEY
AMOCHRIE GLEN

5

Mackiesmill Bridge No 2
Old Patrick Water
SPENCER DR
BEMERSYDE
BRECKSYDE
ELLIOT
ROXBURGH
ABBOTSFORD RD
MAGDALEN WY
GLENALLAN WY
TALISMAN RD
MARMION RD
MONTROSE CR
HERIOT
OLIPHANT
ROADEN AV
ROADEN AV
DURROCKSTOCK CR
Playing Field
AMOCHRIE DR
ROAD
STRAVAIG PTH
STRAVAIG
STLEVIEW
STLEVIEW

6

Foxbar Military Rifle Range
ROWANLEA
ROSEDALE AV
CRESCENT
FOXBAR RD
FOXBAR CRES
FOXBAR DR
Foxbar
HOLLOWS
HOLLOWS CR
AVENUE
Water Works
GLENIFFER ROAD
B775
SERGANT LAN

A B C D

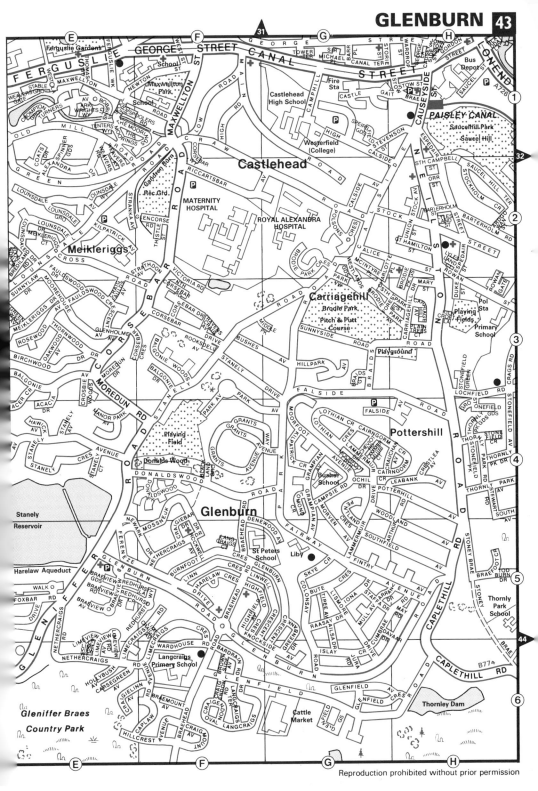

Map grid references: A, B, 32, C, D (top); 1, 43, 2, 3, 4, 5, 6 (left); 54 (bottom)

THORNLY PARK AV
BARCRAIG DR
AVENUE
SOUTH
Shaw Wood
TODBURN DR
B774
CAPLETHILL
Thornly Park School
Playing Field
Playing Field
Caplethill
Harelaw Burn
Harelaw
Harelaw Mount
DYKEBAR HOSPITAL
Playing Field
CALLOWAY CRES
ALLOWAY DRIVE
GRAHAMSTON PL
GRAHAMSTON CR
GRAHAMSTON CT
B771
ROAD
HURLET
A726
ROAD
A736
Oldbarhills Bridge
Oldbar Hills
Oldbar Burn
Logansraes
Fire Sta
Blackbyres
BLACKBYRES
GRAHAMSTON ROAD
PAISLEY ROAD
BROWNSIDE DR
BROWNS DR
BROWNSIDE CRES
GLENIFFER DR
ROWAN
ACACIA
HEATHER AV
MOSS DR
BROOM
BOYLESTONE
BOYLESTONE DR
GORSE AV
WHIN AV
FERN DR
DRIVE
Cross Stobs
Bovelstone Quarries (Disused)
School
QUARRY RD
TREES PARK AV
Fereneze Golf Course
STOBS
SHELL
SEAFORTH CR
LINNHE DRIVE
LEVEN
MORAR
DLOMOND
BURNSIDE AV
DEALSTON RD
B771
VICTORIA
GRAHAMSTON DRIVE
PARK
CRES
GRO
JOHN SMITH
ROAD
VICTORIA PL
VICTORIA AVE
Rec Grd
Sports Ground
SHANKS WAY
SHANKS INDUSTRIAL ESTATE
Crossmill
School
Playing Field
STEWART CT
STEWART
CROSSMILL
TAIT AV
MUIR PL
RUFFLEES AV
WAULKMILL AV
WAULKMILL
WRAES AV
STEWART
CARLIBER BRIDGE
Carliber Bridge
School
MELVIEW
MANSE
FERENEZE GRO
FERENEZE AV
FERENEZE CRES
LAUREL WY
GRAHAM RD
HILLSIDE DR
HILLSIDE GRO
HILLSIDE
GATESIDE RD
NEILSTON RD
LEVERN GDS
CONNEL
BARNES RD
JOHN ST
COGAN ST
ROBERTSON ST
CROSS ARTHURLIE ST
GEORGE ST
MURIEL ST
MURIEL LA
COMMERCIAL RD
CARLIBAR GDNS
CARLIBAR RD
WATER RD
GLEN ST
4TH PK
AVE
BARRHEAD
Football Ground
Levern Nth Bridge
CENTRE
CROSS
Barrhead Sports Centre
Health Centre
Lib
BARRHEAD SHOPPING CENTRE
MAIN STREET
SWAN
LYONCROSS
PRINCES
MANSE

©Estate Publications

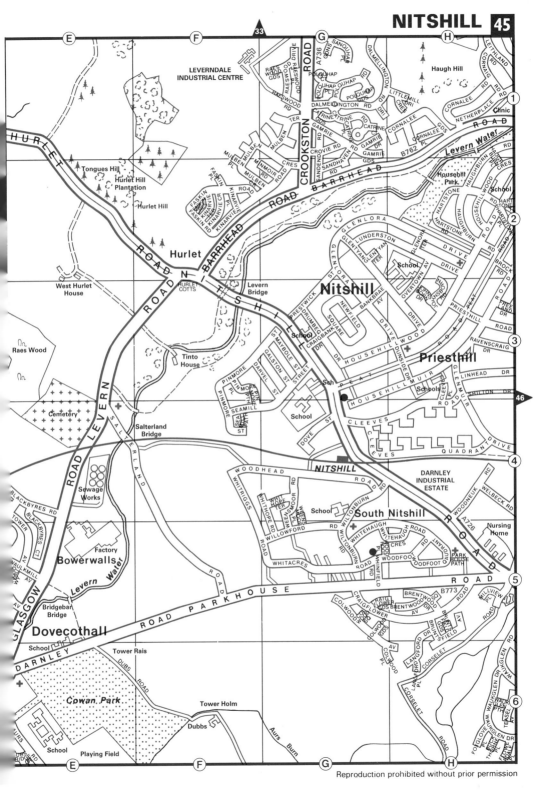

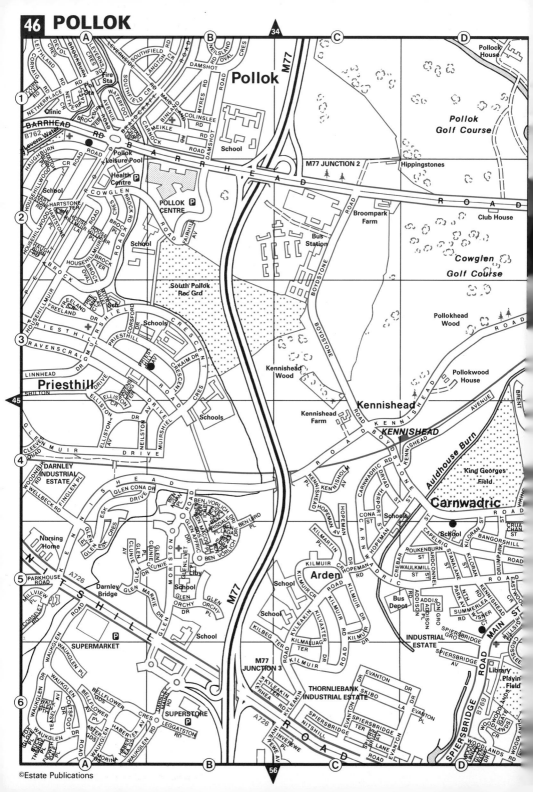

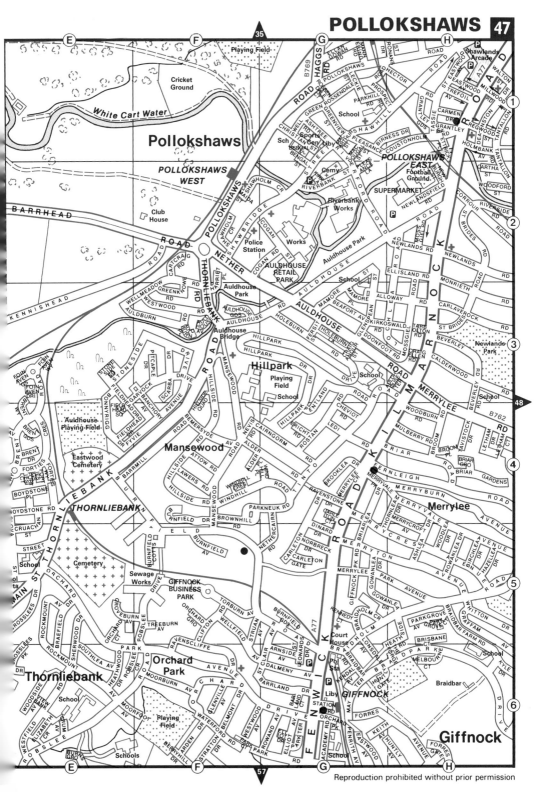

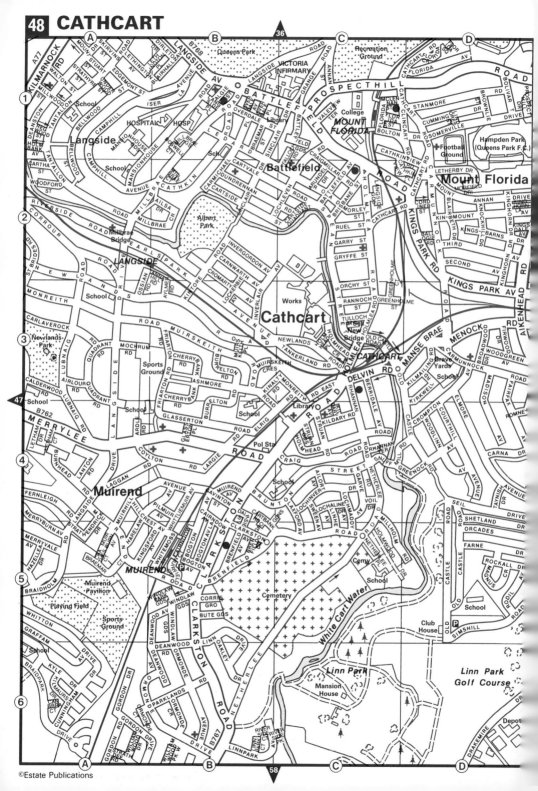

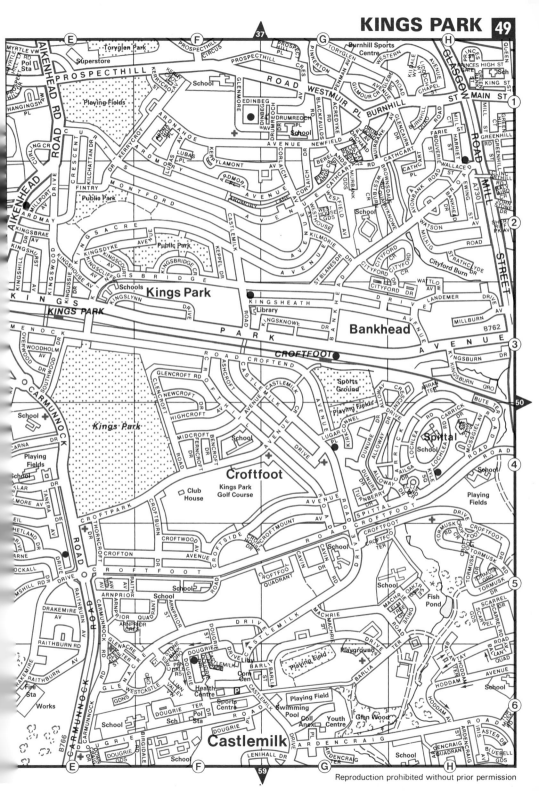

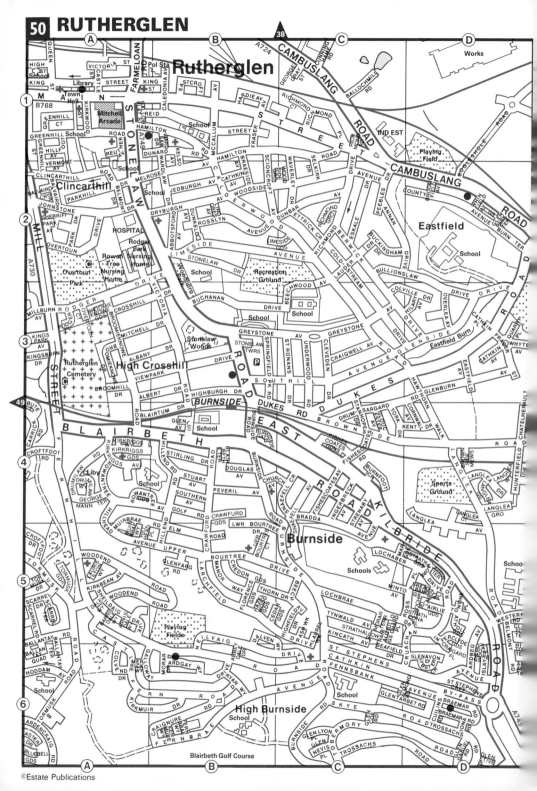

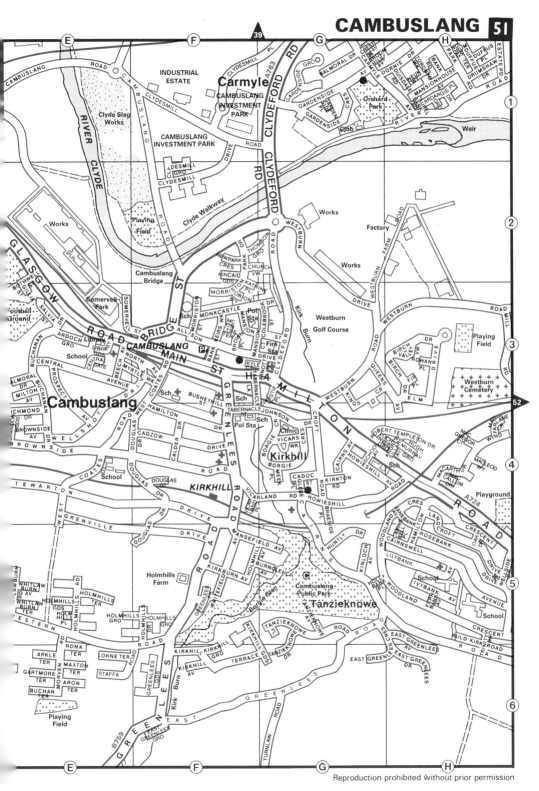

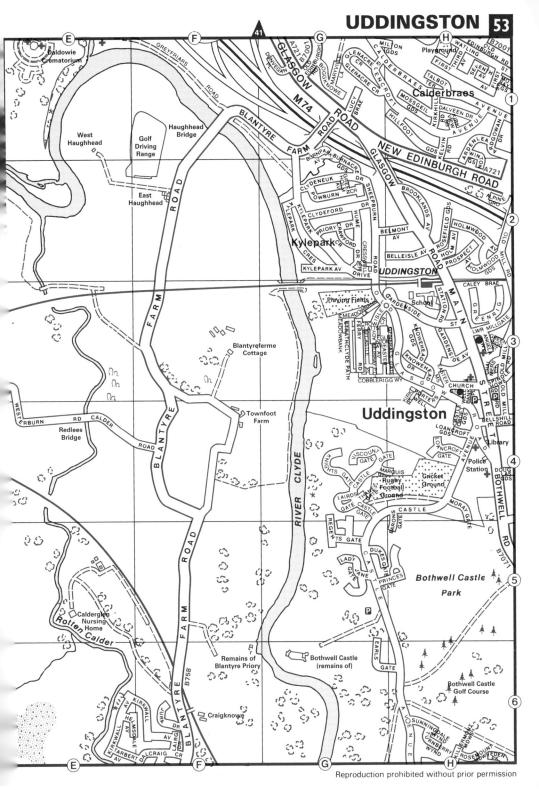

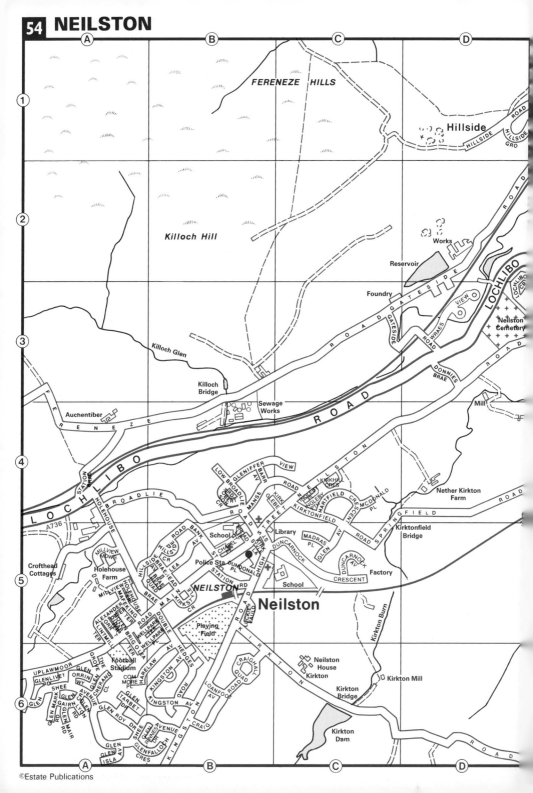

A · B · C · D

1
2
3
4
5
6

FERENEZE HILLS

Hillside

HILLSIDE ROAD

HILLSIDE GRO

Killoch Hill

Works

Reservoir

Foundry

Neilston Cemetery

LOCHLIBO

LOCHLIBO CRE

VIEW

ROWRAES ROAD

ROAD GATESIDE

Killoch Glen

Killoch Bridge

DONNIES BRAE

ROAD

Mill

Auchentiber

FERENEZE

Sewage Works

ROAD

LOCHLIBO

STATION BRAE

A736

BROADLIE

HOLEHOUSE

Crofthead Cottages

Holehouse Farm

MILLVIEW VIEWS

MILLVIEW

HILLSIDE

BROADLIE LEA

ROAD

LOW BROADLIE

GLENIFFER

BARR

VIEW

ROAD

MANSE

KIRK GLEBE

STREET

KIRKHILL CRES

MOSELEY

VESLEY

MARTFIELD

MCDONALD PL

CROMDONALD

KIRKTONFIELD

SPRINGFIELD

Nether Kirkton Farm

ROAD

School

CHAPEL

HIGH STREET

Library

MADRAS PL

GLEN AV

Kirktonfield Bridge

Police Sta

DUNDONALD PL

DUNCARNOCK

DUNCARNOCK AV

CRESCENT

Factory

NEILSTON

Neilston

School

ALEXANDER

HOLEHOUSE ROAD

MARKING

WELLPARK

WELLPARK

BRIG O LEA

MAIN ROAD

KIRKSTYLE CR

DOUBLE HEDGES ROAD

STATION ROAD

HOLM RD

Kirkton Burn

LINTMILL TER

GROVE

THE

Football Stadium

COM MORE PL

HARELAW

KINGSTON AVENUE

KINGSTON ROAD

Playing Field

LOANFOOT AV

KIRKTON

CRAIGHALL QUAD

Neilston House Kirkton

Kirkton Mill

UPLAWMOOR

GLENLIVET

SHEE RD

GLEN

ORRIN WY

GLEN CLERAND CL

AVENUE

GLEN MARK RD

MAGAIRN RD

GLEN LYON

GLENMAIR RD

GLEN ROY DRE

SHEE AV

GLEN INNES DR

GLEN TARBET DR

KINGSTON ROAD

CRAIG

Kirkton Bridge

Kirkton Dam

ROAD

GLEN ISLA AV

GLEN GLENFALLOCH CRES

AVENUE

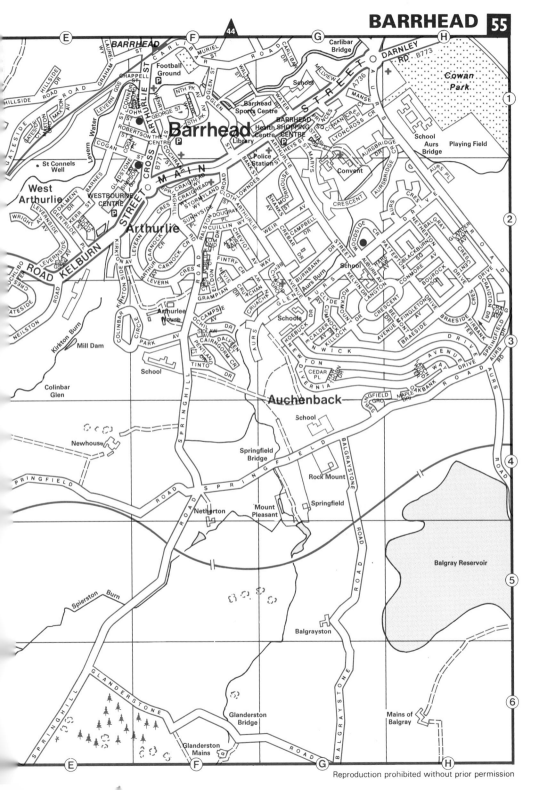

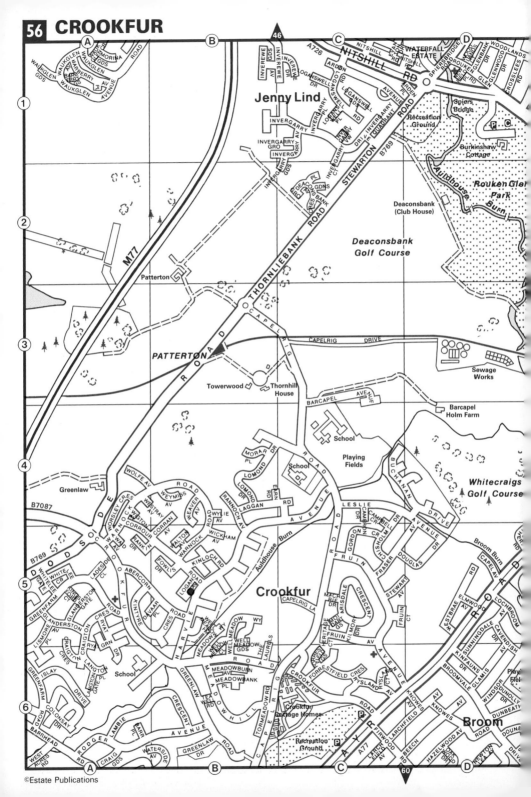

A B C D

46

A726

NITSHILL RD

WATERFALL ESTATE

Jenny Lind

Recreation Ground

Spiers Bridge

P C

Burkinshaw Cottage

Rouken Glen Park

Deaconsbank (Club House)

Deaconsbank Golf Course

Patterton

M77

THORNLIEBANK ROAD

STEWARTON ROAD

B769

CAPELRIG

CAPELRIG DRIVE

Sewage Works

Barcapel Holm Farm

PATTERTON

Towerwood

Thornhill House

BARCAPEL AVENUE

School

Playing Fields

Whitecraigs Golf Course

Greenlaw

B7087

Wolfe Av

School

Broom Burn

B769

Crookfur

CAPELRIG LA

Crookfur Cottage Homes

Recreation Ground

Broom

School

Meadowburn Av

Meadowbank Pl

A77

©Estate Publications

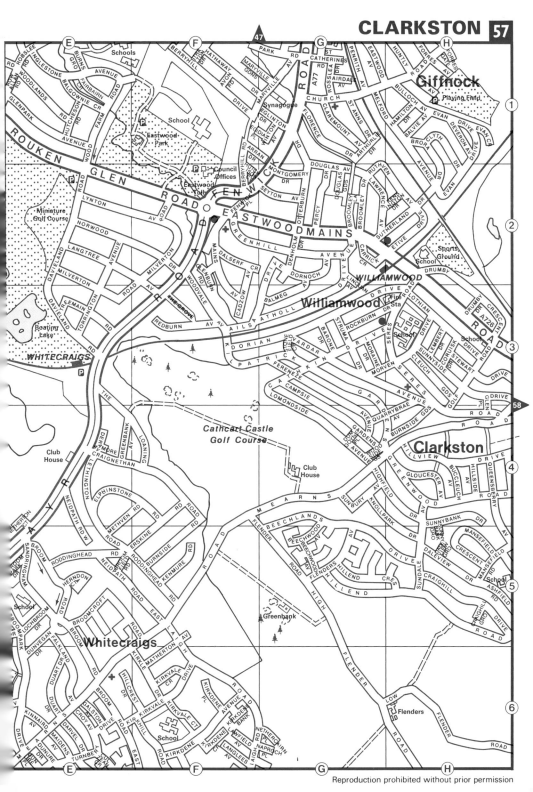

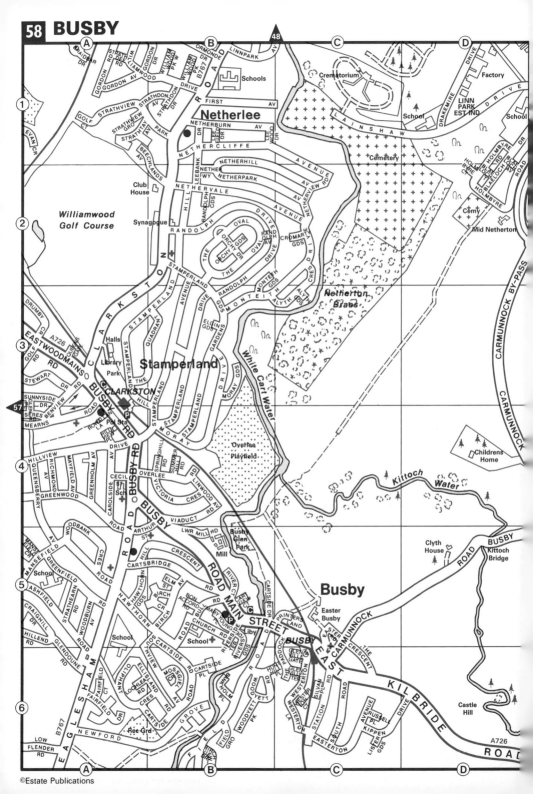

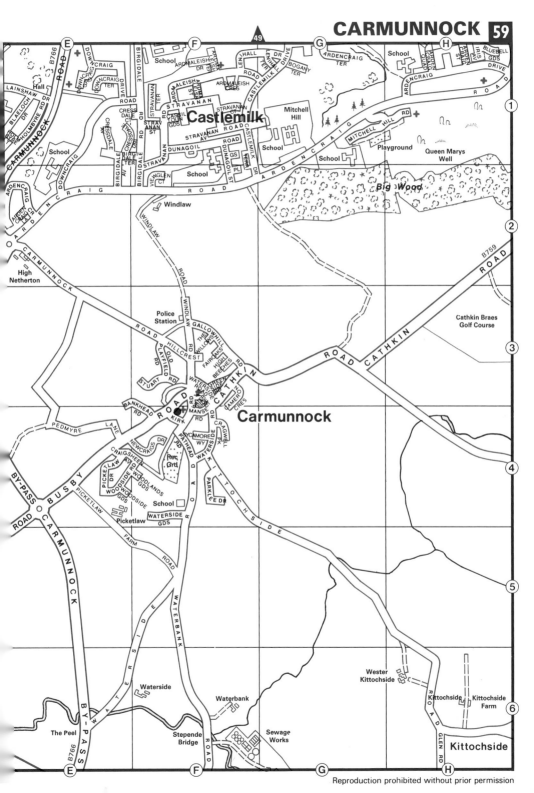

Castlemilk

Carmunnock

Kittochside

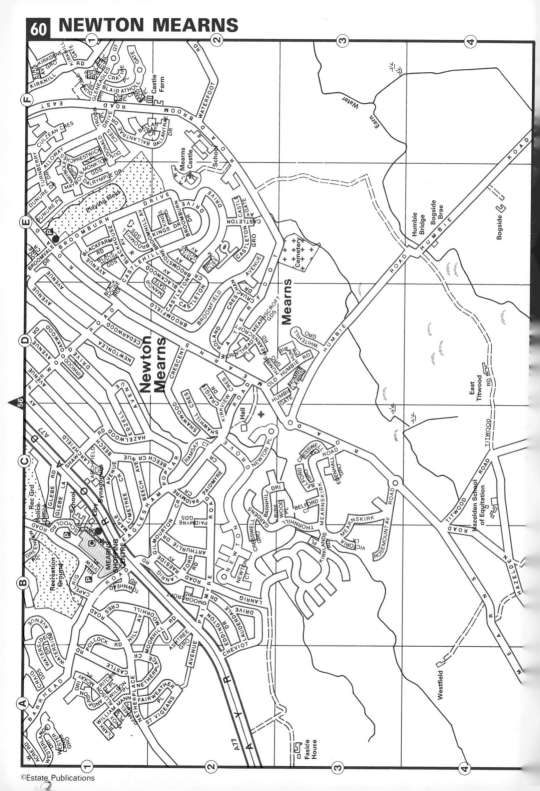

NEWTON MEARNS

Newton Mearns

Mearns

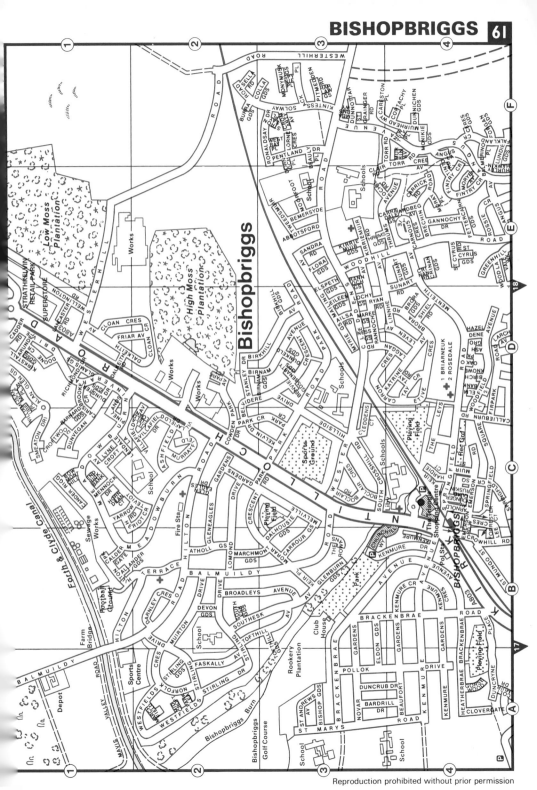

Bishopbriggs

Low Moss Plantation

High Moss Plantation

Strathkelvin Retail Park

SUPERSTORE

Works

Forth & Clyde Canal

Sewage Works

Depot

Fire Sta

Sports Centre

Club House

Rookery Plantation

Bishopbriggs Golf Course

Bishopbriggs Burn

Sports Ground

Playing Field

Playing Field

Playing Field

The Triangle Shopping Centre

WESTERHILL ROAD

KIRKINTILLOCH ROAD

A - Z INDEX TO STREETS

with Postcodes

The Index includes some names for which there is insufficient space on the maps.These names are preceded by an * and are followed by the nearest adjoining thoroughfare.

Abbey Clo. PA1 31 H6
Abbey Dri. G14 22 C1
Abbey Rd. PA5 42 A3
Abbeycraig Rd. G34 29 G4
Abbeydale Dri. G73 50 B6
Abbeyhill St. G32 26 D5
Abbeylands Rd. G81 9 E2
Abbot St. PA3 32 A1
Abbot St. G41 36 A6
Abbotsbur Way. PA3 31 G3
Abbotsford. G64 61 E3
Abbotsford Av. G73 50 B2
Abbotsford Cres. PA2 42 B5
Abbotsford Pl. G5 36 D2
Abbotsford Rd. G61 10 C3
Abbotsford Rd. G81 12 C2
Abbotshall Av. G15 9 G6
Abbotsinch Rd. PA3 31 H1
Abbott Cres. G81 12 D3
Aberconway St. G81 12 C2
Abercorn Av. G52 21 E4
Abercorn Pl. G23 16 A1
Abercorn Rd. G77 56 A5
Abercorn St. G81 9 G1
Abercorn St. PA3 31 H5
Abercromby Ct. G40 37 G2
Abercromby Dri. G40 37 G1
Abercromby St. G40 37 G2
Aberdalgie Path. G34 29 E5
Aberdalgie Rd. G34 29 E4
Aberdour St. G31 26 B5
Aberfeldy St. G31 26 B5
Aberfoyle St. G31 26 B5
Aberlady Rd. G51 22 C6
Abernethy Pl. G77 60 F1
Abernethy St. G31 26 B6
Aberuthven Rd. G32 39 G4
Aboukir St. G51 22 D4
Aboyne Dri. PA2 32 A6
Aboyne St. G51 22 D6
Acacia Dri. G78 44 B4
Acacia Dri. PA2 43 E4
Academy Park. G41 35 G2
Academy Rd. G46 47 G6
Academy St. G32 39 G3
Acer Cres. PA2 43 E3
Achamore Cres. G15 9 G5
Achamore Dri. G15 9 G5
Achamore Rd. G15 9 G4
Achray Dri. PA2 42 D3
Achray Pl. G62 6 B1
Acorn Ct. G40 37 H3
Acorn St. G40 37 H3
Acre Dri. G20 15 F2
Acre Rd. G20 15 F1
Acredyke Cres. G21 18 B4
Acredyke Pl. G21 18 B4
Acredyke Rd. G21 18 B4
Acredyke Rd. G73 49 G1
Adams Ct La. G1 4 D5
Adamswell St. G21 25 G1
Addiewell St. G32 27 F6
Addison Gro. G46 46 D5
Addison Pl. G46 46 D5
Addison Rd. G12 15 H6
Addison Rd. G46 46 D5
Adelaide Ct. G81 8 A3
Adelphi St. G5 37 E2
Admiral St. G41 36 A2
Admiralty Gdns. G60 7 C3
Admiralty Gro. G60 7 C3
Admiralty Pl. G60 7 C3
Afton Cres. G61 11 H5
Afton Dri. PA4 21 E2
Afton St. G41 36 A6
Afton Way. PA2 42 C3
Agamemnon St. G81 8 B6
Agnew La. G42 36 C5
Aikenhead Rd. G42 36 D4
Ailean Dri. G32 40 B2
Ailean Gdns. G32 40 B2
Ailort Av. G44 48 C4
Ailsa Dri. G81 9 E3
Ailsa Dri. PA2 43 G5
Ailsa Dri. G42 48 B2
Ailsa Dri. G73 49 H4
Ailsa Dri. G46 57 F3
Ailsa Rd. G64 61 D3
Ailsa Rd. PA4 20 D3
Ainslie Rd. G52 21 H5
Airdale Av. G46 57 G1
Airgold Dri. G15 10 A4
Airgold Pl. G15 10 A5
Airlie Av. G62 11 E2
Airlie Gdns. G73 50 D5
Airlie La. G12 23 F1
Airlie Rd. G69 40 D4
Airlie St. G12 23 E2
Airlour Rd. G43 48 A3
Airth Dri. G52 34 D4
Airth Pl. G52 34 D4
Airthrey Av. G14 22 C1
Aitken St. G31 26 B5
Alan Glen Gdns. G64 61 D1
Alasdair Ct. G78 55 F2
Albany Av. G32 39 H1
Albany Dri. G73 50 A3
Albany Quad. G32 39 H1
Albany St. G40 38 A3
Albany Ter. G72 50 D6
Albany Way. PA3 31 G3
Albert Av. G42 36 B5
Albert Bri. G5 37 E1
Albert Dri. G61 11 H6
Albert Dri. G41 35 G4
Albert Dri. G73 50 A3
Albert Rd. G81 8 C5
Albert Rd. G42 36 C5
Albert Rd. PA4 20 C2
Albion Gate. G1 5 F5
Albion Gate. PA3 31 G4
Albion St. G69 40 C4
Albion St. G1 5 F5
Albion St. PA3 31 G4
Alcaig Rd. G52 34 C4
Alder Ct. G78 55 F3
Alder Gate. G72 52 B4
Alder Pl. G43 47 F4
Alder Rd. G81 8 C4
Alder Rd. G43 47 F4
Alderman Pl. G13 14 A5
Alderman Rd. G13 13 F3
Alderside Gdns. G71 53 G2
Alexander Cres. G5 36 D3
Alexander St. G81 12 C2
Alexander Ter. G78 54 A5
Alexandra Ct. G31 26 A5
Alexandra Dri. PA2 43 E2
Alexandra Dri. PA4 21 E2
Alexandra Par. G31 25 G4
Alexandra Park St. G31 26 A5
Alford St. G21 25 F1
Alfred La. G12 23 H2
Alfric Dri. PA2 32 B5
Algie St. G41 48 B1
Alice St. PA2 43 G2
Allan Av. PA4 21 E3
Allan Glen Pl. G4 5 F3
Allan Pl. G40 38 A4
Allan St. G40 38 A4
Allander Gdns. G64 61 B1
Allander Rd. G61 10 D6
Allander Rd. G62 6 D2
Allander St. G22 24 D1
Allanton Av. PA1 33 F2
Allanton Dri. G52 34 A2
Allen Way. PA4 21 E4
Allerdyce Ct. G15 13 F1
Allerdyce Dri. G15 13 F1
Allerdyce Pl. G15 13 F1
Allerdyce Rd. G15 13 F1
Allerton Gdns. G69 40 C3
Alleysbank Rd. G73 38 A6
Allison Av. PA8 7 A6
Allison Dri. G72 51 F3
Allison Pl. G42 36 C5
Allison Pl. G77 60 A1
Allison St. G42 36 C5
Allnach Pl. G34 29 G4
Alloway Av. PA2 44 C1
Alloway Cres. PA2 44 C1
Alloway Cres. G73 49 G3
Alloway Dri. PA2 44 C1
Alloway Dri. G81 9 E6
Alloway Dri. G77 60 E1
Alloway Dri. G73 49 G4
Alloway Rd. G43 47 G3
Alma St. G40 38 A1
Almond Av. PA4 21 E2
Almond Bank. G61 14 A1
Almond Cres. PA2 42 C3
Almond Rd. G33 19 H5
Almond St. G33 26 D3
Alness Cres. G52 34 C4
Alpha Centre. G81 12 C3
Alpine Gro. G71 53 H2
Alsatian Av. G81 9 F6
Alton Rd. PA1 32 D3
Altyre St. G32 39 F3
Alva Gdns. G61 10 D1
Alva Gdns. G52 34 C4
Alyth Cres. G76 58 C3
Alyth Gdns. G52 58 C3
Alyth Gdns. G76 34 C4
Ambassador Way. PA4 20 D4
Amisfield St. G20 15 H6
Amochrie Dri. PA2 42 D5
Amochrie Glen. PA2 42 D5
Amochrie Rd. PA2 42 C4
Amochrie Way. PA2 42 C4
Amulree Pl. G32 39 G3
Amulree St. G32 39 G2
Ancaster Dri. G13 14 D5
Anchor Av. PA1 32 B3
Anchor Cres. PA1 32 B3
Anchor Dri. PA1 32 B3
Anchor La. G1 4 D4
Anchor Wynd. PA1 32 B3
Ancroft St. G20 24 C2
Anderson Dri. G77 60 A1
Anderson Dri. PA4 20 D1
Anderson St. G11 23 F3
Anderston Quay. G3 4 A5
Andrew Av. PA4 21 E1
Andrew Dri. G81 12 D2
Andrew Sillars Av. G72 51 H4
Andrews St. PA3 31 G4
*Angela Gate, Lower Millgate. G71 53 H3
Angela Way. G71 53 H3
Angle Gate. G14 22 B1
Angus Av. G64 61 E4
Angus Av. G52 34 A3
Angus La. G64 61 F4
Angus Oval. G52 34 A3
Angus Pl. G52 34 A3
Angus St. G21 25 G1
Angus St. G81 13 E2
Annan Dri. G61 10 C5
Annan Dri. G73 50 C2
Annan St. G42 48 C1
Annandale St. G42 36 D4
Annbank St. G31 25 H6
Anne Av. PA4 13 E6
Annes Ct. G40 37 G3
Annette St. G42 36 C5
Annfield Pl. G31 25 H6
Annick Dri. G61 10 C6
Annick St. G72 52 A4
Annick St. G32 39 G2
Anniesland Cres. G14 13 G6
Anniesland Rd. G13 13 G6
Anstruther St. G32 39 E2
Anthony St. G2 4 B4
Antonine Gdns. G81 8 C2
Antonine Rd. G61 10 B2
Anwoth St. G32 39 F4
Appin Cres. G31 26 B6
Appin Rd. G31 26 B5
Appin Ter. G73 50 D5
Appleby St. G22 24 D1
Applecross St. G22 24 D2
Apsley La. G11 23 E3
Apsley St. G11 23 E3
Aray St. G20 15 H4
Arbroath Av. G52 34 A3
Arcadia Pl. G40 37 G2
Arcadia St. G40 37 G2
Arcan Cres. G15 10 B6
Archerfield Av. G32 39 F5
Archerfield Cres. G32 39 F5
Archerfield Dri. G32 39 F5
Archerfield Gro. G32 39 F5
Archerhill Av. G13 13 G2
Archerhill Cotts. G13 13 G2
Archerhill Cres. G13 13 H3
Archerhill Gdns. G13 13 G2
Archerhill Rd. G13 13 G2
Archerhill Sq. G13 13 G2
Archerhill Ter. G13 13 G2
Ard Rd. PA4 20 C1
Ard St. G32 39 F3
Ardargie Dri. G32 51 H1
Ardargie Gro. G32 51 H1
Ardargie Pl. G32 51 H1
Ardbeg Av. G73 50 D6
Ardbeg Av. G64 61 E4
Ardbeg La. G42 36 C5
Ardbeg St. G42 36 C5
Ardconnel St. G46 46 D5
Arden Av. G46 56 C1
Arden Dri. G46 47 F6
Ardencraig Cres. G45 59 E2
Ardencraig Dri. G45 59 H1
Ardencraig La. G45 59 E2
Ardencraig Pl. G45 49 G6
Ardencraig Quad. G45 49 H6
Ardencraig Rd. G45 49 G6
Ardencraig St. G45 49 H6
Ardencraig Ter. G45 49 G6
Ardenlea. G71 53 H1
Ardenlea St. G40 38 A4
Ardery St. G11 23 E3
Ardessie Pl. G20 15 H5
Ardessie St. G23 15 H1
Ardfern St. G32 39 F4
Ardgay Pl. G32 39 F3
Ardgay St. G32 39 F2
Ardgay Way. G73 50 B6
Ardgowan Av. PA2 32 A4
Ardgowan Dri. G71 53 H1
Ardgowan St. PA2 32 A4
Ardholm St. G32 39 F2
Ardhu Pl. G15 10 A5
Ardlaw St. G51 22 D6
Ardle Rd. G43 48 A4
Ardlui Gdns. G62 6 B2
Ardlui St. G32 39 E2
Ardmaleish Cres. G45 59 F1
Ardmaleish Dri. G45 59 F1
Ardmaleish Rd. G45 59 F1
Ardmaleish St. G45 59 F1
Ardmaleish Ter. G45 59 F1
Ardmay Cres. G44 49 E2
Ardmillan St. G33 27 E4
Ardmore Oval. PA3 30 D4
Ardmory Av. G42 49 F1
Ardmory La. G42 49 F2
Ardmory Pl. G42 49 F2
Ardnahoe Av. G42 49 F1
Ardnahoe Pl. G42 49 F1
Ardniel Rd. G51 22 D6
Ardnish St. G51 22 C6
Ardo Gdns. G51 35 E1
Ardoch Gro. G72 51 E3
Ardoch Rd. G61 11 H3
Ardoch St. G22 16 D6
Ards Dri. G52 34 C4
Ardshiel Rd. G51 22 C6
Ardsloy La. G14 13 G6
Ardsloy Pl. G14 13 H6
Arduthie Rd. G51 22 D6
Ardwell Rd. G52 34 C4
Argyle Arc. G1 4 D5
Argyle St. G2 4 A4
Argyle St. PA1 31 F6
Argyll Av. PA4 12 C6
Argyll Av. PA3 31 G2
Argyll Rd. G61 11 E2
Argyll Rd. G81 12 C2
Arisaig Dri. G61 11 H5
Arisaig Dri. G52 34 C3
Arisaig Pl. G52 34 C4
Arisdale Cres. G77 56 C5
Ark La. G31 25 G6
Arkle Ter. G72 51 E6
Arkleston Cres. PA3 20 C6
Arkleston Rd. PA1 20 B4
Arklet Rd. G51 22 D6
Arkwrights Way. PA1 43 E1
Arlington St. G3 4 A1
Armadale Ct. G31 26 A5
Armadale Pl. G31 26 A5
Armadale St. G31 26 A5
Armour St. G31 5 H6
Arngask Rd. G51 22 D6
Arnhall Pl. G52 34 C4
Arnhem St. G72 52 A4
Arnholm Pl. G52 34 C3
Arnisdale Pl. G34 28 D5
Arnisdale Rd. G34 28 C4
Arnisdale Way. G73 50 A5
Arniston St. G32 27 E6
Arniston Way. PA3 20 A6
Arnol Pl. G33 20 C6
Arnold Av. G64 61 C4
Arnold St. G20 16 C5
Arnott Way. G72 51 G3
Arnprior Cres. G45 49 E5
Arnprior Quad. G45 49 E5
Arnprior Rd. G45 49 E5
Arnprior St. G45 49 F5
Arnside Av. G46 47 G6
Arnwood Dri. G12 15 E6
Aron Ter. G72 51 E6
Arran Av. PA3 31 H1
Arran Dri. G46 57 F1
Arran Dri. PA2 43 G5
Arran Dri. G52 34 D4
Arran Pl. G81 9 E6
Arran Rd. PA4 20 D3
Arran Ter. G73 49 H3
Arranthrue Cres. PA4 20 C1
Arranthrue Dri. PA4 20 C1
Arriden Pl. G33 28 B5
Arrochar Dri. G23 15 H2
Arrochar St. G23 15 G2
Arrol Pl. G40 38 A3
Arrol Rd. G40 38 A3
Arrol St. G52 21 E5
Arrowsmith Av. G13 14 B3
Arthur Av. G78 55 F2
Arthur Rd. PA2 43 H5
Arthur St. G76 58 A5
Arthur St. PA1 31 F6
Arthur St. G3 23 H4
Arthurlie Av. G78 55 F2
Arthurlie Dri. G46 57 G1
Arthurlie Dri. G77 60 B2
Arthurlie St. G78 55 G1
Arthurlie St. G51 22 D6
Arundel Dri. G61 61 D1
Arundel Dri. G42 48 C2
Ascaig Cres. G52 34 C4
Ascog Rd. G61 14 D1
Ascog St. G42 36 C4
Ascot Av. G13 14 D5
Ash Gro. G64 18 A2
Ash Rd. G69 40 D3
Ash Rd. G81 8 C4
Ash Walk. G73 50 C5
Ash Wynd. G72 52 B4
Ashburn Gdns. G62 6 C3
Ashburn Rd. G62 6 C2
Ashburton La. G12 15 F5
Ashburton Rd. G12 15 E5
Ashby Cres. G13 14 C2
Ashcroft Dri. G44 49 F3
Ashdale Dri. G52 34 C4
Ashdene St. G22 16 D4
Ashfield. G64 61 C2
Ashfield Rd. G76 58 A5
Ashfield Rd. G62 6 E3
Ashfield St. G22 17 E5
Ashgill Rd. G22 16 D4
Ashgrove St. G40 38 A5
Ashkirk Dri. G52 34 C3
Ashlea Dri. G46 47 H5
Ashley St. G3 4 A1
Ashmore Rd. G43 48 B3
Ashton La. G12 23 H2
Ashton Rd. G12 23 H2
Ashton Rd. G73 37 H6
Ashton Way. PA2 42 B5
Ashtree Ct. G60 7 B2
Ashtree Gro. G77 60 B2
Ashtree Rd. G43 47 G1
Ashvale Cres. G21 17 F6
Ashwood Gdns. G13 14 D6
Aspen Dri. G21 25 H1
Aspen Pl. G72 52 B4
Aster Dri. G45 49 H6
Aster Gdns. G53 46 A6
Athelstane Rd. G13 14 A4
Athole Gdns. G12 23 G2
Atholl Av. G52 21 E4
Atholl Cres. PA1 33 E1
Atholl Dri. G46 57 G3
Atholl Gdns. G61 11 E2
Atholl Gdns. G64 61 B2
Atholl Gdns. G73 50 D5
Atlas Pl. G21 25 H1
Atlas Rd. G21 25 G1
Atlas St. G81 12 C3
Attlee Av. G81 13 E1
Attow Rd. G43 47 F4
Auburn Av. G78 55 G2
Auchenbothie Cres. G33 18 D5
Auchenbothie Pl. G33 18 D5
Auchencrow St. G34 29 F5
Auchencruive. G62 6 F4

Auchenhowie Rd. G62 6 F4
Auchentorlie Quad. PA1 32 B3
Auchentorlie St. G11 23 E3
Auchentorlie Ter. G21 25 G2
Auchentoshan Av. G81 8 C2
Auchentoshan Ter. G21 25 G2
Auchinairn Rd. G64 18 A3
Auchinden Ct. G61 10 C1
Auchingill Pl. G34 29 G3
Auchingill Rd. G34 29 F4
Auchinlea Rd. G34 28 C3
Auchinlea Av. G33 18 D4
Auchinleck Cres. G33 19 E4
Auchinleck Dri. G33 19 E4
Auchinleck Gdns. G33 18 D5
Auchinleck Rd. G81 9 E2
Auchinleck Rd. G33 19 E3
Auchinleck Ter. G81 9 E2
Auchinloch St. G21 25 H2
Auchmannoch Av. PA1 33 E2
Auchnacraig Rd. G81 9 E1
Auckland Pl. G81 7 D4
Auckland St. G22 24 C1
Auld Kirk Rd. G72 51 H5
Auld Murrach Dri. G62 6 A2
Auld St. G81 8 B6
Auldbar Rd. G52 34 D4
Auldbar Ter. PA2 32 A4
Auldburn Pl. G43 47 F3
Auldburn Rd. G43 47 F3
Auldearn Rd. G21 18 C4
Auldgirth Rd. G52 34 D4
Auldhouse Av. G43 47 F3
Auldhouse Gdns. G43 47 F3
Auldhouse Rd. G43 47 F3
Auldhouse Ter. G43 47 H3
Aultbea St. G22 16 D2
Aultmore Rd. G33 28 C6
Aurs Cres. G78 55 H2
Aurs Dri. G78 55 G3
Aurs Glen. G78 55 F3
Aurs Pl. G78 55 H2
Aurs Rd. G78 55 G1
Aursbridge Cres. G78 55 H2
Aursbridge Dri. G78 55 G1
Austen La. G13 14 C5
Austen Rd. G13 14 C5
Avenel Rd. G13 14 C1
Avenue End Rd. G33 27 G1
Avenue St. G40 38 A2
Avenue St. G73 38 B6
Avenuepark St. G20 16 A6
Aviemore Gdns. G61 11 G4
Aviemore Rd. G52 34 C4
Avoch St. G34 29 E4
Avon Av. G61 11 H5
Avon Dri. G64 17 H3
Avon Rd. G64 17 H2
Avon Rd. G46 57 F1
Avonbank Rd. G73 49 H2
Avondale Dri. PA1 32 C1
Avondale St. G33 27 F3
Avonspark St. G21 26 A1
Aylmer Rd. G43 48 B3
Ayr Rd. G77 56 C6
Ayr St. G21 25 G1
Aytoun Dri. PA8 7 A5
Aytoun Rd. G41 35 H3

Back Causeway. G31 38 D2
Back Law La. PA3 31 H5
Back Sneddon St. PA3 31 H5
Bagnell St. G21 17 G5
Baillie Dri. G61 10 D1
Baillieston Rd. G32 40 A2
Baillieston Rd. G71 41 E4
Bain St. G40 37 F1
Bainsford St. G32 39 E1
Baird Av. G52 21 F4
Baird Dri. G61 10 D4
Baird Dri. PA8 7 A5
Baird St. G81 8 C6
Baird St. G4 5 F1
Bairds Brae. G4 24 D2
Baker St. G41 36 A6
Bakewell Rd. G69 40 D1
Balaclava St. G2 4 A5
Balado Rd. G33 28 B5
Balbeg St. G51 34 D4
Balbeggie St. G32 40 A3
Balblair Rd. G52 34 D4
Balcarres Av. G12 15 F5
Balcomie St. G33 27 F4
Balcurvie Rd. G34 28 C3
Baldernock Rd. G62 6 F3
Baldinnie Rd. G34 28 D5
Baldovan Cres. G33 28 C5
Baldovie Rd. G52 34 A3
Baldragon Rd. G34 29 E4
Baldric Rd. G13 14 A4
Baldwin Av. G13 14 B3

Balerno Dri. G52 34 C4
Balfleurs St. G62 6 F3
Balfluig St. G34 28 C3
Balfour St. G20 15 H5
Balfron Rd. G51 22 C5
Balfron Rd. PA1 32 D2
Balgair Dri. PA1 32 C1
Balgair St. G22 16 D6
Balgair Ter. G32 39 G1
Balglass St. G22 16 C6
Balgonie Av. PA2 42 D3
Balgonie Dri. PA2 43 F3
Balgonie Rd. G52 34 C3
Balgonie Woods. PA2 43 F3
Balgownie Cres. G46 57 E1
Balgray Cres. G78 55 H2
Balgraybank St. G21 17 H6
Balgrayhill Rd. G21 17 G5
Balgraystone Rd. G78 55 G4
Balintore St. G32 39 F2
Baliol St. G3 4 A1
Baljaffray Rd. G61 10 A2
Ballagan Pl. G62 6 B2
Ballaig Av. G61 10 D3
Ballaig Cres. G33 19 H5
Ballantay Quad. G45 49 H6
Ballantay Rd. G45 49 H6
Ballantay Ter. G45 50 A6
Ballantine Av. G52 21 G6
Ballantrae Cres. G77 60 F1
Ballantrae Dri. G77 60 F1
Ballater Dri. G61 14 D1
Ballater Dri. PA2 32 A6
Ballater Pl. G5 37 E2
Ballater St. G5 37 E2
Ballindalloch Dri. G31 26 A5
Ballindalloch La. G31 26 A5
Balliol St. G3 24 B4
Balloch Gdns. G52 34 D3
Ballochmill Rd. G73 50 C1
Ballochmyle Cres. G53 33 G6
Ballochmyle Gdns. G53 33 G6
Ballochmyle Pl. G53 33 G6
Ballogie Rd. G44 48 D2
Balmartin Rd. G23 15 H1
Balmedie. PA8 7 B6
Balmeg Av. G46 57 G3
Balmerino Pl. G64 61 F4
Balmoral Cres. G61 51 E3
Balmoral Dri. G72 51 E3
Balmoral Dri. G32 51 G1
Balmoral St. G14 22 A1
Balmore Pl. G22 16 D5
Balmore Rd. G22 16 C2
Balmore Sq. G22 16 D5
Balmuildy Rd. G23 61 A1
Balnure St. G31 26 C6
Balornock Rd. G21 18 A5
Balruddery Pl. G64 18 C3
Balshagray Av. G11 22 D2
Balshagray Cres. G14 22 D2
Balshagray Dri. G11 22 D2
Balshagray La. G11 22 D2
Baltic Ct. G40 38 A4
Baltic La. G40 38 A4
Baltic Pl. G40 37 H2
Baltic St. G40 38 A3
Balvaird Cres. G73 50 A2
Balvaird Dri. G73 50 A2
Balveny St. G33 28 A3
Balvicar Dri. G42 36 B5
Balvicar St. G42 36 B5
Balvie Av. G15 13 G2
Balvie Av. G46 57 H1
Balvie Cres. G62 6 D2
Banavie Rd. G11 23 F2
Banchory Av. G43 47 F4
Banchory Cres. G61 11 G6
Banff St. G33 27 G2
Bangorshill St. G46 46 D5
Bank Av. G62 6 E1
Bank Rd. G32 51 H1
Bank St. G78 55 F2
Bank St. G72 51 F3
Bank St. G12 24 A2
Bank St. G78 54 B5
Bank St. PA1 32 A2
Bankbrae Av. G53 45 G3
Bankend St. G33 27 F4
Bankfoot Pl. G77 60 F1
Bankfoot Rd. G52 34 A2
Bankfoot Rd. PA3 31 E4
Bankglen Rd. G15 10 B4
Bankhall St. G42 36 D5
Bankhead. G13 13 G4
Bankhead Dri. G73 49 H2
Bankhead Rd. G73 49 G3

Bankhead Rd. G76 59 F4
Bankholm Pl. G76 58 B6
Banknock St. G32 39 E1
Bannatyne Av. G31 26 B5
Banner Dri. G13 14 A1
Banner Rd. G13 14 B1
Bannercross Av. G69 40 D1
Bannercross Dri. G69 40 D1
Bannerman Pl. G81 9 E6
Banton Pl. G33 28 D6
Barberry Av. G53 56 A1
Barberry Gdns. G53 56 A1
Barberry Pl. G53 56 A1
Barcapel Av. G77 56 C3
Barclay Ct. G60 7 B3
Barclay Sq. PA4 20 B3
Barclay St. G21 17 G6
Barclay St. G60 7 C3
Barcraigs Dri. PA2 44 A1
Bard Av. G13 13 H3
Bardowie St. G62 16 D6
Bardrain Rd. PA2 43 F6
Bardrill Dri. G64 61 A3
Bare St. G20 24 C2
Barfillan Dri. G52 34 C2
Bargany Rd. G53 33 G6
Bargaran Rd. G53 33 H4
Bargarran Rd. PA8 7 A6
Bargeddie St. G33 26 D3
Barhill Rd. PA8 7 B6
Barholm Sq. G33 28 A3
Barlanark Av. G32 27 H6
Barlanark Cres. G33 28 A6
Barlanark Pl. G33 28 B6
Barlanark Rd. G33 28 A6
Barland Ct. G46 47 G6
Barlia Dri. G45 49 F6
Barlia St. G45 49 G6
Barlia Ter. G45 49 G6
Barloch Av. G62 6 E2
Barloch Rd. G62 6 F3
Barloch St. G22 16 D6
Barlogan Av. G52 34 C2
Barlogan Quad. G52 34 C2
Barmulloch Rd. G21 26 A1
Barnbeth Rd. G53 34 A4
Barnes Rd. G20 16 C5
Barnes St. G78 55 E2
Barness Pl. G33 27 F5
Barnflat St. G73 38 B6
Barnhill Dri. G77 60 C2
Barnkirk Av. G15 10 A5
Barns St. G81 12 C2
Barnsford Rd. PA3 31 E2
Barnton St. G32 26 D5
Barnwell Ter. G51 22 D6
Barochan Cres. PA3 30 D6
Barochan Pl. G53 33 H4
Barochan Rd. G53 33 H4
Baron Rd. PA3 20 B6
Baron St. PA4 20 D3
Baronald Dri. G12 15 F5
Baronald Gate. G12 15 F5
Baronald St. G73 38 B6
Barone Dri. G76 57 G3
Barons Gate. G71 53 H4
Baronscourt Dri. PA1 42 C1
Baronscourt Gdns. PA1 42 C1
Baronscourt Rd. PA1 42 C1
Barony Ct. G69 41 E1
Barony Dri. G69 41 E1
Barony Gdns. G69 41 E1
Barony Wynd. G69 41 E1
Barr Av. G78 54 B4
Barr Cres. G81 9 E3
Barr Pl. G77 56 A6
Barr Pl. PA1 43 G1
Barra Av. PA4 20 D4
Barra Cres. G60 7 C3
Barra Gdns. G60 7 C3
Barra Rd. G60 7 C3
Barra St. G20 15 G2
Barrachnie Av. G69 40 D1
Barrachnie Cres. G69 40 C1
Barrachnie Dri. G69 40 C1
Barrachnie Gro. G69 40 D1
Barrachnie Rd. G69 40 D1
Barrachnie Rd. G69 40 C2
Barrack St. G4 5 H6
Barrhead Rd. PA2 32 A4
Barrhead Rd. G77 60 A1
Barrhead Rd. G53 45 F2
Barrie Quad. G81 8 C5
Barrie Rd. G52 21 G5
Barrington Dri. G4 24 B3
Barrisdale Rd. G20 15 H3
Barrisdale Way. G73 50 A5
Barrland Dri. G46 47 G6

Barland St. G41 36 C4
Barrmill Rd. G43 47 E4
Barrowfield St. G40 38 A2
Barrwood St. G33 26 D2
Barscube Ter. PA2 32 A4
Barshaw Dri. PA1 32 B1
Barshaw Pl. PA1 32 D1
Barshaw Rd. G52 21 F6
Barskiven Rd. PA1 30 C6
Barterholm Rd. PA2 32 A4
Barterholm St. PA2 43 H2
Bartiebeath Rd. G33 28 A5
Bartholomew St. G40 37 H4
Bassett Av. G13 14 A3
Bassett Cres. G13 14 A3
Bath La. G2 4 B3
Bath St. G2 4 B3
Bathgate St. G31 26 A6
Bathgo Av. PA1 33 E3
Batson St. G42 36 D5
Battlefield Av. G42 48 C2
Battlefield Gdns. G42 48 C1
Battlefield Rd. G42 48 B1
Bavelaw St. G33 28 A2
Bayfield Av. G15 10 A5
Bayfield Ter. G15 10 A5
Beaconsfield Rd. G12 15 F6
Beardmore Pl. G81 8 A5
Beardmore St. G81 8 A5
Beardmore Way. G81 8 A6
Bearford Dri. G52 33 H1
Bearsden Rd. G13 14 D4
Beaton Rd. G41 35 H5
Beattock St. G31 38 D2
Beatty St. G81 8 A5
Beaufort Av. G43 47 G3
Beaufort Gdns. G64 61 A4
Beauly Dri. PA2 42 C3
Beauly Pl. G64 61 F3
Beauly Pl. G20 15 H5
Beauly Rd. G69 40 C4
Beaumont Gate. G12 23 G2
Beckfield Cres. G33 18 C3
Beckfield Dri. G33 18 C3
Beckfield Gate. G33 18 C3
Beckfield Gro. G33 18 C4
Beckfield Pl. G33 18 C4
Beckfield Wk. G33 18 C4
Bedale Rd. G69 40 C3
Bedford Av. G81 13 E1
Bedford La. G5 36 D2
Bedford St. G5 36 D2
Beech Av. G69 40 D2
Beech Av. G61 11 F2
Beech Av. G41 35 F2
Beech Av. PA2 32 B5
Beech Av. G72 51 E3
Beech Av. G77 60 C1
Beech Cres. G72 52 C5
Beech Dri. G81 8 C3
Beech Gdns. G69 40 D2
Beech Pl. G64 18 A3
Beech Rd. G64 18 A3
Beeches Av. G81 8 B2
Beeches Rd. G81 8 B2
Beeches Ter. G81 8 C2
Beechgrove St. G40 38 A4
Beechlands Av. G44 58 B2
Beechlands Dri. G76 57 G4
Beechwood Av. G73 50 C3
Beechwood Av. G76 57 G5
Beechwood Ct. G61 11 F5
Beechwood Dri. G11 22 D1
Beechwood Dri. PA4 20 C3
Beechwood Gro. G78 55 G2
Beechwood La. G61 11 F5
Beechwood Pl. G11 22 D1
Beil Dri. G13 13 F4
Beith St. G11 23 E3
Belford Ct. G77 60 C3
Belgrave La. G12 24 A2
Belhaven Ter. G12 23 G1
Belhaven Ter La. G12 23 G1
Belhaven Ter W. G12 23 G1
Belhaven Ter W La.
G12 23 G1
Bell St. G1 5 F5
Bell St. PA4 20 D3
Bell St. G4 5 H6
Bell St. G81 12 D3
Bell View Ct. PA4 21 E1
Bellahouston Dri. G52 34 C4
Belleisle Av. G71 53 H2
Belleisle St. G42 36 D5
Bellfield Cres. G78 44 B5
Bellfield St. G31 25 H6
Bellflower Av. G53 46 A6

Bellflower Gdns. G53 46 A6
Bellflower Pl. G53 46 A6
Bellrock Ct. G33 27 F4
Bellrock Cres. G33 27 F4
Bellrock St. G33 27 F4
Bellscroft Av. G73 49 G1
Bellshaugh Gdns. G12 15 G6
Bellshaugh La. G12 15 G6
Bellshaugh Pl. G12 15 G6
Bellshaugh Rd. G12 15 G6
Bellshill Rd. G71 53 H4
Belltrees Cres. PA3 30 D6
Bellwood St. G41 48 A1
Belmont Av. G71 53 H2
Belmont Cres. G12 24 A2
Belmont Dri. G78 55 H3
Belmont Dri. G73 50 A2
Belmont Dri. G46 47 F6
Belmont La. G12 24 A2
Belmont Rd. G21 17 G4
Belmont Rd. G72 50 D5
Belmont Rd. PA3 20 B6
Belmont St. G12 24 A2
Belses Dri. G52 34 A2
Belses Gdns. G52 34 A1
Belsyde Av. G15 10 B6
Beltane St. G3 24 B5
Beltrees Av. G53 33 G5
Beltrees Cres. G53 33 G5
Beltrees Rd. G53 33 G5
Belvidere Cres. G64 61 C2
Bemersyde. G64 61 E3
Bemersyde Av. G43 47 F4
Bemersyde Rd. PA2 42 B5
Ben Alder Dri. PA2 32 D5
Ben Buie Way. PA2 32 D5
Ben Donich Pl. G53 46 B4
Ben Edra Pl. G53 46 B5
Ben Garisdale Pl. G53 46 B4
Ben Glas Pl. G53 46 B4
Ben Hope Av. PA2 32 D5
Ben Laga Pl. G53 46 B5
Ben Lawers Dri. PA2 32 D5
Ben Ledi Av. PA2 33 E5
Ben Lui Dri. PA2 32 D6
Ben Lui Pl. G53 46 B4
Ben Macdui Gdns. G53 46 B5
Ben More Dri. PA2 32 D5
Ben Nevis Rd. PA2 32 C6
Ben Rigan Pl. G53 46 B4
Ben Uird Pl. G53 46 B4
Ben Vane Av. PA2 32 D6
Ben Vorlich Dri. G53 46 B4
Ben Wyvis Dri. PA2 32 D6
Benalder St. G11 23 G3
Benarty Gdns. G64 61 D3
Benbow Rd. G81 8 B6
Bencroft Dri. G44 49 F4
Bengairn St. G31 26 C6
Bengal Pl. G43 47 G1
Bengal St. G43 47 G1
Benhar Pl. G33 27 E5
Benholm St. G32 39 E4
Benmore St. G21 17 G5
Bennan Sq. G42 36 D5
Benny Lynch Ct. G5 37 E2
Benthall St. G5 37 F3
Bentinck St. G3 23 H4
Bents Rd. G69 40 D1
Benvenue Way. PA2 32 D5
Benvie Gdns. G64 61 D3
Benview Rd. G76 58 A4
Benview St. G20 16 B6
Benview Ter. PA2 32 C5
Berelands Cres. G73 49 G2
Berelands Pl. G73 49 G1
Beresford Av. G14 22 C1
Berkeley St. G3 24 A4
Berkeley Ter La. G3 24 B4
Bernard St. G40 38 A3
Bernard Ter. G40 37 H2
Berneray St. G22 17 E4
Berridale Av. G44 48 C3
Berriedale Av. G69 40 D3
Berryburn Rd. G21 26 B1
Berryhill Dri. G46 57 F1
Berryhill Rd. G46 57 F2
Berryknowes Av. G52 34 B2
Berryknowes La. G52 34 B2
Berryknowes Rd. G52 34 B2
Bertram St. G41 36 A6
Bervie St. G51 22 D6
Berwick Dri. G73 50 C2
Berwick Dri. G52 34 A3
Betula Dri. G81 8 C3
Beverley Rd. G43 47 H3
Bevin Av. G81 13 E1
Bideford Rd. G32 40 A4

Biggar St. G40 38 B1
Bigton St. G33 27 G2
Bilsland Ct. G20 16 C5
Bilsland Dri. G20 16 B6
Binland Rd. G53 46 B1
Binns Rd. G33 28 A2
Birch Av. G76 58 B5
Birch Cres. G76 58 B5
Birch Dri. G72 51 H3
Birch Knowe. G64 18 A2
Birch Pl. G72 52 C4
Birch Rd. G81 8 C4
Birch St. G5 37 F3
Birch View. G61 11 G4
Birchfield Dri. G14 14 A6
Birchead Dri. G21 26 A2
Birchead Pl. G21 26 A2
Birchlea Dri. G46 47 H5
Birchview Dri. G76 58 B6
Birchwood Av. G32 40 B3
Birchwood Dri. PA2 43 E3
Birchwood Pl. G32 40 B3
Birdston Rd. G21 18 B4
Birgidale Av. G45 59 E2
Birgidale Rd. G45 59 F1
Birgidale Ter. G45 59 E1
Birkenshaw Way. PA3 31 G3
Birkhall Av. G52 33 G2
Birkhall Dri. G61 11 F6
Birkhill Av. G64 61 D2
Birkhill Gdns. G64 61 D3
Birkmyre Rd. G51 23 E6
Birkwood Pl. G77 60 C3
Birkwood St. G40 38 A5
Birmingham Rd. PA4 20 B3
Birnam Av. G64 61 D2
Birnam Gdns. G64 61 D3
Birness Dri. G43 47 G1
Birnam Cres. G61 11 H4
Birnam Pl. G77 60 F1
Birnam Rd. G31 38 D3
Birnie Ct. G21 26 B1
Birnie Rd. G21 26 B1
Birnock Av. PA4 21 F3
Birnyhill Ct. G81 8 C1
Birrell Rd. G62 6 C1
Birsay Rd. G22 16 D3
Bishop Gdns. G64 61 A3
Bishop La. G2 4 B4
Bishopmill Pl. G21 18 C6
Bishopmill Rd. G21 18 C6
Bishopsgate Rd. G21 17 G4
Bisset Cres. G81 8 B2
Black St. G4 5 G2
Blackburn Sq. G78 55 H2
Blackburn St. G51 35 H1
Blackbyres Ct. G78 45 E4
Blackbyres Rd. G78 44 C3
Blackcraig Av. G15 10 B5
Blackcroft Gdns. G32 40 A3
Blackcroft Rd. G32 40 A3
Blackfarm Rd. G77 60 E1
Blackford Cres. G32 39 H3
Blackford Rd. G32 39 H3
Blackford Rd. PA2 32 B4
Blackfriars St. G1 5 F5
Blackhall La. PA1 32 A3
Blackhall St. PA1 32 A3
Blackhill Pl. G33 26 D3
Blackhill Rd. G23 15 H1
Blackhouse Av. G77 60 E1
Blackhouse Gdns. G77 60 E1
Blackhouse Rd. G77 60 D1
Blackie St. G3 23 H4
Blackland Gro. PA4 43 F4
Blackmuir Rd. G61 10 B4
Blackstone Av. G53 34 A6
Blackstone Cres. G53 34 A6
Blackstone Rd. PA1 30 D3
Blackstoun Oval. PA3 31 E6
Blackstoun Rd. PA3 30 D4
Blackthorn St. G22 17 F5
Blackwood Av. G77 60 D2
Blackwood Rd. G62 6 C1
Blackwood St. G13 14 C4
Blackwood St. G78 55 E2
Bladda La. PA1 31 H6
Bladnock Dri. G15 14 A1
Blaeloch Av. G45 58 D2
Blaeloch Dri. G45 58 D2
Blaeloch Ter. G45 58 D2
Blair Atholl Cres. G77 60 F1
Blair Atholl Gate. G77 60 F1
Blair Ct. G81 8 D6
Blair Cres. G69 40 D3
Blair Pa. PA1 33 E1
Blair St. G32 39 E2
Blairatholl Av. G11 23 E2
Blairatholl Gdns. G11 23 E2

Blairbeth Dri. G44 48 D2
Blairbeth Rd. G73 50 A4
Blairbeth Ter. G73 50 B4
Blairdardie Rd. G13 14 A1
Blairgowrie Rd. G52 34 A2
Blairhall Av. G41 48 B1
Blairlogie St. G33 27 G3
Blairmore Av. PA1 32 D2
Blairtum Dri. G73 50 B4
Blairtummock Rd. G33 27 H4
Blairtummock Rd. G33 28 B4
Blane Dri. G62 6 F1
Blantyre Ct. PA8 7 B5
Blantyre Cres. G81 8 B2
Blantyre Farm Rd. G71 53 F4
Blantyre St. G3 23 H4
Blaven Ct. G69 41 F3
Blawart Hill St. G14 13 G6
Bleachfield. G62 6 D1
Bleasdale Ct. G81 12 B1
Blenheim Ct. PA1 31 G5
Blochairn Rd. G21 26 A3
Bluebell Gdns. G45 49 H6
Bluevale St. G31 26 A6
Blyth Pl. G33 28 B6
Blyth Rd. G33 28 B6
Blythswood Av. PA4 12 D6
Blythswood Dri. PA3 31 G4
Blythswood Av. PA4 12 D6
Blythswood Sq. G2 4 B3
Blythswood St. G2 4 B5
Bobbins Gate. PA2 43 E1
Boclair Av. G61 11 F4
Boclair Cres. G61 11 G4
Boclair Cres. G64 61 C3
Boclair Rd. G61 11 G4
Boclair Rd. G64 61 C3
Boclair St. G13 14 C3
Boden St. G40 38 A3
Bogany Ter. G45 59 G1
Bogbain Rd. G34 28 D4
Boggknowe. G71 53 G1
Boghall Rd. G71 40 D4
Boghall St. G33 27 G3
Boghead Rd. G21 17 H6
Bogleshole Rd. G72 50 D2
Bogmoor Pl. G51 22 A4
Bogmoor Rd. G51 22 A5
Bogside Rd. G65 19 F5
Bogside St. G40 38 B3
Bogton Av. G44 48 B5
Bogton Av La. G44 48 B5
Boleyn Rd. G41 36 A5
Bolivar Ter. G42 48 D1
Bolton Dri. G42 48 C1
Bon Accord Rd. G76 58 B5
Bon Accord Sq. G81 12 C3
Bonawe St. G20 24 B1
Bonhill St. G22 24 D1
Bonnar St. G40 37 H4
Bonnaughton Rd. G61 10 B2
Bonnyholm Av. G53 33 G4
Bonnyrigg Dri. G43 47 E3
Bonyton Av. G13 13 G4
Boon Dri. G15 10 B6
Boquhanran Pl. G81 8 C5
Boquhanran Rd. G81 8 C6
Borden La. G13 14 C5
Borden Rd. G13 14 C5
Boreland Dri. G13 13 H4
Boreland Pl. G13 13 H4
Borgie Cres. G72 51 G4
Borland Rd. G61 11 G5
Borron St. G4 24 D2
Borthwick St. G33 27 G3
Boswell Ct. G42 48 B1
Boswell Sq. G52 21 F6
Botanic Cres. G20 23 H1
Botanic Cres La. G20 23 H1
Bothwell La. G12 4 C4
Bothwell Pl. PA2 42 B5
Bothwell Rd. G71 53 H4
Bothwell St. G72 51 E2
Bothwell St. G2 4 B4
Bourock Sq. G78 55 H2
Bouverie St. G14 13 F6
Bouverie St. G73 49 H1
Bouverie St. G14 13 E4
Bowden Dri. G52 33 H1
Bower St. G12 24 A2
Bowerwalls St. G78 45 E5
Bowes Cres. G69 40 C3
Bowfield Av. G52 33 F1
Bowfield Cres. G52 33 F1
Bowfield Dri. G52 33 G1
Bowfield Path. G52 33 F1
Bowfield Pl. G52 33 F1
Bowling Green La. G14 22 B2
Bowling Green Rd. G32 40 A3

Bowling Green Rd. G14 22 B2
Bowling Green Vw. G72 52 C4
Bowman St. G42 36 C5
Bowmont Gdns. G12 23 G1
Bowmont Hill. G64 61 C1
Bowmont Ter. G12 23 G2
Bowmore Gdns. G73 50 D6
Bowmore Rd. G52 34 C2
Boyd St. G42 36 D5
Boydstone Pl. G46 47 E4
Boydstone Rd. G46 46 C3
Boyle St. G81 12 D2
Boylestone Rd. G78 44 B4
Boyndie Path. G34 29 E5
Boyndie St. G34 29 E5
Brabloch Cres. PA3 20 A6
Bracadale Dri. G69 41 F3
Bracadale Gdns. G69 41 F3
Bracadale Gro. G69 41 F3
Bracadale Rd. G69 41 F3
Bracken St. G22 16 D4
Brackenbrae Av. G64 61 A3
Brackenbrae Rd. G64 61 B3
*Brackenrig Rd,
  Nitshill Rd. G46 56 C1
Brackla Av. G81 13 E3
Bradan Av. G81 13 E3
Bradda Av. G73 50 C4
Bradfield Av. G12 15 G5
Braefield Dri. G46 47 E5
Braefoot Av. G62 6 E4
Braefoot Cres. PA2 43 H5
Braehead Av. G81 8 C2
Braehead Av. G62 6 C3
Braehead Rd. G78 54 B5
Braehead Cres. G81 8 D2
Braehead Quad. G78 54 B5
Braehead Rd. G81 8 C2
Braehead Rd. PA2 43 F5
Braehead St. G5 37 E4
Braemar Av. G81 8 C4
Braemar Ct. G44 48 A5
Braemar Cres. G61 11 F6
Braemar Cres. PA2 32 A6
Braemar Rd. G73 50 D6
Braemar St. G42 48 B1
Braemar View. G81 8 C4
Braemore Gdns. G22 17 F6
Braemount Av. PA2 43 F6
Braes Av. G81 12 D2
Braeside Av. G62 6 D4
Braeside Dri. G78 55 H3
Braeside Pl. G72 51 G4
Braeside St. G20 24 B1
Braeview Av. PA2 43 E5
Braeview Dri. PA2 43 E5
Braeview Gdns. PA2 43 E5
Braeview Rd. PA2 43 E5
Braid Sq. G4 24 C3
Braid St. G4 24 C3
*Braidbar Ct,
  May Ter. G46 47 G6
Braidbar Farm Rd. G46 47 H5
Braidbar Rd. G46 47 H5
Braidcraft Pl. G53 46 A1
Braidcraft Rd. G53 34 A5
Braidfauld Gdns. G32 39 E4
Braidfauld Pl. G32 39 E4
Braidfauld St. G32 39 E4
Braidfield Gro. G81 9 E4
Braidfield Rd. G81 9 E3
Braidholm Cres. G46 47 G5
Braidholm Rd. G46 47 G6
Braidpark Dri. G46 47 G6
Braids Dri. G53 33 G6
Braids Gait. PA2 43 G3
Braids Rd. PA2 43 G3
Branchock Av. G72 52 A5
Brand Pl. G51 35 G1
Brand St. G51 35 G1
Brandon Dri. G61 11 E1
Brandon Gdns. G72 51 E4
Brandon St. G31 37 H1
Brassey St. G20 16 A4
Breadalbane Gdns. G73 50 D5
Breadalbane St. G3 24 A4
Breadie Dri. G62 6 C4
Brechin Rd. G64 61 E4
Brechin St. G3 24 A4
Breck Av. PA2 42 B4
Bredaland PA2 42 B4
Bredisholm Rd. G69 41 F2
Bredisholm Ter. G69 41 F2
Brenfield Av. G44 48 B5
Brenfield Dri. G44 48 B5
Brenfield Rd. G44 48 B5
Brent Av. G46 47 E4

Brent Dri. G46 47 E4
Brent Gdns. G46 47 E4
Brent Rd. G46 47 E4
Brent Way. G6 47 E4
Brentham Av. G53 45 H5
Brentwood Dri. G53 45 H5
Brentwood Sq. G53 45 H5
Brereton St. G42 37 E5
Bressay Rd. G33 28 B6
Breval Cres. G81 8 C2
Brewster Av. PA3 20 B5
Briar Dri. G81 8 D4
Briar Gdns. G43 47 H4
Briar Gro. G43 47 H4
Briar Rd. G43 47 H4
Briarcroft Dri. G33 18 D4
Briarcroft Pl. G33 18 D4
Briarcroft Rd. G33 18 D4
Briarlea Rd. G46 47 G5
Briar Neuk. G64 61 D4
Briarneuk. G64 18 A2
Briarwell La. G62 6 F3
Briarwell Rd. G62 6 F3
Briarwood Ct. G32 40 B4
Bricht Rd. G43 47 G4
Brick La. PA3 31 H5
Bridge St. G72 51 F3
Bridge St. G81 8 B6
Bridge St. G5 36 D1
Bridge St. PA1 31 H6
Bridge Way. PA8 7 A4
Bridgegate. G1 5 E6
Brig o Lea Ter. G78 54 A5
Brigham Pl. G23 16 A2
Bright St. G21 25 G3
Brighton Pl. G51 23 F6
Brighton St. G51 23 F6
Brisbane Ct. G46 47 H5
Brisbane St. G42 48 C2
Brisbane St. G81 7 D4
Briton St. G51 23 F6
Brittania Way. PA4 20 D4
Brittania Way. G81 12 C1
Broad St. G40 37 H2
Broadford St. G4 25 E2
Broadholm St. G22 16 D5
Broadleys Av. G64 61
Broadloan. PA4 20 C3
Broadwood Dri. G44 48 C3
Brock Oval. G53 46 A2
Brock Pl. G53 46 A2
Brock Rd. G53 46 A2
Brock Ter. G53 46 A2
Brockburn Rd. G53 33 G5
Brockburn Ter. G53 46 A1
Brockville St. G32 39 E1
Brodick Sq. G64 18 B3
Brodick St. G21 25 H3
Brodie Park Av. PA2 43 G3
Brodie Park Cres. PA2 43 G2
Brodie Park Gdns. PA2 43 H2
Brodie Rd. G21 18 C4
Brook St. G40 37 H2
Brook St. G81 8 B5
Brookfield Av. G33 18 C3
Brookfield Cnr. G33 18 D4
Brookfield Dri. G33 18 D3
Brookfield Gdns. G33 18 D3
Brookfield Gate. G33 18 D3
Brookfield Pl. G33 18 D3
Brooklands Av. G71 53 H2
Brooklea Dri. G46 47 H5
Brookside St. G40 38 A2
Broom Cres. G78 44 B4
Broom Dri. G81 8 D4
Broom La. G43 47 H4
Broom Park Dri. G77 57 E5
Broom Rd. G43 47 H4
Broom Rd East. G77 60 F2
Broomburn Dri. G77 60 E1
Broomcliff. G77 60 E1
Broomcroft Rd. G77 57 E5
Broomdyke Way. PA3 31 G3
Broomfield Av. G72 50 D2
Broomfield Av. G77 60 D2
Broomfield La. G21 17 H6
Broomfield Pl. G21 17 G5
Broomfield Rd. G21 17 G5
Broomfield Rd. G46 57 G5
Broomhill Av. G11 22 D3
Broomhill Av. G77 51 G1
Broomhill Av. G77 60 E2
Broomhill Dri. G11 22 D2
Broomhill Dri. G73 50 A3
Broomhill Gdns. G11 22 D2
Broomhill Gdns. G77 60 E1

Broomhill La. G11 22 D2
Broomhill Pl. G11 22 D2
Broomhill Ter. G11 22 D2
Broomieknowe Dri.
  G73 50 A3
Broomieknowe Gdns.
  G73 50 A3
Broomielaw. G1 4 B5
Broomknowes Rd. G21 18 A6
Broomlands St. PA1 31 F6
Bromley La. G46 57 G2
Bromley La. G46 57 G2
Broomloan Ct. G51 35 E1
Broomloan Pl. G51 35 E1
Broomloan Rd. G51 35 E1
Broompark Circus. G31 25 H5
Broompark Dri. G31 25 G5
Broompark La. G31 25 H5
Broomstone Av. G77 60 E2
Broomton Rd. G21 18 B3
Broomvale Dri. G77 56 D4
Brora Dri. G61 11 G5
Brora Dri. G46 57 H1
Brora Dri. PA4 21 E2
Brora Gdns. G64 61 D4
Brora Rd. G64 61 D4
Brora St. G33 26 C4
Broughton Dri. G23 16 A2
Broughton Gdns. G23 16 A1
Broughton Rd. G23 16 A1
Brown Av. G81 13 E2
Brown Pl. G72 51 F3
Brown St. G2 4 B5
Brown St. PA1 31 F5
Brown St. PA4 20 C2
Brownhill Rd. G43 47 F4
Brownlie St. G42 48 D1
Browns La. PA1 31 H6
Brownsdale Rd. G73 49 G2
Brownside Av. G72 51 E4
Brownside Av. PA2 43 F6
Brownside Cres. G78 44 B4
Brownside Dri. G78 44 B4
Brownside Dri. G13 13 F4
Brownside Gro. G78 44 B4
Brownside Mews. G72 50 D4
Brownside Rd. G72 50 C4
Bruce Av. PA3 20 B6
Bruce Rd. PA3 20 A6
Bruce Rd. G41 36 A3
Bruce St. G81 12 B4
Brucefield Pl. G34 29 G4
Brunstane Rd. G34 28 D4
Brunswick La. G1 5 E5
Brunswick St. G1 5 E5
Brunton St. G44 48 B4
Bruntsfield Av. G53 45 H5
Bruntsfield Gdns. G53 45 H5
Bryson St. G81 9 G2
Buccleuch Av. G76 57 H4
Buccleuch Av. G52 21 E4
Buccleuch Dri. G61 11 E1
Buccleuch La. G3 4 B1
Buccleuch St. G3 4 B1
Buchan Ter. G72 51 E6
Buchanan Cres. G64 18 B3
Buchanan Dri. G64 18 B3
Buchanan Dri. . G61 11 F4
Buchanan Dri. G72 51 E3
Buchanan Dri. G77 56 C4
Buchanan Dri. G73 50 B3
Buchanan Gdns. G32 40 B4
Buchanan Gro. G69 41 E2
Buchanan St. G69 41 E2
Buchanan St. G1 4 D5
Buchanan St. G62 6 E3
Buchlyvie Gdns. G64 17 G3
Buchlyvie Path. G34 29 E5
Buchlyvie Rd. PA1 33 F1
Buchlyvie St. G34 29 E5
Buckie. PA8 7 B5
Buckingham Dri. G32 39 G6
Buckingham Dri. G73 50 C2
Buckingham Ter. G12 24 A1
Bucklaw Gdns. G52 34 B3
Bucklaw Pl. G52 34 A3
Bucklaw Ter. G52 34 A3
Buckley St. G22 17 F5
Bucksburn Rd. G21 18 C6
Buckthorne Pl. G53 46 A6
Buddon St. G40 38 B3
Budhill Av. G32 39 G1
Bull Rd. G76 58 B5
Bulldale Ct. G14 13 F5
Bulldale Rd. G14 13 F5
Bulldale St. G14 13 F5

Bullionslaw Dri. G73 50 C2
Bulloch Av. G46 57 H1
Bullwood Av. G53 33 G6
Bullwood Ct. G53 33 G6
Bullwood Dri. G53 33 G6
Bullwood Gdns. G53 33 G6
Bullwood Pl. G53 33 G6
Bunessan St. G52 34 D2
Bunhouse Rd. G3 23 G3
Burbank Highland Rd.
G62 6 D2
Burgh Hall La. G11 23 F3
Burgh La. G11 23 H2
Burghead Pl. G51 22 C5
Burgher St. G31 38 C2
Burkenshaw St. G31 26 B5
Burleigh St. G51 23 E5
Burlington Av. G12 15 F5
Burmola St. G22 16 D6
Burn Crooks Ct. G81 8 C3
Burn Ter. G72 50 D2
Burnacre Gdns. G71 53 G2
Burnawn Gdns. G33 18 D3
Burnawn Pl. G33 18 C3
Burnbank Dri. G78 55 G2
Burnbank Gdns. G20 24 B2
Burnbank Pl. G20 24 B2
Burnbank Ter. G20 24 B2
Burnbrae. G81 8 C3
Burnbrae Av. G61 11 G1
Burnbrae St. G21 26 A1
Burnbrae St. G81 9 F1
Burncleuch Av. G72 51 G5
Burncrooks Av. G61 10 D1
Burndyke Ct. G51 23 G5
Burndyke Sq. G51 23 G6
Burndyke St. G51 23 F5
Burnett Rd. G33 28 B6
Burnfield Av. G46 47 F5
Burnfield Cotts. G46 47 F5
Burnfield Dri. G43 47 F4
Burnfield Gdns. G46 47 G5
Burnfield Rd. G43 47 F4
Burnfoot Cres. PA2 43 F5
Burnfoot Cres. G73 50 C4
Burnfoot Dri. G52 33 H2
Burnham Rd. G14 13 G6
Burnhead Rd. G43 48 A4
Burnhill Quad. G73 49 H1
Burnhill St. G73 49 H1
Burnhouse St. G20 15 G4
Burnhouse St. G20 15 G4
Burnmouth Pl. G61 11 G3
Burnmouth Rd. G33 40 C1
Burnpark Av. G71 53 G1
Burns Gro. G46 57 E1
Burns St. G4 24 D2
Burns St. G81 8 A5
Burnside. G61 10 C2
Burnside Av. G78 44 C4
Burnside Ct. G81 10 C2
Burnside Cres. G81 8 D2
Burnside Gdns. G76 57 H4
Burnside Gate. G73 50 B4
Burnside Rd. PA5 42 A3
Burnside Rd. G73 50 B4
Burnside Rd. G46 57 E1
Burnside Wk. G61 10 D2
Burntbroom Dri. G69 40 C4
Burntbroom Gdns. G69 40 C4
Burntbroom Rd. G69 40 D4
Burntbroom St. G33 28 A5
Burra Gdns. G64 61 F2
Burrell Ct. G41 35 G5
Burrell's La. G4 5 G3
Burrelton Rd. G43 48 B3
Burton La. G42 36 C6
Busby Rd,
Carmunnock. G76 58 D5
Busby Rd,
Clarkston. G76 58 A3
Bushes Av. PA2 43 F3
Busheyhill St. G72 51 F3
Bute Av. PA4 20 D3
Bute Cres. G60 7 D3
Bute Cres. G61 14 D1
Bute Cres. PA2 43 G5
Bute Dri. G61 7 D3
Bute Gdns. G12 23 H2
Bute Gdns. G44 48 B5
Bute La. PA3 31 E4
Bute La. G12 23 H2
Bute Rd. PA3 31 F2
Bute Ter. G71 53 G1
Butterbiggins Rd. G42 36 C4
Butterfield Pl. G41 36 B4
Byrebush Rd. G53 34 A5
Byres Av. PA3 32 A1
Byres Cres. PA3 32 A1

Byres Rd. PA5 42 A2
Byres Rd. G11 23 G3
Byron St. G81 8 C4
Byron St. G11 22 D3
Byshot St. G22 25 F1

Cable Depot Rd. G81 12 A1
Cadder Pl. G20 16 A4
Cadder Rd. G64 61 D1
Cadder Rd. G20 16 A3
Cadoc St. G72 51 G4
Cadogan St. G2 4 B4
Cadrow St. G2 4 B4
Cadzow Av. G46 57 F3
Cadzow Dri. G72 51 F4
Caird Dri. G11 23 F2
Caird Ter. G61 10 D1
Cairn Av. PA4 21 E4
Cairn St. G21 17 G4
Cairnban St. G51 22 B6
Cairnbrook Rd. G34 29 E4
Cairncraig St. G40 38 B3
Cairndow Av. G44 48 B5
Cairndow Ct. G44 48 B5
Cairngorm Cres. G78 55 F3
Cairngorm Cres. G61 10 B2
Cairngorm Cres. PA2 43 G4
Cairngorm Rd. G443 47 G4
Cairnhill Circus. G52 33 F4
Cairnhill Dri. G52 33 G3
Cairnhill Pl. G52 33 F3
Cairnhill Rd. G61 14 D1
Cairnlea Dri. G51 35 F1
Cairnlea Rd. G62 6 B3
Cairns Av. G72 51 G4
Cairns Dri. G62 6 E2
Cairns Rd. G72 51 G4
Cairnsmore Dri. G61 10 B1
Cairnsmore Rd. G15 9 H6
Cairnswell Av. G72 51 H5
Cairnswell Pl. G72 51 H5
Cairntoul Dri. G14 13 G5
Cairntoul Pl. G14 13 G5
Caithness St. G4 24 D2
Caithness St. G20 16 B6
Calcots Path. G34 29 F4
Calcots Pl. G34 29 F4
Caldarvan St. G22 24 C1
Calder Av. G78 55 G3
Calder Dri. G72 51 F4
Calder Gate. G64 61 B1
Calder Pl. G69 41 E3
Calder Rd. PA4 30 D6
Calder Rd. G72 53 E4
Calder St. G42 36 C4
Calderbank View. G69 41 E3
Calderbraes Av. G71 41 G6
Caldercuilt Rd. G20 15 G3
Calderpark Av. G71 41 E4
Calderpark Cres. G71 41 E4
Calderwood Av. G69 40 D4
Calderwood Dri. G69 40 D3
Calderwood Gdns. G69 40 D4
Calderwood Rd. G43 47 H3
Calderwood Rd. G73 50 B2
Caldwell Av. G13 13 G4
Caledon La. G12 23 G2
Caledon St. G12 23 G2
Caledonia Av. G5 37 E4
Caledonia Av. G73 50 B1
Caledonia Ct. PA3 31 G4
Caledonia Dri. G69 41 E3
Caledonia Rd. G69 40 D4
Caledonia Rd. G5 37 E3
Caledonia St. G81 8 B6
Caledonia St. PA3 31 G4
Caledonia St. G5 37 E4
Caledonia Way. PA3 31 G2
Caledonia Way East.
PA3 31 G2
Caledonia Way West.
PA3 31 G2
Caley Brae. G71 53 H3
Calfhill Rd. G53 33 H4
Calgary St. G4 5 E2
Callander St. G20 24 C2
Callieburn Rd. G64 18 A2
Cally Av. G15 10 A5
Calside. PA2 43 G2
Calside Av. PA2 43 G2
Calvay Cres. G33 28 A6
Calvay Pl. G33 28 B6
Calvay Rd. G33 28 A6
Cambridge Av. G81 9 E6
Cambridge Rd. PA1 20 D2
Cambridge St. G4 4 C2
Camburn St. G32 39 E1
Cambus Pl. G33 27 H3
Cambusdoon Rd. G33 27 H3
Cambuskenneth Gdns.
G32 40 A2

Cambuskenneth Pl.
G33 27 H2
Cambuslang Rd. G72 51 E1
Cambuslang Rd. G72 50 D2
Cambusmore Pl. G33 27 H3
Camden Ter. G5 37 E3
Camelon St. G32 39 E1
Cameron Ct. G81 12 C2
Cameron Cres. G76 59 F3
Cameron Dri. G61 11 G5
Cameron Dri. G77 56 C4
Cameron Sq. G81 9 E2
Cameron St. G52 21 F5
Cameron St. G81 12 C3
Camlachie St. G31 38 A1
Camp Rd. G69 40 D2
Camp Rd. G5 37 G5
Campbell Av. G62 6 D3
Campbell Dri. G78 55 G2
Campbell Dri. G61 10 D3
Campbell Dri. G77 56 C4
Campbell St. G20 15 H4
Campbell St. PA4 13 E6
Camphill. PA1 43 G1
Camphill Av. G41 48 A1
Camphill Ho (flats).
G41 36 A6
Camps Cres. PA4 21 E3
Campsie Av. G78 55 F3
Campsie Dri. G61 10 D1
Campsie Dri. G62 6 F2
Campsie Dri. PA4 20 B4
Campsie Dri. PA3 31 H1
Campsie Dri. PA2 43 G4
Campsie Gdns. G76 57 G3
Campsie Pl. G33 27 G3
Campsie St. G21 17 H6
Campsie Vw. G72 52 B6
Campston Pl. G33 27 G3
Camstradden Dri East.
G61 10 D4
Camstradden Dri West.
G61 10 C4
Camus Pl. G15 10 A4
Canal Gdns. PA5 42 A1
Canal St. PA5 42 A1
Canal St. G4 5 E1
Canal St. PA1 43 F1
Canal St. PA4 21 E1
Canal Ter. PA1 43 G1
Canberra Av. G81 7 D4
Canberra Ct. G46 48 A6
Cander Rigg. G64 61 C1
Candleriggs. G1 5 E5
Candren Rd. PA3 30 A5
Candren Rd. PA3 30 D5
Candren Way. PA3 30 D5
Canmore Pl. G31 38 C3
Canmore St. G31 38 C3
Cannich Dri. PA2 32 B6
Canniesburn Rd. G61 10 C6
Canonbie St. G34 29 G4
Canting Way. G51 23 G6
Capel Av. G77 56 D5
Capelrig Dri. G77 56 C3
Capelrig La. G77 56 C5
Capelrig Rd. G46 46 D5
Capelrig Rd. G77 56 B3
Caplaw Rd. PA2 43 F6
Caplethill Rd. PA2 43 H5
Caprington St. G33 27 F4
Cara Dri. G51 22 C5
Caravelle Way. PA4 20 D4
Carberry Rd. G41 35 H5
Carbeth Rd. G62 6 C3
Carbeth St. G22 16 D6
Carbisdale St. G22 17 F5
Carbost St. G23 15 H1
Carbrook St. PA1 31 F6
Carbrook St. G21 25 H4
Cardarrach St. G21 18 A6
Cardell Av. PA2 42 D2
Cardell Dri. PA2 42 D2
Cardell Rd. PA2 42 D2
Cardonald Dri. G52 33 H3
Cardonald Gdns. G52 33 H3
Cardonald Pl Rd. G52 33 H3
Cardow Rd. G21 26 C1
Cardowan St. G32 27 E6
Cardrona St. G33 27 G2
Cardross Ct. G31 25 H6
Cardross St. G31 25 H6
Cardwell St. G5 36 C3
Cardyke St. G21 26 A1
Careston Pl. G64 61 F3
Carfin St. G42 36 D5
Carfrae St. G3 23 G4
Cargill Sq. G64 18 B3
Cargill St. G31 38 D3
Carham Cres. G52 34 B1
Carham Dri. G52 34 A2

Carillon Rd. G51 35 F2
Carinthia Sq. G81 12 C1
Carisbrooke Cres. G64 61 C1
Carlaverock Rd. G43 48 A3
Carleith Av. G81 8 B2
Carleith Quad. G51 22 B5
Carleith Ter. G81 8 B2
Carleston St. G21 17 G6
Carleton Ct. G46 47 G4
Carleton Dri. G46 47 G4
Carleton Gate. G46 47 G4
Carlibar Av. G13 13 F4
Carlibar Dri. G78 44 D6
Carlibar Gdns. G78 44 D6
Carlibar Rd. G78 44 C6
Carlisle St. G21 25 F1
Carlock Walk. G32 39 H1
Carlton Ct. G5 4 C6
Carlton Pl. G5 4 C6
Carlyle Av. G52 21 F5
Carlyle Ter. G73 38 B6
Carmaben Rd. G33 28 B4
Carment Dri. G41 47 H1
Carmichael Pl. G42 48 B2
Carmichael St. G51 35 F1
Carmunnock By-Pass.
G76 58 D3
Carmunnock Rd,
Busby. G76 58 C6
Carmunnock Rd,
Carmunnock. G76 59 E2
Carmunnock Rd,
Cathcart. G44 48 D2
Carmyle Av. G32 39 G4
Carna Dri. G44 48 D4
Carnarvon St. G3 4 A1
Carnegie Rd. G52 21 G6
Carnoch St. G23 15 H1
Carnock Cres. G78 55 F2
Carnock Gdns. G62 6 B2
Carnock Rd. G53 46 B1
Carnoustie Cres. G64 61 E4
Carnoustie St. G5 36 B2
Carntyne Pl. G32 26 D6
Carntyne Rd. G32 26 C6
Carntynehall Rd. G32 27 E5
Carnwadric Rd. G46 46 C4
Carnwath Av. G43 48 B2
Caroline St. G31 38 D2
Carolside Av. G76 58 A4
Carolside Dri. G15 10 B5
Carradale Gdns. G64 61 E4
Carrbridge Dri. G20 15 H5
Carriagehill Dri. PA2 43 H3
Carriagehill Dri. PA2 43 H3
Carrick Cres. G46 57 G2
Carrick Dri. G33 40 B2
Carrick Dri. G73 49 H4
Carrick Gro. G32 40 B3
Carrick Rd. G64 61 E4
Carrick Rd. G73 49 H4
Carrick St. G2 4 B5
Carrickarden Rd. G61 11 E5
Carrington St. G4 24 B3
Carroglen Gdns. G32 40 A2
Carroglen Gro. G32 40 A2
Carron Cres. G61 10 C6
Carron Cres. G64 61 D4
Carron Cres. G22 17 F5
Carron Cres. G22 17 F5
Carron St. G22 17 G5
Carron Way. PA3 20 B5
Carrour Rd. G64 61 B3
Carsaig Dri. G52 34 C2
Carse View Dri. G61 11 G2
Carsegreen Av. PA2 43 E6
Carstairs St. G40 37 H4
Carswell Gdns. G41 36 A5
Cart La. PA3 31 H5
Cart St. G81 12 C3
Cartbank Gdns. G44 48 C4
Cartbank Gro. G44 48 B4
Cartbank Rd. G44 48 B4
Cartcraigs Rd. G43 47 F2
Cartha St. G41 48 A2
Cartsbridge Rd. G76 58 A5
Cartside Av. G73 58 B6
Cartside Dri. G76 58 B6
Cartside Pl. G76 58 B6
Cartside Quad. G42 48 C2
Cartside Rd. G76 58 B6
Cartside St. G42 48 B2
Cartvale La. PA3 31 H4
Cartvale Rd. G42 48 B2
Cartview Ct. G76 58 B6
Cassiltoon Gdns. G45 59 F1
Cassley Av. PA4 21 F3
Castle Av. G71 53 G5
Castle Chimmins Av.
G72 52 A5

Castle Chimmins Rd.
G72 52 A6
Castle Gait. PA1 43 G1
Castle Gdns. PA2 42 D1
Castle Gate. G77 60 E2
Castle Gate. G71 53 G4
Castle Mains Rd. G62 6 B2
Castle Pl. G71 53 G3
Castle Rd. G77 60 A1
Castle Sq. G81 8 A5
Castle St. G11 23 G3
Castle St. G69 40 C4
Castle St. G81 8 A5
Castle St. G4 5 G3
Castle St. PA1 31 F6
Castle St. G73 50 A1
Castlebank Ct. G13 14 C4
Castlebank Cres. G11 23 E4
Castlebank Gdns. G13 14 C4
Castlebank St. G11 23 E4
Castlebank Villas. G13 14 C4
Castlebay Dri. G22 17 E2
Castlebay Pl. G22 17 E2
Castlebay St. G22 16 D2
Castlecroft Gdns. G71 53 H4
Castlefern Rd. G73 50 A5
Castlehill Cres. PA4 13 E6
Castlehill Dri. G77 60 E2
Castlehill Rd. G61 10 B2
Castlelaw Gdns. G32 39 G1
Castlelaw St. G32 39 G1
Castlemilk Arc. G45 49 F6
Castlemilk Cres. G44 49 G3
Castlemilk Dri. G45 59 F1
Castlemilk Rd. G44 49 F2
Castlemilk Ter. G45 59 F1
Castlemount Av. G77 60 E2
Castleton Av. G64 17 G3
Castleton Av. G77 60 E2
Castleton Cres. G77 60 D2
Castleton Dri. G77 60 D2
Castleton Gro. G77 60 E2
Castleview Av. PA2 42 D5
Castleview Dri. PA2 42 D5
Castleview Pl. PA2 42 D5
Cathay St. G22 17 E2
Cathcart Cres. PA2 32 B4
Cathcart La. G73 49 G1
Cathcart Pl. G73 49 H2
Cathcart Rd. G73 49 G2
Cathcart Rd. G42 36 D4
Cathedral Sq. G4 5 G4
Cathedral St. G4 5 E3
Cathkin Av. G72 50 D3
Cathkin Av. G73 50 B2
Cathkin By-Pass. G73 50 C6
Cathkin Dri. G76 57 G3
Cathkin Gdns. G71 41 G6
Cathkin Pl. G72 50 D3
Cathkin Rd. G71 41 G6
Cathkin Rd. G42 48 B2
Cathkin Vw. G32 39 G6
Cathkinview Pl. G42 48 C2
Cathkinview Rd. G42 48 C1
Catrine Av. G81 9 F6
Catrine Ct. G53 45 G1
Catrine Pl. G53 45 G1
Catrine Rd. G53 45 G1
Catter Gdns. G62 6 B2
Cauldstream Pl. G62 6 B3
Causewayside Cres.
G32 39 F4
Causewayside St. G32 39 F5
Causeyside St. PA1 31 H6
Cavendish Dri. G77 56 D5
Cavendish Pl. G5 36 D3
Cavendish St. G5 36 C3
Cavin Dri. G45 49 G5
Cavin Rd. G45 49 G5
Cayton Gdns. G69 40 C3
Cecil St. G12 23 H2
Cecil St. G76 58 A4
Cedar Av. G81 8 A4
Cedar Ct. G20 24 C2
Cedar Ct. G72 52 B4
Cedar Gdns. G73 50 B5
Cedar Pl. G78 55 G3
Cedar Rd. G64 18 B2
Cedar St. G20 24 C2
Cedar Walk. G64 18 B2
Cedarwood Av. G77 60 D1
Cemetery Rd. G52 34 B2
Centenary Ct. G81 12 B2
Central Av. G32 40 A3
Central Av. G72 51 E3
Central Av. G81 8 C6
Central Av. G11 22 D2
Central Gate. G72 51 E3

Central Gro. G32 40 B3
Central Path. G32 40 B2
Central Rd. PA1 31 H5
Centre St. G5 4 C6
Centre Way. G78 55 F1
Ceres Gdns. G64 61 F4
Cessnock Rd. G33 19 G6
Cessnock St. G51 35 G1
Chalmers Ct. G71 53 H3
Chalmers St. G40 37 G1
Chalmers St. G81 12 C2
Chamberlain La. G13 14 C5
Chamberlain Rd. G13 14 C5
Chancellor St. G11 23 F3
Chapel Pl. G78 54 B5
Chapel Rd. G81 8 C2
Chapel St. G20 16 A5
Chapel St. G73 49 H1
Chapelhill Rd. PA2 32 A5
Chapelton Av. G61 11 F5
Chapelton Gdns. G61 11 F4
Chapelton St. G22 16 D4
Chaplet Av. G13 14 A2
*Chapman St,
  Allison St. G42 36 C5
Chappell St. G81 55 F1
Charing Cross La. G3 4 A2
Charles Av. PA4 21 E1
Charles St. G21 25 G3
*Charlotte La Sth,
  London Rd. G1 5 F6
*Charlotte La West,
  London Rd. G1 5 F6
Charlotte Pl. PA2 43 G2
Charlotte St. G1 5 F6
Chatelherault Av. G72 50 D4
Chatton St. G23 15 G2
Cheapside St. G3 4 A5
Chelmsford Dri. G12 15 F5
Cherry Cres. G81 8 C4
Cherry Pl. G64 18 A2
Cherry Tree Dri. G72 52 B4
Cherrybank Rd. G43 48 B3
Chester St. G32 39 F2
Chesterfield Av. G12 15 E5
Chesters Rd. G61 10 C4
Chestnut Dri. G81 8 C3
Chestnut La. G62 6 B3
Chestnut St. G22 17 E5
Chestnut Way. G72 52 B5
Cheviot Av. G78 55 F2
Cheviot Dri. G77 60 A2
Cheviot Gdns. G61 10 D1
Cheviot Rd. PA2 43 G4
Cheviot Rd. G43 47 G4
Chirmorie Pl. G53 33 G6
Chirnside Pl. G52 33 H1
Chirnside Rd. G52 21 G6
Chisholm Dri. G77 56 C5
Chisholm St. G1 5 F6
Christian St. G43 47 G1
Christie La. PA3 31 H5
Christie Pl. G72 51 G3
Christie St. PA1 32 A2
Church Av. G73 50 B4
Church Hill. PA1 31 G6
Church Pl. G60 7 B2
Church Rd. G76 58 B5
Church Rd. G46 57 G1
Church St. G81 8 D5
Church St. G69 41 E2
Church St. G11 23 G3
Church St. G71 53 H3
Church View. G72 51 F2
Churchill Dri. G11 23 E1
Churchill Way. G64 61 B3
Circus Dri. G31 25 H5
Circus Pl. G31 25 H5
Cityford Cres. G73 49 G2
Cityford Dri. G73 49 G2
Civic St. G20 24 D3
Clachan Dri. G51 22 C4
Claddens Quad. G22 16 D5
Claddens St. G22 16 D4
Clair Rd. G64 61 E3
Clairinch Gdns. PA4 20 C4
Clare St. G21 25 H3
Claremont Dri. G62 6 D3
Claremont Gdns. G3 24 B4
Claremont Gdns. G62 6 D3
Claremont St. G3 24 A4
Claremont Ter. G3 24 B4
Claremont Ter La. G3 24 B4
Claremount Av. G46 57 G1
Clarence Dri. PA1 32 B2
Clarence Gdns. G11 23 E1
Clarence La. G12 23 F2
Clarence St. G81 9 E5
Clarence St. PA1 32 B2

Clarendon Pl. G20 24 C3
Clarendon St. G20 24 C3
Clarion Cres. G13 13 H3
Clarion Rd. G13 13 H3
Clark Pl. G77 60 A1
Clark St. G81 8 B4
Clark St. PA3 31 F4
Clark St. PA4 20 C2
Clarkston Av. G44 48 B5
Clarkston Rd. G44 48 B5
Claud Rd. PA3 32 B1
Claude Av. G72 52 B5
Clavens Rd. G52 21 F6
Claverhouse Pl. PA2 32 B4
Claverhouse Rd. G52 21 G6
Clavering St East. PA1 31 F6
Clavering St West. PA1 31 F6
Claypotts Pl. G33 27 F3
Claypotts Rd. G33 27 F3
*Clayslaps Rd,
  Dumbarton Rd. G11 23 H4
Claythorn Av. G40 37 F1
Claythorn Park. G40 37 F1
Claythorn St. G40 5 H6
Claythorn Ter. G40 37 G1
Clayton Ter. G31 25 H5
Cleddans Cres. G81 9 E3
Cleddans Rd. G81 9 E3
Cleddans View. G81 9 E5
Cleddens Ct. G64 61 C3
Cleeves Pl. G53 45 H3
Cleeves Quad. G53 45 G4
Cleeves Rd. G53 45 G4
Cleish Av. G61 10 C1
Cleland La. G5 36 D2
Cleland St. G5 36 D2
Clelland Av. G64 17 H3
Clerwood St. G32 26 C6
Cleuch Gdns. G76 57 H3
Cleveden Cres. G12 15 F6
Cleveden Cres La. G12 15 F6
Cleveden Dri. G12 15 F6
Cleveden Dri. G73 50 C3
Cleveden Gdns. G12 15 G6
Cleveden La. G12 15 F4
Cleveden Pl. G12 15 F4
Cleveden Rd. G12 15 F4
Cleveland La. G3 4 A3
Cleveland St. G3 4 A3
Cliff Rd. G3 24 B3
Clifford Gdns. G51 35 F2
Clifford La. G51 35 G1
Clifford Pl. G51 35 F2
Clifford St. G51 35 F2
Clifton Rd. G46 47 F5
Clifton St. G3 24 A4
Clifton Ter. G72 50 D5
Clincart Rd. G42 48 C1
Clincarthill Rd. G73 50 A2
Cloan Av. G15 10 B6
Cloan Cres. G64 61 D1
Clober Farm La. G62 6 C2
Clober Rd. G62 6 D1
Cloberfield. G62 6 D1
Cloberfield Gdns. G62 6 D1
Cloch St. G33 27 F4
Clochbar Av. G62 6 D2
Clochbar Gdns. G62 6 D2
Clonbeith St. G33 28 B3
Closeburn St. G22 16 D6
Cloth St. G78 55 F2
Clouston La. G20 24 A1
Clouston St. G20 15 H6
Clova St. G46 47 E5
Cloverbank St. G21 26 A4
Clovergate. G64 61 A4
Clunie Rd. G52 34 C3
Cluny Av. G61 11 G6
Cluny Av. G81 9 E1
Cluny Dri. G61 11 G6
Cluny Dri. PA3 20 B6
Cluny Dri. G77 56 A6
Cluny Gdns. G69 40 D3
Clutha St. G51 35 H1
Clyde Av. G78 55 G3
Clyde Holm Ter. G81 13 E4
Clyde Pl. G72 52 A5
Clyde Pl. G5 4 B6
Clyde Rd. PA3 20 C5
Clyde St. G1 4 C6
Clyde St. PA4 13 E5
Clyde St. G81 12 C3
Clyde Tunnel. G51 22 C4
Clyde View. G71 52 C5
Clyde Way. PA3 20 C5
Clydebrae St. G51 23 F5
Clydeford Dri. G32 38 D3
Clydeford Dri. G71 53 G2
Clydeford Rd. G72 51 G1
Clydeholm Rd. G14 22 B3

Clydeneuk Dri. G71 53 G2
Clydesdale Av. PA3 20 A4
Clydeside Expressway.
  G14 22 B1
Clydeside Rd. G5 37 G5
Clydesmill Dri. G32 51 F2
Clydesmill Gro. G32 51 F2
Clydesmill Pl. G32 51 F1
Clydesmill Rd. G32 51 F1
Clydeview Ter. G32 39 H6
Clynder St. G51 23 F6
Clyth Dri. G46 57 H1
Coalhill St. G31 38 B1
Coatbridge Rd. G69 41 F2
Coats Cres. G69 40 D2
Coats Dri. PA2 43 E1
Cobblerigg Way. G71 53 G3
Cobden Rd. G21 25 G2
Cobington Pl. G33 27 G3
Cobinshaw St. G32 39 F1
Coburg St. G5 36 D1
Cochno Rd. G81 8 D1
Cochno St. G81 12 C2
Cochran St. PA1 32 A3
Cochrane St. G78 55 F1
Cochrane St. G1 5 E4
Cockels Loan. PA4 20 C4
Cockenzie St. G32 39 F1
Cockmuir St. G21 17 H6
Cogan Pl. G78 55 E1
Cogan Rd. G43 47 G2
Cogan St. G78 55 E1
Cogan St. G43 47 G2
Colbert St. G40 37 G3
Colbreggan Ct. G81 9 E2
Colbreggan Gdns. G81 9 E2
Colchester Dri. G12 15 E4
Coldingham Av. G14 13 H4
Coldstream Dri. G73 50 C2
Coldstream Dri. PA2 42 D4
Coldstream Rd. G81 12 C1
Colebrooke Pl. G12 24 A2
Colebrook St. G72 51 G3
Colebrooke St. G12 24 A2
Colfin St. G34 29 F4
Colgrain St. G20 16 B5
Colgrave Cres. G32 39 E4
Colinbar Circle. G78 55 E3
Colinslee Av. G53 46 A1
Colinslee Cres. PA2 32 A6
Colinslee Dri. PA2 32 A5
Colintraive Av. G33 27 E1
Colintraive Cres. G33 27 E1
Coll Pl. G21 26 B2
Coll St. G21 26 A3
Colla Gdns. G64 61 F3
College Gate. G61 10 C2
College La. G1 5 F4
College La. PA1 31 G6
College St. G1 5 F4
Collessie Dri. G33 27 H2
Collina St. G20 15 G4
Collins St. G81 9 E2
Collins St. G4 5 G4
Collinton Pl. G32 27 G6
Collylinn Rd. G61 11 E4
Colmonell Av. G13 13 F4
Colonsay Av. PA4 20 D4
Colonsay Rd. G52 34 C2
Colonsay Rd. G77 56 A6
Colquhoun Av. G52 21 G6
Colquhoun Dri. G61 10 D3
Colquhoun Rd. G52 21 G5
Colston Av. G64 17 G4
Colston Dri. G64 17 G3
Colston Gdns. G64 17 G3
Colston Path. G64 17 G3
Colston Pl. G64 17 G3
Colston Rd. G64 17 F3
Coltmuir Cres. G64 17 E2
Coltmuir Dri. G64 17 G2
Coltmuir Gdns. G64 17 F2
Coltmuir St. G22 16 D4
Coltness St. G33 27 H5
Coltpark Av. G64 17 G3
Coltpark La. G64 17 G3
Coltsfoot Dri. G53 46 A6
Columba St. G51 23 F6
Colvend Dri. G73 50 A6
Colvend St. G40 37 H4
Colville Dri. G73 50 C3
Colwood Av. G53 45 G5
Colwood Gdns. G53 45 G5
Colwood Pl. G53 45 G6
Colwood Sq. G53 45 G5
Comelypark St. G31 37 H1
Commerce St. G5 4 C6
Commercial Ct. G5 37 E2
Commercial Rd. G78 44 D6

Commercial Rd. G5 37 E2
Commonhead Rd. G34 29 G5
Commore Av. G78 55 H2
Commore Dri. G13 13 G3
Commore Pl. G78 54 A6
Comrie Rd. G33 19 H6
Comrie St. G32 39 G3
Cona St. G46 46 C4
Congress Rd. G51 23 H6
Congress Way. G51 24 A5
*Conisborough Pth,
  Conisborough Rd. G34 28 C3
Conisborough Rd. G34 28 C3
Coniston Cres. G69 40 C3
Connal St. G40 38 A4
Connel Cres. G62 6 F3
Conniston St. G32 27 E5
Connor Rd. G78 55 E1
Conon Av. G61 10 C5
Conquhorn St. G41 35 G3
Consett La. G32 27 H5
Consett St. G32 27 H5
Contin Pl. G20 15 H5
Conval Way. PA3 31 G3
Cook St. G5 36 C2
Cooperage Ct. G81 13 E4
Cooperage Pl. G3 23 G4
Coopers Well St. G11 23 G3
Copland Pl. G51 23 F6
Copland Quad. G51 23 F6
Copland Rd. G51 23 F6
Corbett Ct. G32 39 F4
Corbett St. G32 39 F4
Corbie Pl. G62 6 B3
Cordiner St. G44 48 D2
Corkerhill Gdns. G52 34 C3
Corkerhill Pl. G52 34 C5
Corkerhill Rd. G52 34 B6
Corlaich Av. G42 49 G1
Corlaich Dri. G42 49 G2
Corn St. G20 24 D3
Cornaig Rd. G53 45 H1
Cornalee Gdns. G53 45 H1
Cornalee Rd. G53 45 H1
Cornhill St. G21 17 H5
Cornock Cres. G81 8 D5
Cornock St. G81 8 D5
Cornwall Av. G73 50 D4
Cornwall St. G41 35 H2
Coronation Way. G61 11 F6
Corpach Pl. G34 29 F1
Corran Av. G77 56 B5
Corran St. G33 27 F5
Correen Gdns. G61 10 B1
Corrie Dri. PA1 33 E2
Corrie Gro. G44 48 B5
Corrour Rd. G77 56 A5
Corrour Rd. G43 48 A2
Corse Rd. G52 33 E1
Corsebar Cres. PA2 43 E3
Corsebar Dri. PA2 43 F3
Corsebar Rd. PA2 43 E3
Corsebar Way. PA2 43 F1
Corsehill Pl. G34 29 F5
Corsehill St. G34 29 F5
Corselet Rd. G53 45 H6
Corseford Av. G53 46 A3
Corsock St. G31 36 B6
Corston St. G33 26 C5
Cortachy Pl. G64 61 F4
Coruisk Dri. G76 57 H3
Corunna St. G3 24 A4
Coshneuk Rd. G33 19 G6
Cottar St. G20 15 H3
Cotton St. G40 37 H5
Cotton St. PA1 31 H6
Coulin Gdns. G22 17 F4
County Av. G72 50 D2
County Pl. PA1 31 H5
County Sq. PA1 31 H5
Couper Pl. G4 5 F2
Couper St. G4 5 F2
Courthill. G61 10 D2
Courthill Av. G44 48 D4
Coustonholm Rd. G43 47 H1
Coventry Dri. G31 26 A4
Cowal Dri. PA3 20 A6
Cowal Rd. G20 15 G4
Cowal St. G20 15 G4
Cowan Cres. G78 55 H3
Cowan La. G12 24 B1
Cowan St. G12 24 B1
Cowcaddens Rd. G4 4 C2
Cowcaddens St. G4 4 C2
Cowden Dri. G64 61 C2
Cowden St. G51 33 H1
Cowdenhill Circus. G13 14 B2
Cowdenhill Pl. G13 14 B2
Cowdenhill Rd. G13 14 B3

Cowday Cres. PA4 21 E2
Cowglen Rd. G53 46 A2
Cowlair Way. PA4 20 D3
Cowlairs Rd. G21 25 F1
Coxhill St. G21 25 E2
Coxton Pl. G33 28 A4
Coylton Rd. G43 48 A4
Craggan Dri. G14 13 G5
Crags Av. PA2 32 A5
Crags Cres. PA2 32 A5
Crags Rd. PA2 32 A6
Cragwell Park. G76 59 F4
Craig Gdns. G77 56 A6
Craig Rd. G44 48 C4
Craig Rd. G78 54 B6
Craigallian Av. G72 52 A5
Craigallian Av. G62 6 D1
Craiganoue St. G43 47 G3
Craigash Quad. G62 6 C2
Craigash Rd. G62 6 C2
Craigbank Dri. G53 45 G3
Craigbanzo St. G81 9 F1
Craigbarnet Cres. G33 19 G6
Craigbarnet Rd. G62 6 B3
Craigbo Av. G23 15 H2
Craigbo Ct. G23 15 H2
Craigbo Dri. G23 15 H2
Craigbo Pl. G23 15 H2
Craigbo Rd. G23 15 H2
Craigbo St. G23 15 H2
Craigbog Av. PA2 31 F5
Craigdhu Av. G62 6 C3
Craigdhu Rd. G62 6 B4
Craigellen Rd. G43 47 H3
Craigenbay St. G21 26 A1
Craigencart Ct. G81 8 C3
Craigend Cres. G62 6 C2
Craigend Dri West. G62 6 C2
Craigend Pl. G13 14 C4
Craigend St. G13 14 C4
Craigendmuir St. G33 26 C3
Craigendon Oval. PA2 43 F6
Craigendon Rd. PA2 43 F6
Craigfaulds Av. PA2 43 E3
Craigflower Gdns. G53 45 G5
Craigflower Rd. G53 45 G5
Craighall St. G4 24 D2
Craighaw St. G81 9 F1
Craighead Av. G33 26 C2
Craighead Dri. G62 6 A2
Craighead Way. G78 55 F2
Craighill Dri. G76 57 H5
Craighill Gro. G76 57 H5
Craighirst Rd. G62 6 A2
Craighouse St. G33 27 F4
Craighurst Dri. G81 8 C1
Craigie Dri. G77 60 D2
Craigie St. G42 36 C5
Craigiebar Dri. PA2 43 F5
Craigieburn Gdns. G20 15 F3
Craigiehall Pl. G51 35 H1
Craigiehall St. G51 35 H1
Craigielea Ct. PA4 20 C1
Craigielea Cres. G62 6 C2
Craigielea Dri. PA3 31 E4
Craigielea Pk. PA4 20 C1
Craigielea Rd. G81 8 B2
Craigielea Rd. PA4 20 C1
Craigielea St. G31 26 A5
Craigielinn Av. PA2 43 E6
Craigievar Av. G64 61 F4
Craigievar St. G33 28 B3
Craigleith St. G32 27 E6
Craiglockhart St. G33 28 A3
Craigmillar Av. G62 6 E2
Craigmillar Rd. G42 48 C1
Craigmont Dri. G20 16 A5
Craigmont St. G20 16 A5
Craigmore Rd. G61 10 B2
Craigmore St. G31 26 B6
Craigmount Av. PA2 43 F6
Craigmuir Cres. G52 33 F1
Craigmuir Pl. G52 33 F1
Craigmuir Rd. G52 33 F1
Craigneil St. G33 28 B3
Craignestock Pl. G40 37 G2
Craignestock St. G40 37 G2
Craignethan Rd. G46 57 E4
Craignure Rd. G73 50 B6
Craigpark. G31 25 H6
Craigpark Dri. G31 25 H5
Craigpark St. G81 9 F1
Craigs Av. G81 9 E2
Craigton Av. G78 55 H3
Craigton Av. G62 6 D2
Craigton Cres. G77 56 A5
Craigton Dri. G78 55 H3
Craigton Dri. G51 34 D1
Craigton Gdns. G62 6 D1

Craigton Rd. G51 34 D1
Craigton Rd. G62 6 A1
Craigton St. G81 9 F1
Craigvicar Gdns. G32 40 A2
Craigwell Av. G73 50 C3
Crail St. G31 38 D2
Cramond Av. PA4 21 F3
Cramond St. G5 37 F4
Cramond Ter. G32 39 G1
Cranborne Rd. G12 15 E5
Cranbrooke Dri. G20 15 H3
Cranston St. G3 24 B5
Cranworth La. G12 23 H2
Cranworth St. G12 23 H2
Crarae Av. G61 14 C1
Crathes Ct. G44 48 A5
Crathie Dri. G11 23 E3
Crathie Pl. G77 60 F1
Craw Rd. PA2 43 F1
Crawford Cres. G71 53 G2
Crawford Dri. G15 13 G3
Crawford Rd. G73 50 B5
Crawford St. G11 23 E3
Crawfurd Dri. PA2 31 E5
Crawfurd Gdns. G73 50 B4
Crawfurd Rd. G62 6 C1
Crebar Dri. G78 55 G2
Crebar St. G46 46 B5
Credon Gdns. G73 50 B5
Cree Av. G64 61 F4
Cree Gdns. G32 39 E2
Creran Dri. PA4 20 C1
Crescent Gdns. G21 25 G1
Crescent Rd. G13 13 H5
Cressdale Av. G45 59 E1
Cressdale Ct. G45 59 E1
Cressdale Dri. G45 59 E1
Cresswell Gro. G77 60 B2
Cresswell La. G12 23 H2
Cresswell Pl. G77 60 C3
Cresswell St. G12 23 H2
Cresswell Ter. G71 53 G2
Cressy St. G51 22 C4
Crest Av. G13 13 H2
Crestlea Av. PA2 43 H4
Crichton St. G21 25 F1
Crichton St. G21 25 F1
Crimea St. G2 4 B5
Crinan Gdns. G64 61 E4
Crinan Rd. G64 61 E4
Crinan St. G31 26 B4
Cripps Av. G81 12 D1
Crodie Pl. PA4 20 C3
Croft Rd. G72 51 E4
Croft Way. PA4 21 E4
Croftbank St. G21 17 H6
Croftburn Dri. G44 49 F4
Croftcroighn Rd. G33 27 G4
Croftend Av. G44 49 G3
Croftfoot Cres. G45 49 H5
Croftfoot Dri. G45 49 G5
Croftfoot Quad. G45 49 G5
Croftfoot Rd. G44 49 G5
Croftfoot St. G45 49 H5
Croftfoot Ter. G45 49 G5
Crofthead Pl. G77 60 D2
Crofthill Rd. G44 49 F3
Crofthouse Dri. G44 49 F5
Croftmount Av. G44 49 G5
Crofton Av. G44 49 E5
Croftpark Av. G44 49 E4
Croftpark Rd. G81 8 D2
Croftside Av. G44 49 F5
Croftspar Av. G32 28 A6
Croftspar Ct. G32 40 A1
Croftspar Dri. G32 28 A6
Croftspar Gate. G32 40 A1
Croftspar Gro. G32 39 H1
Croftspar Pl. G32 39 H1
Croftwood. G64 61 E4
Croftwood Av. G44 49 F5
Cromalt Cres. G61 6 A4
Cromarty Av. G43 48 D4
Cromarty Av. G43 48 D4
Cromarty Cres. G61 11 E1
Cromarty Gdns. G76 58 C2
Crombie Gdns. G69 40 C3
Cromdale St. G51 22 C6
Cromer St. G20 16 B5
Cromer Way. PA3 31 G3
Crompton Av. G44 49 F4
Cromwell La. G20 16 B5
Cromwell St. G20 16 B5
Cronberry Quad. G52 33 F4
Cronberry Ter. G52 33 F4
Crookfur Rd. G77 56 A5
Crookston Av. G52 33 G3
Crookston Ct. G52 33 G3
Crookston Dri. G52 33 F3
Crookston Gdns. G52 33 F3

Crookston Gro. G52 33 G3
Crookston Pl. G52 33 G3
Crookston Quad. G52 33 G3
Crookston Rd. G52 33 G6
Crosbie Dri. PA2 42 B5
Crosbie La. G20 15 G3
Crosbie St. G20 15 G3
Crosbie Woods. PA2 43 E3
Cross Arthurlie St. G78 55 F2
Cross Rd. PA2 43 E2
Cross St. G32 39 H6
Cross St. PA1 31 F6
Crossbank Av. G42 37 F6
Crossbank Dri. G42 37 F6
Crossbank Rd. G42 37 F6
Crossbank Ter. G42 37 F6
Crossburn Av. G62 6 D3
Crossflat Cres. PA1 32 A2
Crossford Dri. G23 16 A2
Crosshill Av. G42 36 D6
Crosshill Dri. G73 50 A3
Crosslee St. G52 34 C2
Crosslees Dri. G46 46 D6
Crosslees Park. G46 47 E6
Crosslees Rd. G46 56 D1
Crossloan Rd. G51 22 D5
Crossloan Ter. G51 23 E5
Crossmill Av. G78 44 D5
Crossmyloof Gdns. G41 35 G6
Crosspoint Dri. G23 16 A2
Crossstobs Rd. G53 33 H5
Crossveggate. G62 6 E3
Crossview Av. G69 41 G2
Crossview Pl. G69 41 G2
Crovie Rd. G53 45 G1
Crow Rd. G11 14 D6
Crowflats Rd. G71 53 G3
Crowhill Rd. G64 17 H3
Crowhill St. G22 17 E5
Crowlin Cres. G33 27 G5
Crown Av. G81 8 D5
Crown Circus. G12 23 G2
Crown Gdns. G12 23 G2
Crown Rd Nth. G12 23 F2
Crown Rd Sth. G12 23 F2
Crown St. G69 40 C4
Crown St. G5 36 D2
Crown Ter. G12 23 F2
Crownhall Pl. G32 39 H2
Crownpoint Rd. G40 37 G2
Croy Av. G77 57 E6
Croy Pl. G21 18 B5
Croy Rd. G21 18 B5
Cruachan Av. PA4 20 C4
Cruachan Av. PA2 43 G4
Cruachan Dri. G78 55 F3
Cruachan Dri. G77 60 D2
Cruachan Rd. G61 10 B1
Cruachan Rd. G73 50 D6
Cruachan St. G46 47 E5
Cruachan Way. G78 55 F3
Cruden St. G51 22 B6
Crum Av. G46 47 E6
Crusader Av. G13 14 B2
Cuillin Way. G78 55 F2
Culbin Dri. G13 13 G3
Cullen. PA8 7 B5
Cullen St. G32 39 F3
Cullen Gdns. G22 17 E6
Cullins Rd. G73 50 D6
Culloden St. G31 26 A4
Culrain Gdns. G32 39 F2
Culrain St. G32 39 F2
Culross St. G32 39 H3
Cults St. G51 22 D6
Culvain Av. G61 10 C1
Culzean Cres. G69 40 D3
Culzean Cres. G77 60 F1
Culzean Dri. G32 40 A2
Cumberland Pl. G5 37 E3
*Cumberland St,
  Crown St. G5 36 D2
Cumberland St. G5 37 E3
Cumbernauld Rd. G31 26 B5
Cumbrae Ct. G81 9 E6
Cumbrae Rd. PA2 43 G5
Cumbrae Rd. PA4 20 D4
Cumbrae St. G33 27 F4
Cumlodden Dri. G20 15 G3
Cumming Dri. G42 48 D1
Cumnock Dri. G33 18 D4
Cumnock Dri. G78 55 G3
Cunard Ct. G81 12 C3
Cunard St. G81 12 C3
Cunningham Dri. G81 8 B2
Cunningham Dri. G46 48 A6
Cunningham Rd. G52 21 F4
Cunninghame Rd. G73 50 C1
Curfew Rd. G13 14 B1
Curle St. G14 22 B2

Curle St. G14 22 C3
Curling Cres. G44 49 E1
Currie St. G20 16 A4
Curtis Av. G44 49 E1
Curzon St. G20 16 A4
Cuthbertson St. G42 36 C4
Cuthelton Dri. G31 38 D3
Cuthelton St. G31 38 D3
Cuthelton Ter. G31 38 D3
Cypress St. G22 17 E5
Cypress Way. G72 52 C4
Cyril St. PA1 32 B2

Daer Av. PA4 21 F3
Dairsie Gdns. G64 18 C2
Dairsie St. G44 48 B4
Daisy St. G42 36 D5
Dalbeth Pl. G32 39 F4
Dalbeth Rd. G32 39 F4
Dalcharn Dri. G34 28 D5
Dalcraig Cres. G72 53 F6
Dalcross St. G11 23 G3
Dalgarroch Av. G81 13 E3
Dalgleish Av. G81 8 B2
Dalhousie Gdns. G64 61 B3
Dalhousie La. G3 4 B2
Dalhousie St. G3 4 B2
Dalilea Dri. G34 29 F4
Dalilea Pl. G34 29 F4
Dalintober St. G5 36 C1
Dalkeith Av. G41 35 F2
Dalkeith Av. G64 61 D2
Dalkeith Rd. G64 61 D1
Dalmahoy St. G20 27 E5
Dalmally St. G20 24 B1
Dalmarnock Bri. G40 38 A5
Dalmarnock Rd. G40 38 A4
Dalmary Dri. PA1 32 C1
Dalmellington Rd. G53 45 G1
Dalmeny Av. G46 47 G6
Dalmeny Dri. G78 55 E2
Dalmeny St. G5 37 F5
Dalnair Pl. G62 6 B3
Dalnair St. G3 23 G4
Dalness St. G32 39 F3
Dalnottar Av. G60 7 C3
Dalnottar Dri. G60 7 C3
Dalnottar Gdns. G60 7 C3
Dalnottar Hill Rd. G60 7 C3
Dalnottar Ter. G60 7 B3
Dalreoch Av. G69 41 E1
Dalriada St. G64 38 B2
Dalry St. G32 39 G3
Dalrymple Dri. G77 60 E1
Dalserf Cres. G46 57 F2
Dalserf St. G31 38 A2
Dalsetter Av. G15 13 G1
Dalsetter Pl. G15 13 G1
Dalsholm Av. G20 15 F3
Dalsholm Rd. G20 15 F3
Dalskeith Av. PA3 30 D6
Dalskeith Cres. PA3 30 D5
Dalskeith Rd. PA3 30 D5
Dalswinton St. G34 29 F5
Dalton Av. G81 13 E1
Dalton St. G31 38 D2
Dalveen Dri. G78 55 F3
Dalveen St. G32 39 E2
Dalveen Way. G73 50 B5
Dalziel Dri. G41 35 G3
Dalziel Quad. G41 35 G3
Dalziel Rd. G52 21 F4
Damshot Cres. G53 34 B6
Damshot Rd. G53 46 B1
Danby Rd. G69 40 C3
Danes Av. G14 14 A6
Danes Cres. G14 14 A6
Danes Dri. G14 13 H6
*Danes Dri Footpath,
  Norse Pl. G14 14 A6
Danes La Sth. G14 22 B1
Dargarvel Av. G41 35 F3
Darkwood Ct. PA3 31 E4
Darkwood Cres. PA3 31 E4
Darkwood Dri. PA3 31 E4
Darleith St. G32 39 F2
Darnaway Av. G33 28 A2
Darnaway St. G33 28 A2
Darnick St. G21 26 A2
Darnley Cres. G64 61 C2

Darnley Gdns. G41 36 A5
Darnley Mains Rd. G53 46 A6
Darnley Rd. G78 45 E6
Darnley Rd. G. G41 36 A5
Darroch Dri. PA8 7 A5
Darvel Cres. PA1 33 E2
Darvel Dri. G77 57 E6
Darvel St. G53 45 F3
Darwin Pl. G81 8 A5
Dava St. G51 23 E6
Davaar Dri. PA2 43 G5
Davaar Pl. G77 56 B5
Davaar Rd. PA4 20 D3
Davaar St. G40 38 B2
Daventry Dri. G12 15 E5
David Pl. G12 40 C3
David Pl. PA3 20 C6
David St. G40 38 A2
David Way. PA3 20 C6
Davidson Quad. G81 8 B2
Davidson Pl. G32 39 H1
Davidson St. G40 38 A4
Davidson St. G81 13 E2
Davieland Rd. G46 57 E2
Davies Sq. G81 8 C2
Daviot St. G51 22 B6
Dawson Pl. G4 24 D2
Dawson Rd. G4 24 D2
Deacons Bank Av. G46 56 C2
Deacons Bank Cres.
  G46 56 C2
Deacons Bank Gdns.
  G46 56 C2
Deacons Bank Gro. G46 56 C2
Deacons Bank Pl. G46 56 C2
Dealston Rd. G78 44 C5
Dean Park Rd. PA4 21 E2
Dean St. G81 12 D2
Deanfield Quad. G52 21 F6
Deanpark Dri. G72 52 A6
Deans Av. G72 52 A5
Deanside Rd. G52 21 G4
Deanston Dri. G41 48 A1
Deanwood Av. G44 48 B5
Deanwood Rd. G44 48 B6
Dechmont Av. G72 52 A6
Dechmont Pl. G72 52 A6
Dechmont St. G31 38 C2
Dee Av. PA2 42 C2
Dee Dri. PA2 42 C3
Dee St. G33 26 C4
Deepdene Rd. G61 10 D6
Delhi Av. G81 7 D4
Delny Path. G33 28 B6
Delvin Rd. G44 48 C3
Denbeck St. G32 39 E2
Denbrae St. G32 39 E2
Denewood Av. PA2 43 F5
Denham St. G22 24 C1
Denholm Dri. G46 57 G2
Denmark St. G22 17 E6
Denmilne Gdns. G34 29 F5
Denmilne Path. G34 29 F5
Denmilne Rd. G34 29 F5
Denmilne St. G34 29 F5
Deramore Av. G46 57 E4
Derby St. G3 24 A4
Derwent St. G22 24 D1
Despard Av. G32 40 B2
Despard Gdns. G32 40 B2
Deveron Av. G46 57 H1
Deveron Rd. G61 10 D6
Deveron St. G33 26 C4
Devol Cres. G53 33 H6
Devon Gdns. G64 61 B2
Devon Pl. G41 36 D3
Devon St. G5 36 D3
Devonshire Ter. G12 15 F6
Devonshire Ter La. G12 15 F6
Diana Av. G13 13 H3
Dick St. G20 24 B2
Dickens Av. G81 8 C4
Dilwara Av. G14 22 C3
Dinard Dri. G46 47 G5
Dinart St. G33 26 C4
Dinduff St. G34 29 F3
Dinmont Av. PA2 42 C4
Dinmont Pl. G41 36 A5
Dinmont Rd. G41 35 H6
Dinmont Way. PA2 42 B4
Dinwiddie St. G21 26 B2
Dipple Pl. G15 13 H3
Dirleton Dri. PA2 42 D3
Dirleton Dri. G41 36 A6
Dirleton Gate. G61 10 D6
Divernia Way. G78 55 G3
Dixon Av. G42 36 C5
Dixon Rd. G42 36 D6

Dixon St. G1 4 D6
Dixon St. G46 37 E6
Dixon St. PA1 32 A2
Dochart Av. PA4 21 F3
Dochart St. G33 26 D3
Dodhill Pl. G13 13 H4
Dodside Gdns. G32 39 H2
Dodside Pl. G32 39 H2
Dodside Rd. G77 56 A5
Dodside St. G32 39 H2
Dolan St. G69 41 E2
Dolphin Rd. G41 35 H5
Don Av. PA4 21 F2
Don Dri. PA2 42 C3
Don St. G33 26 C4
Donaldsons Dri. PA4 20 D1
Donaldswood Pk. PA2 43 F4
Donaldswood Rd. PA2 43 F4
Doncaster St. G20 24 B1
Donnies Brae. G78 54 D3
Doon Cres. G61 10 D5
Doon St. G81 9 F6
Doone Cres. G64 61 D1
Doonfoot Rd. G43 47 G3
Dora St. G40 38 A2
Dorchester Av. G12 15 E5
Dorchester Pl. G12 15 E5
Dorian Dri. G76 57 F3
Dormanside Ct. G53 33 H4
Dormanside Gate. G53 33 H4
Dormanside Gro. G53 33 H4
Dormanside Pl. G53 34 B5
Dormanside Rd. G53 34 A4
Dornal Av. G13 13 F3
Dornford Av. G32 40 A4
Dornford Rd. G32 40 A4
Dornie Dri. G32 51 H1
Dornoch Av. G46 57 G2
Dornoch Pl. G64 61 F3
Dornoch Rd. G61 10 D6
Dornoch St. G40 37 G2
Dorset Sq. G3 24 B5
Dorset St. G3 4 A3
Dosk Av. G13 13 F3
Dosk Pl. G13 13 F3
Double Hedges Rd. G78 54 B5
Dougalston Av. G62 6 F3
Dougalston Cres. G62 6 F3
Dougalston Gdns Nth.
  G62 6 F3
Dougalston Gdns Sth.
  G62 6 F3
Dougalston Rd. G23 15 H2
Douglas Av. G73 50 B4
Douglas Av. G32 39 G6
Douglas Av. G46 57 G2
Douglas Cres. PA8 7 A5
Douglas Dri. G72 40 C2
Douglas Dri. G72 51 F4
Douglas Dri. G15 13 G2
Douglas Dri. G73 56 D5
Douglas Gdns. G61 11 F4
Douglas Gdns. G46 57 G2
Douglas La. G2 4 C3
*Douglas La, Gleneagles
  La Nth. G14 22 A1
Douglas Muir Dri. G62 6 A1
Douglas Muir Gdns. G62 6 A1
Douglas Muir Pl. G62 6 A1
Douglas Muir Rd. G62 6 A2
Douglas Pl. G61 9 F1
Douglas Pl. G61 11 E3
Douglas Rd. PA4 20 B4
Douglas Rd. G71 53 H4
Douglas St. G62 6 D3
Douglas St. PA1 31 F5
Douglas St. G2 4 B3
Dougray Pl. G78 55 F2
Dougrie Dri. G45 49 F6
Dougrie Dri La. G45 49 F6
Dougrie Gdns. G45 49 E6
Dougrie Pl. G45 49 F6
Dougrie Rd. G45 49 E6
Dougrie St. G45 49 F6
Dougrie Ter. G45 49 F6
Doune Cres. G77 57 E6
Doune Gdns. G20 24 A1
Doune Gdns La. G20 24 A1
Doune Quad. G20 24 A1
Dove St. G53 45 G4
Dowanhill St. G11 23 G3
Dowanside La. G12 23 G2
Dowanside Rd. G12 23 G2
Downcraig Dri. G45 59 E1
Downcraig Gro. G45 59 E1
Downcraig Rd. G45 59 E1
Downcraig Ter. G45 59 E1

Downfield St. G32 39 E4
Downiebrae Rd. G73 38 B5
Downs St. G21 17 H6
Dowrie Cres. G53 34 A6
Drake St. G40 37 G2
Drakemire Av. G45 49 E5
Drakemire Dri. G45 48 D6
Drive Rd. G51 22 C5
Drochil St. G34 28 D4
Drumbeg Dri. G53 45 G3
Drumbeg Ter. G62 6 A2
Drumbottie Rd. G21 17 H6
Drumbrock Rd. G62 6 A3
Drumby Cres. G76 57 H2
Drumby Dri. G76 57 H3
Drumcarn Dri. G62 6 C3
Drumchapel Gdns. G15 13 H1
Drumchapel Pl. G15 13 H1
Drumchapel Rd. G15 10 B6
Drumclog Av. G62 6 D1
Drumclog Gdns. G33 19 E5
Drumcross Rd. G53 34 A6
Drumhead La. G32 39 E6
Drumhead Pl. G32 39 E6
Drumhead Rd. G32 39 E6
Drumilaw Rd. G73 50 A4
Drumilaw Way. G73 50 A4
Drumlaken Av. G23 15 G2
Drumlaken Ct. G23 15 G2
Drumlaken Pl. G23 15 G2
Drumlaken St. G23 15 G2
Drumlanrig Av. G34 29 F4
Drumlanrig Pl. G34 29 G4
Drumlanrig Quad. G34 29 F4
Drumlin Dri. G62 6 D4
Drumlochy Rd. G33 27 F3
Drummond Av. G73 49 G1
Drummond Dri. PA1 33 E2
Drummore Rd. G15 10 B4
Drumover Dri. G31 38 D2
Drumoyne Av. G51 22 C5
Drumoyne Circus. G51 34 C1
Drumoyne Pl. G51 34 C1
Drumoyne Quad. G51 22 C6
Drumoyne Rd. G51 22 C6
Drumoyne Sq. G51 22 C6
Drumpark St. G46 46 D5
Drumpellier Av. G69 40 D3
Drumpellier Pl. G69 40 D3
Drumpellier Rd. G69 40 D3
Drumpellier St. G33 26 D3
Drumreoch Dri. G42 49 G1
Drumreoch Pl. G42 49 G1
Drumry Pl. G15 9 G6
Drumry Rd. G81 9 E5
Drumry Rd East. G81 9 G6
Drums Av. PA3 31 E5
Drums Cres. PA3 31 F5
Drums Rd. G53 33 H4
Drumsargard Rd. G73 50 C4
Drumshaw Dri. G32 51 H1
Drury St. G2 4 D4
Dryad St. G46 46 C4
Dryburgh Av. PA2 42 D4
Dryburgh Av. G73 50 B2
Dryburgh Gdns. G20 24 B1
Dryburgh Rd. G61 10 C2
Dryburn Av. G52 33 G2
Drygate. G4 5 G4
Drygrange Rd. G33 27 H2
Drymen Rd. G61 10 D2
Drymen Wynd. G61 11 F5
Duart Dri. G77 57 E6
Duart St. G20 15 G3
Dubs Rd. G78 45 E6
Dubton St. G34 29 E4
Duchall Pl. G14 13 H6
Duchess Pl. G73 38 B6
Duchess St. G73 38 B6
Duchray Dri. PA1 33 F3
Duchray La. G33 26 C4
Duchray St. G33 26 C4
Ducraig St. G32 39 F2
Dudhope St. G33 28 A3
Dudley Dri. G12 23 E2
Dudley La. G12 23 E1
Duffus Pl. G32 51 H1
Duffus St. G34 28 C3
Duffus Ter. G32 39 H6
Duich Gdns. G23 15 H1
Duisdale Rd. G32 51 H1
Duke St. PA2 43 H3
Duke St. G31 26 A6
Duke St. G4 5 G4
Dukes Gate. G71 53 G5
Dukoc Rd. G73 50 B4
Dulnain St. G72 52 B4
Dulsie Rd. G21 18 B4
Dumbarton Rd, Clydebank. G81 12 A1
Dumbarton Rd, Duntocher. G81 8 B2
Dumbarton Rd, Old Kilpatrick. G60 7 A1
Dumbarton Rd, Partick. G11 23 E3
Dumbarton Rd, Whiteinch. G14 22 B2
Dumbarton Rd, Yoker. G13 13 E4
Dumbreck Av. G41 35 E3
Dumbreck Ct. G41 35 E3
Dumbreck Pl. G41 35 E3
Dumbreck Rd. G41 35 F4
Dumbreck Sq. G41 35 E3
Dumgoyne Av. G62 6 C3
Dumgoyne Dri. G61 10 D1
Dumgoyne Gdns. G62 6 C3
Dumgoyne Pl. G46 57 G4
Dunagoil Gdns. G45 59 F1
Dunagoil Pl. G45 59 F2
Dunagoil Rd. G45 59 F1
Dunagoil St. G45 59 F1
Dunalistair Av. G33 19 G5
Dunan Path. G33 28 B6
Dunard Rd. G73 50 B1
Dunard St. G33 24 B1
Dunard Way. PA3 31 G3
Dunaskin St. G11 23 G3
Dunbar Av. G73 50 C2
Dunbar Rd. PA2 42 D3
Dunbeath Av. G77 56 D6
Dunbeith Pl. G20 15 H5
Dunblane St. G4 4 D1
Dunblane St. G4 4 D2
Duncan Av. G14 22 B1
Duncan La. G14 22 B1
*Duncan La N, Norse La Nth. G14 22 B1
*Duncan La S, Gleneagles La Nth. G14 22 A1
Duncan St. G81 8 D5
Duncansby Rd. G33 28 B6
Duncarnock Av. G78 54 C4
Duncarnock Cres. G78 54 C4
Dunchattan St. G31 25 G5
Dunchurch Rd. PA1 32 D2
Dunclutha St. G40 38 B4
Duncolm Pl. G62 6 B2
Duncombe Av. G81 8 D1
Duncombe St. G20 15 H3
Duncombe Vw. G81 9 F5
Duncrub Dri. G64 61 A3
Duncruin St. G20 15 G3
Duncruin Ter. G20 15 H3
Duncryne Av. G32 40 B3
Duncryne Gdns. G32 40 B3
Duncryne Pl. G64 61 A4
Dundas St. G1 4 D3
Dundasvale Ct. G4 4 C2
Dundee Dri. G52 34 A3
Dundee Path. G52 34 A4
Dundonald Cres. G77 60 F1
Dundonald Pl. G78 54 B5
Dundonald Rd. G12 23 G1
Dundonald Rd. PA3 20 A5
Dundrennan Rd. G42 48 B2
Dunearn Pl. PA2 32 B4
Dunearn St. G4 24 B3
Dunedin Ter. G81 12 D3
Dunellan Dri. G81 8 D2
Dunellan Rd. G62 6 A2
Dunellan St. G52 34 C2
Dunera Av. G14 22 B3
Dungeonhill Rd. G34 29 G5
Dunglass Av. G14 22 A1
*Dunglass La, Norse La Sth. G14 22 A1
Dunglass Pl. G62 6 B1
Dungoyne St. G20 15 G3
Dunholme Park. G81 8 A5
Dunira St. G32 39 E4
Dunkeld Av. G73 50 B2
Dunkeld Dri. G61 11 H4
Dunkeld Gdns. G64 61 D3
Dunkeld Pl. G77 60 F1
Dunkeld St. G31 38 C3
Dunkenny Pl. G15 9 H5
Dunkenny Rd. G15 9 H5
Dunlin. G12 15 E4
Dunlop Pl. G62 6 D1
*Dunlop St, Hairst St. PA4 20 D1
Dunlop St. G1 4 D6
Dunlop S. G72 52 B3
Dunmore St. G81 12 D2
Dunn Sq. PA1 31 H6
Dunn St, Bridgeton. G40 38 A3
Dunn St, Clydebank. G81 8 A5
Dunn St, Duntocher. G81 8 C2
Dunn St, Paisley. PA1 32 B2
Dunnichen Gdns. G64 61 F4
Dunnottar St. G64 61 F3
Dunnottar St. G33 27 G3
Dunolly Dri. G77 56 D6
Dunolly St. G21 25 H3
Dunphail Dri. G34 29 G4
Dunragit St. G31 26 B6
Dunrobin Ct. G81 8 C6
Dunrobin St. G31 38 B1
Dunrod St. G32 39 G3
Dunside Dri. G53 45 H3
Dunskaith Pl. G34 29 G5
Dunskaith St. G34 29 F5
Dunsmuir St. G51 23 F6
Dunster Gdns. G64 61 D1
Dunswin Av. G81 8 B5
Dunsyre Pl. G23 16 A1
Dunsyre St. G33 27 E5
Duntarvie Av. G34 29 E5
Duntarvie Clo. G34 29 E5
Duntarvie Cres. G34 29 E5
Duntarvie Dri. G34 29 E5
Duntarvie Gdns. G34 29 E5
Duntarvie Gro. G34 29 E5
Duntarvie Pl. G34 29 E4
Duntarvie Rd. G34 29 E4
Dunterlie Av. G13 13 H5
Dunterlie Ct. G13 44 D5
Duntiglennan Rd. G81 8 C2
Duntocher Rd. G81 8 C3
Duntocher Rd. G61 10 A2
Duntreath Av. G13 13 F2
Duntreath Dri. G15 13 G1
Duntreath Gdns. G15 13 G1
Duntreath Gro. G15 13 G1
Duntroon St. G31 26 B4
Dunure Dri. G77 60 E1
Dunure Dri. G73 49 G4
Dunure Pl. G77 60 E1
Dunure St. G20 15 H4
Dunvaig St. G33 28 B5
Dunvegan Pl. G71 53 G1
Dunvegan Dri. G64 61 C1
Dunvegan Dri. G77 57 E6
Dunvegan Quad. PA4 20 C1
Dunwan Av. G13 13 F4
Dunwan Pl. G13 13 G4
Durban Av. G81 7 D4
Durness Av. G61 11 H4
Durno Path. G33 28 B6
Duror St. G32 39 F1
Durris Gdns. G32 40 A4
Durrockstock Cres. PA2 42 C5
Durrockstock Rd. PA2 42 C5
Durrockstock Way. PA2 42 C5
Durward Av. G41 35 H6
Durward Cres. PA2 42 C4
Durward Gdns. G41 35 H6
Durward Way. PA2 42 C4
Duthil St. G51 22 C6
Dyce La. G11 23 F2
Dyers La. G1 5 F6
Dyers Wynd. PA1 31 H6
Dyke Rd. G14 13 F5
Dykebar Av. G13 13 H4
Dykebar Cres. PA2 32 C5
Dykehead La. G33 28 A5
Dykehead St. G33 28 A5
Dykemuir Pl. G21 26 A1
Dykemuir Quad. G21 25 H1
Dykemuir St. G21 25 H1
Eagle Cres. G61 10 B3
Eagle St. G4 24 D2
Eaglesham Pl. G51 35 H1
Eaglesham Rd. G76 58 A6
Eaglesham Rd. G77 60 B1
Earl Haig Rd. G52 21 G5
Earl La. G14 22 A1
Earl Pl. G14 22 A1
Earl St. G14 22 A1
Earlbank Av. G14 22 A1
Earlbank La Nth. G14 22 A1
Earlbank La Sth. G14 22 B2
Earlbank La St. G14 22 A1
Earls Gate. G71 53 G6
Earn Av. G61 11 H5
Earn Av. PA4 21 E3
Earn Rd. G77 56 B4
Earn St. G33 26 D3
Earnock St. G33 26 C1
Earnside St. G32 39 G2
Earslpark Av. G42 48 A2
Easdale Dri. G32 39 F2
East Av. PA4 20 D2
East Barns St. G81 12 D3
East Bath La. G2 4 D3
East Buchanan St. PA1 32 A2
East Campbell St. G1 5 G6
East Greenlees Av. G72 51 H5
East Greenleas Cres. G72 51 G6
East Greenlees Dri. G72 51 H6
East Greenlees Gro. G72 51 F6
East Greenlees Rd. G72 51 F6
East Hallhill Rd. G69 28 D6
East Kilbride Rd. G73 50 B4
East Kilbride Rd. G76 58 C6
East La. PA1 32 B1
East Rd. PA3 31 H4
East Springfield Ter. G64 18 A2
East Thomson St. G81 9 E5
East Wellington St. G31 38 C1
Eastbank Dri. G32 39 H2
Eastbank Pl. G32 39 H2
Eastbank Rise. G32 39 H2
Eastburn Cres. G21 18 B5
Eastburn Pl. G21 18 A5
Eastburn Rd. G21 18 A5
Eastcote Av. G14 22 C1
Eastcroft. G73 50 B1
Eastcroft Ter. G21 25 H1
Easter Av. G71 53 G3
Easter Craigs. G31 26 B5
Easter Mews. G71 53 H3
Easter Queenslie Rd. G33 28 B4
Easter Rd. G76 58 C5
Easterhill Pl. G32 39 E4
Easterhill St. G32 39 E4
Easterhouse Pl. G34 29 F4
Easterhouse Quad. G34 29 F5
Easterhouse Rd. G34 29 F4
Easterton Av. G76 58 C6
Eastfield Av. G72 50 D3
Eastfield Rd. G21 17 F6
Easthall Pl. G69 28 C6
Eastmuir St. G32 39 G2
Eastvale Pl. G3 23 G4
Eastwood Av. G46 57 G1
Eastwood Av. G41 47 H1
Eastwood Cres. G46 46 D5
Eastwood View. G72 52 B3
Eastwoodmains Rd. G76 57 F2
Eccles St. G22 17 F5
Eckford St. G32 39 F2
Eday St. G22 17 E4
Edderton Pl. G34 28 D5
Eddington Dri. G77 60 B2
Eddlewood Ct. G33 28 C6
Eddlewood Path. G33 28 C6
Eddlewood Pl. G33 28 C6
Eddlewood Rd. G33 28 C6
Eden La. G33 26 C4
Eden Park. G71 53 H6
Eden Pl. PA4 21 F3
Eden St. G33 26 C3
Edenhall Gro. G77 60 C3
Edenwood St. G31 38 D2
Edgefauld Av. G21 25 H1
Edgefauld Dri. G21 25 H1
Edgefauld Pl. G21 17 G6
Edgefauld Rd. G21 17 G6
Edgehill La. G11 23 E1
Edgehill Rd. G61 11 E2
Edgehill Rd. G11 23 E1
Edgemont St. G41 48 A1
Edgham Dri. G52 34 A2
Edinbeg Av. G42 49 F1
Edinbeg Pl. G42 49 G1
Edinburgh Rd. G33 26 C5
Edington St. G20 24 D3
Edison St. G52 21 E5
Edmiston Dri. G51 34 D1
Edrom Ct. G32 39 E2
Edrom St. G32 39 E2
Edward Av. PA4 21 E1
Edward St. G81 13 E3
Edwin St. G51 35 H1
Edzell Ct. G14 22 B2
Edzell Dri. PA5 42 A2
Edzell Dri. G77 60 C1
Edzell Gdns. G64 18 B2
Edzell Pl. G14 22 B2
Edzell St. G14 22 B2
Egidia Av. G46 57 G1
Egilsay Cres. G22 16 D3
Egilsay Pl. G22 17 E3
Egilsay St. G22 17 E3
Egilsay Ter. G22 16 D3
Eglinton Av. G71 53 G3
Eglinton Ct. G5 36 D2
Eglinton Dri. G76 57 G1
Eglinton St. G5 36 C3
Eider. G13
Eighth St. G71 41 G6
Eildon Dri. G78 55 F3
Eileen Gdns. G64 61 D3
Elcho St. G40 37 G1
Elder Cres. G72 52 B5
Elder St. G51 23 E5
Elderbank. G61 11 E6
Elderpark Gdns. G51 22 D5
Elderpark Gro. G51 22 D5
Elderpark St. G51 22 D6
Elderslie St. G3 24 B4
Eldon Gdns. G64 61 A3
Eldon St. G3 24 A3
Elgin Gdns. G76 58 B3
Elgin Rd. G61 11 F1
Elibank St. G33 27 F4
Elie St. G11 23 G3
Elizabeth Cres. G46 47 E6
Elizabeth St. G51 35 G1
Elizabethan Way. PA4 20 D4
Ellangowan Rd. G62 6 E2
Ellangowan Rd. G41 35 G6
Ellergreen Rd. G61 11 E4
Ellesmere St. G22 24 C1
Elliot Av. PA2 42 B5
Elliot Av. G46 47 G6
Elliot Dri. G46 47 G6
Elliot Pl. G3 24 A5
Elliot St. G3 24 A6
Ellisland Av. G81 9 E5
Ellisland Cres. G73 49 H4
Ellisland Rd. G76 58 A6
Ellisland Rd. G43 47 H2
Ellismuir Pl. G69 41 F3
Ellismuir Rd. G69 41 F2
Elliston Av. G53 46 A4
Elliston Cres. G53 46 A4
Elliston Dri. G53 46 A4
Ellon Gro. PA3 20 A6
Ellon Way. PA3 20 A6
Elm Av. PA4 12 D6
Elm Bank. G64 18 A2
Elm Dri. G72 51 H3
Elm Gdns. G61 11 E2
*Elm La East, Earlbank La Sth. G14 22 B2
*Elm La West, Earlbank La Sth. G14 22 B2
Elm Rd. G81 8 C4
Elm Rd. PA2 32 B5
Elm Rd. G73 50 B5
Elm St. G76 58 B5
Elm St. G14 22 B2
Elm Way. G72 52 B5
Elmtree Gdns. G45 49 H5
Elm Walk. G61 11 E2
Elmbank St. G2 4 B3
Elmbank St La. G2 4 A3
Elmfoot St. G5 37 F4
Elmore Av. G44 48 D4
Elmslie Ct. G69 41 E3
Elmvale Row. G21 17 F6
Elmvale St. G21 17 F6
Elmwood Av. G77 56 D5
Elmwood Av. G11 22 D1
Elmwood La. G11 22 D1
Elphin St. G23 15 H1
Elphinstone Pl. G51 23 G6
Elphinstone Rd. G46 57 E4
Elrig Rd. G44 48 B4
Elspeth Gdns. G64 61 D3
Eltham St. G20 24 D1
Elvan St. G32 39 E2
Embo Dri. G13 14 A5
Emerson Rd. G64 61 C4
Emerson Rd West. G64 61 B4
Emerson St. G20 16 C5
Endfield Av. G12 15 F5
Endrick Bank. G64 61 C1
Endrick Dri. G61 11 F5
Endrick Dri. PA1 32 C1
Endrick Gdns. G63 6 B2
Endrick St. G21 25 F1
Ensay St. G22 17 E3
Enterkin St. G32 39 E2
Eriboll Pl. G22 16 C4
Eriboll St. G22 16 C4
Eriska Av. G14 13 H5
Eriskay Dri. G60 7 D2
Eriskay Pl. G60 7 D2
Erradale St. G22 16 B4
Errogie St. G34 29 E4
Errol Gdns. G5 37 E2
Erskine Av. G41 35 F3
Erskine Ferry Rd. G60 7 B3
Erskine Rd. G46 57 F5
Erskine Vw. G60 7 B2
Ervie St. G34 29 F5
Esk Av. PA4 21 E2

Esk Dri. PA2 42 B4
Esk St. G13 13 F5
Esk Way. PA2 42 B3
Eskbank St. G32 39 F1
Eskdale Dri. G73 50 C2
Eskdale Rd. G61 10 D6
Eskdale St. G42 36 D6
Esmond St. G3 23 G4
Espedair St. PA2 43 H1
Essenside Av. G15 10 C6
Essex Dri. G14 22 C1
Essex La. G14 22 C1
Esslemont Av. G14 14 A6
Estate Quad. G32 39 H6
Estate Rd. G32 39 H6
Etive Av. G61 11 H5
Etive Ct. G81 9 E3
Etive Cres. G64 61 D4
Etive Dri. G46 57 H2
Etive St. G32 39 F2
Ettrick Av. PA4 21 F3
Ettrick Cres. G73 50 C2
Ettrick Dri. G61 10 C1
Ettrick Oval. PA2 42 B4
Ettrick Pl. G43 47 H1
Evan Cres. G46 57 H1
Evan Dri. G46 57 H1
Evanton Dri. G46 46 C6
Evanton Pl. G46 46 D6
Everard Ct. G21 17 F4
Everard Dri. G21 17 F4
Everard Quad. G21 17 F4
Everton Rd. G53 34 B4
Ewing Pl. G31 38 C2
Ewing St. G73 49 H2
Exeter Dri. G11 23 E3
*Exeter La, Exeter Dri. G11 23 E3
Eynort St. 16 C4
Eyrepoint Ct. G33 27 F5
Faifley Rd. G81 9 E1
Fairbairn Cres. G46 57 E1
Fairbairn St. G40 37 H3
Fairburn St. G32 39 F3
Fairfax Av. G44 48 D3
Fairfield Ct. G76 58 A6
Fairfield Dri. G76 58 A6
Fairfield Dri. PA4 21 E3
Fairfield Gdns. G51 22 D5
Fairfield Pl. G51 22 D5
Fairfield St. G51 22 D5
Fairhaven Rd. G23 15 H2
Fairhill Av. G53 46 B2
Fairley St. G51 35 F1
Fairlie Park Dri. G11 23 E3
Fairoaks. G76 59 F3
Fairview Ct. G62 6 E3
Fairway. G60 10 C3
Fairway Av. PA2 43 G5
Fairways View. G81 9 F2
Fairweather Pl. G77 60 A1
Falcon Cres. PA3 31 E5
Falcon Ter. G20 15 G3
Falcon Ter La. G20 15 G3
Falfield St. G5 36 C2
Falkland La. G12 23 F1
Falkland Av. G77 57 E6
Falkland Cres. G64 61 G4
Falkland St. G12 23 F1
Falloch Rd. G62 6 B2
Falloch Rd. G64 48 C1
Falside Av. PA2 43 G4
Falside Rd. PA2 43 G3
Falside Rd. G32 39 F5
Fara St. G23 16 B3
Farie St. G73 49 H1
Farm Rd, Bellahouston. G41 35 F2
Farm Rd, Dalmuir. G81 8 A5
Farm Rd, Duntocher. G81 8 C1
Farmeloan Rd. G73 38 A6
Farmington Av. G32 40 A2
Farmington Gdns. G32 40 A2
Farmington Gate. G32 40 A2
Farmington Gro. G32 40 A2
Farne Dri. G44 48 D5
Farnell St. G4 24 D2
Faskally Av. G64 61 A2
Faskin Cres. G53 45 F2
Faskin Pl. G53 45 F2
Fasque Pl. G15 9 G4
Fastnet St. G33 27 F4
Fauldhouse St. G5 37 F4
Faulds. G69 41 F2
Faulds Gdns. G69 41 F1
Faulds Park Cres. G69 41 F1
Fauldshead Rd. PA4 20 D2
Fauldswood Cres. PA4 43 E3
Fauldswood Dri. PA2 43 E3
Fearnmore Rd. G20 15 H3
Felton Pl. G13 13 F4
Fendoch St. G32 39 F3
Fenella St. G32 39 G2
Fennsbank Av. G73 50 C6
Fenwick Dri. G78 55 G3
Fenwick Pl. G46 57 F2
Fenwick Rd. G46 47 G6
Ferclay St. G81 9 F1
Fereneze Av. G78 44 B5
Fereneze Av. PA4 20 B4
Fereneze Av. G76 57 G3
Fereneze Cres. G13 13 G4
Fereneze Dri. PA2 43 E5
Fereneze Gro. G78 44 C5
Fereneze Rd. G78 54 A3
Fergus Av. PA3 30 D5
Fergus Dri. PA3 30 D5
Fergus Dri. G20 24 A1
Fergus Hill. PA3 30 D5
Fergus La. G20 24 B1
Ferguslie. PA1 42 D1
Ferguslie Pk Av. PA3 30 D6
Ferguslie Pk Cres. PA3 30 D6
Ferguslie Walk. PA1 31 E6
Ferguson Av. G62 6 D3
Ferguson Av. PA4 20 D2
Ferguson St. PA4 20 D1
Fergusson Rd. G61 11 F5
Fern Av. G64 18 A3
Fern Dri. G78 44 B4
Fern La. G13 14 D5
Fernan St. G32 39 E2
Fernbank Av. G72 51 H5
Fernbank Rd. G21 17 G6
Fernbank St. G21 17 G6
Fernbrae Av. G73 50 B6
Fernbrae Way. G73 50 B6
Ferncroft Dri. G44 49 F4
Ferndale Ct. G23 15 H3
Ferndale Dri. G23 15 G2
Ferndale Gdns. G23 15 G2
Ferndale Pl. G23 15 H2
Ferness Oval. G21 18 C4
Ferness Pl. G21 18 B4
Ferness Rd. G21 18 C4
Ferngrove Av. G12 15 F5
Fernhill Rd. G73 50 A4
Fernie Gdns. G20 16 A4
Fernlea. G61 11 E6
Fernleigh Rd. G43 47 G4
Ferry Rd. PA4 13 E6
Ferry Rd. G71 53 G3
Ferry Rd. G3 23 F4
Ferry View Cres. G13 13 F5
Ferryden St. G14 22 C3
Fersit St. G43 47 G4
Fetlar Dri. G44 49 E4
Fettercairn Av. G15 9 G5
Fettercairn Gdns. G64 61 E4
Fettes St. G33 27 E4
Fidra St. G33 27 E5
Field Gro. G76 58 B6
Field Rd. G76 58 B6
Field Rd. G81 9 F1
Fielden Pl. G40 38 A2
Fielden St. G40 38 A2
Fieldhead Dri. G43 47 E3
Fieldhead Sq. G43 47 E4
Fife Av. G52 34 A3
Fife Way. G64 18 C2
Fifth Av. G12 14 D5
Fifth Av. G33 20 C3
Fifty Pitches Pl. G52 22 A6
Fifty Pitches Rd. G52 22 A6
Finart Dri. PA2 32 B6
Finaven Gdns. G61 10 C1
Finch Dri. G13 13 G3
Findhorn. PA8 7 B6
Findhorn Av. PA4 21 F2
Findhorn St. G33 26 C4
Findochty. PA8 7 B5
Findochty St. G33 28 A3
Fingal La. G20 15 G4
Fingal St. G20 15 G4
Fingask St. G32 39 H2
Finglas Av. PA2 32 B6
Finglen Gdns. G62 6 B2
Finglen Pl. G53 46 A4
Fingleton Av. G78 55 H3
Finhaven St. G32 38 D4
Finlarig St. G34 29 F5
Finlas St. G22 17 E6
Finlay Dri. G31 26 A6
Finlay Rise. G62 6 F4
Finlock St. G81 8 A2
Finnart St. G40 37 H3
Finnieston Quay. G3 24 A6
Finnieston Sq. G3 24 A5
Finnieston St. G3 24 A6
Finsbay St. G51 22 C6
Fintry Av. PA2 43 G5
Fintry Cres. G78 55 F2
Fintry Cres. G64 61 E4
Fintry Dri. G44 49 E2
Fintry Gdns. G61 6 A4
Fir Cover. G72 52 B5
Fir Pl. G69 40 D3
Fir Pl. G72 51 H3
Firbank Ter. G78 55 H3
Firdon Cres. G15 13 G1
Firhill Rd. G20 24 B1
Firhill St. G20 24 B1
Firpark Rd. G64 18 A2
Firpark St. G31 25 G5
Firpark Ter. G31 25 G5
First Av. G44 11 F6
First Av. G71 53 H1
First Av. G33 19 G6
First Av. PA4 20 D3
First Av. G44 58 B1
First Gdns. G41 35 E3
First St. G71 53 H1
First Ter. G81 8 C5
Firwood Cts. G77 60 D1
Firwood Dri. G44 48 D3
Firwood Rd. G77 60 D1
Fischer Av. PA1 30 C6
Fischer Dri. PA1 30 C6
Fischer Gdns. PA1 30 C6
Fischer Way. PA1 30 C6
Fisher Cres. G81 8 D3
Fishers Rd. PA4 12 D5
Fishescoates Av. G73 50 C4
Fishescoates Gdns. G73 50 C4
Fishescoates Rd. G73 50 C4
Fitzalan Rd. PA4 20 B4
Fitzallan Pl. PA3 32 A1
Fitzroy La. G3 24 A4
*Fitzroy Pl, Fitzroy La. G3 24 A4
Flanders St. G81 9 E1
Fleet Av. PA4 21 E4
Fleet Av. G32 39 G2
Fleming Av. G81 12 D2
Fleming Ct. G81 8 D6
Fleming St. G31 26 B6
Fleming St. PA3 31 H3
Flemington St. G21 25 G1
Flender Rd. G76 57 G5
Flenders Av. G76 57 G5
Fleurs Av. G41 35 F3
Fleurs Rd. G41 35 F3
Flora Gdns. G64 61 E3
Florence Dri. G46 57 G1
Florence Gdns. G73 50 B5
Florence St. G5 37 E2
Florida Av. G42 48 D1
Florida Cres. G42 48 D1
Florida Dri. G42 48 C1
Florida Gdns. G69 40 D2
Florida Sq. G42 48 D1
Florida St. G42 48 C1
Flowerdale Pl. G53 46 A6
Fochabers Dri. G52 34 A1
Fogo Pl. G20 15 H5
Foinaven Dri. G46 47 E3
Foinaven Gdns. G46 47 E3
Foinaven Way. G46 47 E3
Forbes Dri. G40 37 G1
Forbes Pl. PA1 31 H6
Forbes St. G40 37 G1
Ford Rd. G12 15 G6
Ford Rd. G77 60 B2
Fordneuk St. G40 37 H2
Fordoun St. G34 29 F5
Fordyce St. G11 23 F3
Fore St. G14 22 A1
Foremount Ter La. G12 23 F2
Forest Pl. PA2 43 G3
Foresthall Cres. G21 25 H1
Foresthall Dri. G21 25 H2
Forfar Av. G52 33 H3
Forfar Cres. G64 18 C2
Forgan Gdns. G64 61 F4
Forge St. G21 26 B2
Forge St. G21 26 A3
Forglen St. G34 29 E4
Formby Dri. G23 15 H2
Forres Av. G46 47 G6
Forres Gate. G46 47 H6
Forres St. G23 15 H2
Forrest St. G40 37 H2
Forrester Ct. G64 61 B4
Forrestfield Cres. G77 56 C6
Forrestfield Gdns. G77 56 C6
Forteviot Av. G69 41 E1
Forteviot Pl. G69 41 E1
Forth Av. PA2 42 C3
Forth Rd. G61 10 D6
Forth St. G41 36 B4
Forties Ct. G46 47 E4
Forties Cres. G46 47 E4
Forties Gdns. G46 47 E4
Forties Way. G46 47 E4
Fortingall Av. G12 15 G5
Fortingall Pl. G12 15 G5
Fortrose St. G11 23 F2
Foswell Pl. G15 9 H4
Fotheringay La. G41 35 H5
Fotheringay Rd. G41 35 H5
Foulis La. G13 14 D4
Foulis St. G13 14 D4
*Foundry La, Main St. G78 55 F1
Foundry St. G21 25 H1
Fountainwell Av. G21 25 F2
Fountainwell Dri. G21 25 F2
Fountainwell Pl. G21 25 F2
Fountainwell Rd. G21 25 F2
Fountainwell Sq. G21 25 F2
Fountainwell Ter. G21 25 F2
Fourth Av. G33 19 G6
Fourth Av. PA4 20 C3
Fourth Gdns. G41 35 E3
Fourth St. G71 41 H6
Fowlis Dri. G77 56 B5
Fox La. G1 4 D6
Fox St. G1 4 D6
Foxbar Cres. PA2 42 B6
Foxbar Dri. PA2 42 B6
Foxbar Dri. G13 13 H5
Foxbar Rd. PA2 42 B6
Foxglove Pl. G53 46 A6
Foxhills Pl. G23 16 A1
Foxley St. G32 39 H6
Foyers Ter. G21 25 H1
Francis St. G5 36 C3
Franconia Sq. G81 12 C1
Frankfield St. G33 26 C2
Frankfort St. G41 36 A6
Franklin St. G40 37 G3
Fraser Av. G77 56 C5
Fraser Av. G73 50 B1
Fraser St. G72 50 D3
Frazer St. G40 38 A2
Freeland Ct. G53 46 A3
Freeland Cres. G53 46 A3
Freeland Dri. G53 45 H3
Freelands Cres. G60 7 C4
Freelands Pl. G60 7 C4
Freelands Rd. G60 7 C4
French St. G40 37 G4
French St. G81 8 A5
French St. PA4 20 C2
Freuchie St. G34 29 E5
Friar Av. G64 61 D1
Friars Pl. G13 14 B3
Friarscourt Av. G13 14 B2
Friarton Rd. G43 48 A1
Friendship Way. PA4 20 D4
Fruin Av. G77 56 C5
Fruin Ct. G77 56 C5
Fruin Pl. G22 17 E6
Fruin Rd. G15 13 G2
Fruin St. G22 17 E6
Fulbar Av. PA4 12 D6
Fulbar Ct. PA4 12 D6
Fulbar Cres. PA2 42 C2
Fulbar Gdns. PA2 42 D2
Fulbar La. PA4 12 D6
Fulbar Rd. PA2 42 C2
Fulbar Rd. G51 22 B6
Fulbar Rd. PA4 20 D1
Fullarton Av. G32 39 F5
Fullarton Dri. G32 39 F5
Fullarton La. G32 39 F5
Fullarton Rd. G32 39 F6
Fullers Gate. G81 9 E1
Fullerton Ter. PA3 31 G3
Fulmar Ct. G64 17 H3
Fulton Rd. G62 6 E3
Fulwood Av. G13 13 F3
Fulwood Pl. G13 13 G4
Fyvie Av. G43 47 F4
Gadie Av. PA4 21 F3
Gadie St. G33 26 C4
Gadloch St. G22 16 D5
Gadsburn Ct. G21 18 B5
Gadshill St. G21 25 G4
Gailes St. G40 38 B1
Gairbraid Av. G20 15 G5
Gairbraid Ct. G20 15 G5
Gairbraid Pl. G20 15 G5
Gairbraid Ter. G20 15 G5
Gala Av. PA4 21 F2
Gala St. G33 26 D3
Galbraith Dri. G51 22 C5
Galbraith Dri. G62 6 D4
Galdenoch St. G33 27 G3
Gallacher Av. PA2 42 D4
Gallan Av. G23 15 H2
Galloway Dri. G73 50 A6
Galloway St. G21 17 G4
Gallowflat St. G73 50 A1
Gallowgate. G1 5 F6
Gallowgate. G1 38 A1
Gallowhill Rd. G76 59 F3
Gallowhill Rd. PA3 20 B6
Galston St. G53 45 G3
Gamrie Dri. G53 45 G1
Gamrie Gdns. G53 45 G1
Gamrie Rd. G53 45 G1
Gannochy Dri. G64 61 E4
Gantock Cres. G33 27 G5
Garden Veterans Cotts. PA8 7 A3
Gardenside Av. G32 51 G1
Gardenside Av. G71 53 H3
Gardenside Cres. G32 51 G1
Gardenside Gro. G32 51 G1
Gardenside Pl. G32 51 G1
Gardenside St. G71 53 H3
Gardner St. G11 23 F2
Gardyne St. G34 28 D3
Gareloch Av. PA2 42 D3
Garfield St. G31 25 H6
Gargrave Av. G69 40 C3
Garion Dri. G13 13 H5
Garlieston Rd. G33 40 C1
Garmouth Ct. G51 23 E5
Garmouth Gdns. G51 23 E5
Garmouth St. G51 22 D5
Garnet St. G3 4 B2
Garnethill St. G3 4 B2
Garnock St. G21 25 H3
Garrioch Cres. G20 15 H6
Garrioch Dri. G20 15 H6
Garrioch Mill Rd. G20 24 B2
Garriochmill Rd. G20 23 H1
Garrioch Mill Way. G20 24 B2
*Garrioch Pl, Garrioch Rd. G20 15 H5
Garrioch Rd. G20 15 H5
Garrioch Quad. G20 15 H6
Garrowhill Dri. G69 40 C2
Garry Av. G61 11 G6
Garry Dri. PA2 42 D2
Garry St. G44 48 C2
Garscadden Rd. G15 13 G1
Garscadden Rd Sth. G13 13 G3
Garscadden Vw. G81 9 F5
Garscube Rd. G4 4 C1
Garscube Rd. G20 24 B1
Gartconnell Dri. G61 11 E3
Gartconnell Gdns. G61 11 E3
Gartconnell Rd. G61 11 E3
Gartcosh Rd. G33 27 F3
Gartcraig Path. G33 27 F3
Gartcraig Pl. G33 27 F3
Gartcraig Rd. G33 27 E4
Gartferry St. G69 17 H6
Garth St. G1 5 E5
Garthamlock Rd. G33 28 B3
Garthland Dri. G31 26 A6
Garthland La. PA1 32 A2
Gartloch Rd, Gartloch. G33 28 A3
Gartmore La. PA1 32 C2
Gartmore Ter. G72 51 H3
Gartocher Dri. G32 39 H2
Gartocher Rd. G32 39 H2
Gartocher Ter. G32 39 H1
Gartons Rd. G21 18 B6
Garturk St. G42 36 C5
Garvald Ct. G40 38 A4
Garvald St. G40 38 A4
Garve Av. G44 48 C4
Garvel Cres. G33 28 B6
Garvel Pl. G62 6 B2
Garvel Rd. G62 6 B2
Garvel Rd. G33 28 B6
Garvock Dri. G43 47 F3
Garwhitter Dri. G62 6 F3
Gask Pl. G13 13 F3
Gateside Av. G72 52 A4
Gateside Ct. G78 55 E1
Gateside Cres. G78 55 E1
Gateside Rd. G78 55 E1

Gateside St. G31 26 B6
Gauldry Av. G52 34 A3
Gauze St. PA1 31 H6
Gavinburn Gdns. G60 7 A1
Gavinburn Pl. G60 7 A2
Gavinburn St. G60 7 B2
Gavins Mill Rd. G62 6 E3
Gavins Rd. G81 8 D3
Gavinton St. G44 48 B4
Gear Ter. G40 38 A4
Geary St. G23 15 H1
Geddes Rd. G21 18 B4
Gelston St. G32 39 G2
Gemmel Pl. G77 60 A1
Generals Gate. G71 53 H3
Gentle Row. G81 8 C3
George Av. G81 9 E5
George Cres. G81 9 E5
George Gray St. G52 50 C1
George Mann Ter. G73 50 A4
George La. PA2 43 H1
George Pl. PA1 31 H6
George Reith Av. G12 14 D5
George Sq. G1 5 E4
George St. G78 55 F1
George St. G1 5 E4
George St. PA1 43 F1
George St. G1 5 E4
George St. G69 41 E3
George V Bri. G2 4 C6
Gertrude Pl. G78 55 E2
Gibson Rd. PA4 20 C4
Gibson St. G40 37 F1
Gibson St. G12 24 A2
Giffnock Park Rd. G43 47 G5
Gifford Dri. G52 33 G2
Gifford Wynd. PA2 42 C2
Gilbert Field Pl. G33 27 G2
Gilbert St. G3 23 G4
Gilbertfield Rd. G72 52 A6
Gilbertfield St. G33 27 G3
Gilfillan Way. PA2 42 B5
Gillhill St. G20 15 H4
Gillia St. G72 51 E3
Gillies La. G69 41 F2
Gilmerton St. G32 39 F3
Gilmour Av. G81 8 D3
Gilmour Cres. G73 49 G1
Gilmour Pl. G5 37 E3
Gilmour St. G81 9 E5
Gilmour St. PA1 31 H6
Gilmourton Cres. G77 60 B2
Girthon St. G32 39 H2
Girvan St. G33 26 C4
Gladney Av. G13 13 E3
Gladsmuir Rd. G52 33 G1
Gladstone Av. G78 55 E2
Gladstone St. G81 8 B6
Gladstone St. G4 24 C4
Glamis Av. G77 56 D6
Glamis Gdns. G64 61 D1
Glamis Rd. G31 38 C3
Glanderston Av. G68 55 H2
Glanderston Av. G77 56 A5
Glanderston Ct. G13 13 G3
Glanderston Dri. G13 13 G3
Glanderston Gate. G77 56 A5
Glanderston Rd. G68 55 E6
Glasgow Bri. G1 4 C6
Glasgow Rd. G69 40 C2
Glasgow Rd. G72 51 E2
Glasgow Rd. G78 45 E5
Glasgow Rd. G81 8 D2
Glasgow Rd. G62 6 E4
Glasgow Rd. G5 37 G4
Glasgow Rd. PA4 21 F2
Glasgow Rd. G71 53 G1
Glasgow Rd. PA1 12 C2
Glasgow Rd. PA1 32 A2
Glasgow St. G12 24 A2
Glassel Rd. G34 29 F4
Glasserton Pl. G43 48 B4
Glasserton Rd. G43 48 B4
Glassford St. G1 5 E5
Glassford St. G62 6 E3
Glavie Rd. G13 14 B1
Glebe Ct. G4 5 G2
Glebe La. G77 60 C1
Glebe Pl. G72 51 G4
Glebe Pl. G73 49 G1
Glebe Rd. G77 60 C1
Glebe St. PA4 20 D1
Glebe St. G4 5 G2
Gleddoch Rd. G52 33 E1
Glen Affric Av. G53 46 B5
Glen Affric Dri. G53 46 B5
Glen Av. G78 54 C5
Glen Av. G32 27 G6
Glen Cairn Cres. G78 54 A6
Glen Clunie Av. G53 46 A5
Glen Clunie Dri. G53 46 A5

Glen Clunie Pl. G53 46 B5
Glen Coe Rd. G73 50 C6
Glen Cona Dri. G53 46 A4
Glen Craran Clo. G78 54 A6
Glen Cres. G13 13 E4
Glen Esk Dri. G53 46 A5
Glen Esk Pl. G53 46 A5
Glen Isla Av. G78 54 A6
Glen Livet Pl. G53 46 B5
Glen Luce Dri. G32 40 A3
Glen Lyon Pl. G73 50 C6
Glen Lyon Rd. G78 54 A6
Glen Mair Rd. G78 54 A6
Glen Malloch Pl. PA5 42 A2
Glen Mark Rd. G78 54 A6
Glen Markie Dri. G53 46 A5
Glen Mavis St. G4 4 C1
Glen Moriston Rd. G53 46 B5
Glen Nevis Pl. G73 50 C6
Glen Ogle St. G32 40 A3
Glen Orchy Dri. G53 46 B5
Glen Orchy Pl. G53 46 B5
Glen Orrin Way. G78 54 A6
Glen Park Ter. G72 50 D2
Glen Pl. G46 57 H3
Glen Rinnes Dri. G78 54 B6
Glen Rd. G76 59 H6
Glen Rd. G60 7 C3
Glen Rd. G32 27 G6
Glen Roy Dri. G78 54 A6
Glen Sax Dri. PA4 21 E4
Glen Shee Av. G78 54 A6
Glen St. G78 55 F1
Glen St. G72 52 A5
Glen St. PA3 31 G5
Glenacre Cres. G71 53 G1
Glenacre Dri. G45 49 E6
Glenacre St. G45 49 E6
Glenacre Ter. G45 49 E5
Glenallan Way. PA2 42 B5
Glenalmond Rd. G73 50 D6
Glenalmond St. G32 39 F3
Glenapp Av. PA2 32 B6
Glenapp Rd. PA2 32 B6
Glenapp St. G41 36 B4
Glenarklet Dri. PA2 32 B6
Glenashdale Way. PA2 32 B6
Glenavon Rd. G20 15 H3
Glenbank Dri. G46 56 D1
Glenbank Av. G33 19 E4
Glenbarr St. G33 19 E4
Glenbervie Pl. G23 15 H2
Glenbrittle Dri. PA2 32 A6
Glenbrittle Way. PA2 32 A6
Glenbuck Av. G33 19 E4
Glenbuck Dri. G33 19 E4
Glenburn Av. G72 50 D3
Glenburn Av. G69 41 F1
Glenburn Cres. PA2 43 F5
Glenburn Gdns. G64 61 B3
Glenburn Rd. G61 10 D3
Glenburn Rd. PA2 43 E5
Glenburn Rd. G46 57 F2
Glenburn St. G20 16 A3
Glenburn Wk. G69 41 F1
Glenburnie Pl. G34 28 C5
Glencairn Ct. G73 49 H1
Glencairn Dri. G73 49 H1
Glencairn Dri. G41 36 A4
Glencairn Gdns. G41 35 H4
Glencairn Gdns. G72 52 A4
Glencairn La. G41 36 A4
Glencally Av. PA3 32 C6
Glenclora Dri. PA2 32 B6
Glencoats Cres. PA3 31 E6
Glencoats Dri. PA3 30 D6
Glencoe Pl. G13 14 D4
Glencoe St. G13 14 D4
Glencorse Rd. PA2 43 F2
Glencorse St. G32 26 D5
Glencroy St. G20 15 G3
Glencroft Av. G71 53 G1
Glencroft Rd. G44 49 F3
Glendale Cres. G64 18 B3
Glendale Pl. G64 18 B3
Glendale Pl. G31 26 A6
Glendale St. G31 26 A6
Glendaruel Av. G61 11 H4
Glendaruel Rd. G73 50 D6
Glendarvel Gdns. G21 17 E6
Glendee Gdns. PA4 20 D2
Glendee Rd. PA4 20 D2
Glendevon Pl. G81 8 C5
Glendevon Sq. G33 27 G3
Glendinning Rd. G13 14 C1
Glendore St. G14 22 C2
Glendoune Rd. G76 58 A6

Glendower Way. PA2 42 B5
Glenduffhill Rd. G69 40 C2
Gleneagles Dri. G64 61 C2
Gleneagles Dri. G77 60 F1
Gleneagles Gate. G77 60 F1
Gleneagles La Nth. G14 22 A1
Gleneagles La Sth. G14 22 A1
Glenelg Quad. G34 29 F2
Glenetive Pl. G73 50 D6
Glenfalloch Cres. G78 54 A6
Glenfarg Cres. G61 11 H4
Glenfarg Rd. G73 50 B5
Glenfield Av. PA2 43 G6
Glenfield Cres. PA2 43 G6
Glenfield Gdns. PA2 43 G6
Glenfield Rd. PA2 43 G6
Glenfinnan Dri. G20 11 H5
Glenfinnan Rd. G20 15 H5
Glenfruin Cres. PA2 32 6
Glengarry Dri. G52 34 A2
Glengavel Cres. G33 19 E4
Glengyre St. G34 29 F4
Glenhead Cres. G81 8 C1
Glenhead Cres. G22 17 E5
Glenhead Rd. G81 8 C3
Glenhead St. G22 17 E5
Glenholme Av. PA2 43 E3
Glenhove Rd. G33 27 E2
Gleniffer Av. G13 13 G4
Gleniffer Dri. G78 44 B4
Gleniffer Rd. PA4 20 B4
Gleniffer Rd. PA2 42 C6
Gleniffer Vw. G78 54 A6
Gleniffer Vw. G81 9 F5
Glenisla St. G31 38 D3
Glenkirk Dri. G15 10 B6
Glenlivet Rd. G78 54 A6
Glenlora Dri. G53 45 G2
Glenlora Ter. G53 45 H2
Glenloy Pl. G53 46 B5
Glenlui Av. G73 50 B4
Glenluce Dri. G42 49 F1
Glenluss Pl. G53 45 H3
Glenmanor Av. G69 41 F1
Glenmavis St. G4 4 C1
Glenmuir Dri. G53 45 H3
Glenpark Av. G46 57 E1
Glenpark Gdns. G72 50 D2
Glenpark Rd. G31 38 A1
Glenpark St. G31 26 A6
Glenpatrick Rd. PA5 42 A3
Glenraith Rd. G33 27 G2
Glenraith Walk. G33 27 G2
Glenshee St. G31 38 D3
Glenshiel Av. PA2 32 B6
Glenshira Av. PA2 32 B6
Glenside Av. G53 33 H5
Glenspean Pl. G43 47 G3
Glenspean St. G43 47 G3
Glentanar Ct. PA1 32 B3
Glentanar Pl. G22 16 D3
Glentanar Rd. G22 16 D3
Glentarbert Rd. G73 50 D6
Glenturret St. G32 39 F3
Glentyan Dri. G53 45 G2
Glentyan Ter. G53 45 G2
Glenville Av. G46 47 F6
Glenville Gate. G76 58 C6
Glenville Ter. G76 58 C6
Glenwood Dri. G46 57 F2
Glenwood Gdns. G21 17 E6
Glenwood Path. G45 49 G6
Glenwood Pl. G45 49 G6
Glenwood Rd. G45 49 G6
Gloucester Av. G73 50 C4
Gloucester Av. G76 57 H4
Gloucester St. G5 36 B1
Gockston Rd. PA3 31 G3
Gogar Pl. G33 26 D5
Gogar St. G33 26 D5
Goldberry Av. G14 14 A6
Goldenhill Ct. G81 9 E2
Golf Ct. G44 58 A1
Golf Dri. G15 13 F2
Golf Dri. PA1 32 C3
Golf Pl. G73 50 B4
Golf Rd. G73 50 B4
Golf Rd. G76 57 H3
Golf View. G81 8 B4
Golfhill Dri. G31 25 H5
Golfview. G61 10 C3
Golspie St. G51 23 E4
Gorbals St. G5 36 D2
Gordon Av. G69 40 C2
Gordon Av. G44 58 A1
Gordon Cres. G77 56 C5
Gordon Dri. G44 48 A6
Gordon La. G1 4 D5
Gordon Rd. G44 48 A6
Gordon St. G1 4 C4
Gordon St. PA1 31 H6
Gorebridge St. G32 26 D4
Gorget Av. G13 14 A2
Gorget Pl. G13 14 A2

Gorget Quad. G13 14 A2
Gorse Dri. G78 44 B5
Gorse Wood. G64 61 A4
Gorstan Pl. G23 15 G5
Gorstan St. G23 15 H2
Gosford La. G14 13 G6
Goudie St. PA3 31 F3
Gough St. G33 26 C4
Gourlay St. G21 25 F1
Gourock St. G5 36 C3
Govan Rd. G51 22 C4
Govanhill St. G42 36 C5
Gowanlea Av. G15 13 G1
Gowanlea Dri. G46 47 G5
Gower St. G41 35 G3
Gower Ter. G41 35 G2
Goyle Av. G15 10 C5
Grace St. G3 24 B5
Graffham Av. G46 47 H5
Grafton Pl. G1 5 E3
Graham Av. G81 8 D6
Graham Av. G72 52 A4
Graham Dri. G62 6 C2
Graham Sq. G31 37 G1
Graham St. G78 44 B4
Graham Ter. G64 18 B3
Grahamston Ct. PA2 44 C1
Grahamston Cres. PA2 44 C1
Grahamston Park. PA2 44 C1
Grahamston Pl. PA2 44 C1
Grahamston Rd. PA2 44 C1
Grainger Rd. G64 61 F3
Grampian Av. PA2 43 G4
Grampian Ct. G61 10 C1
Grampian Cres. G32 39 G3
Grampian Pl. G32 39 G3
Grampian St. G32 39 G3
Grampian Way. G78 55 F3
Grampian Way. G61 10 B1
Gran St. G81 13 E2
Granby La. G12 23 H2
Grandtully Dri. G12 15 G5
Grange Av. G62 6 E3
Grange Rd. G61 11 F3
Grange Rd. G42 48 C1
Grant St. G3 4 A1
Grantlea Gro. G32 40 A3
Grantlea Ter. G32 40 A3
Grantley Gdns. G41 47 H1
Grantley St. G41 47 H1
Granton St. G5 37 F5
Grants Av. PA2 43 F3
Grants Way. PA2 43 F3
Granville St. G81 8 D5
Granville St. G3 4 A2
Gray Dri. G61 11 F5
Gray St. G3 24 A4
Great Dovehill. G31 5 G6
Great George St. G12 23 H2
Great Hamilton St. PA2 43 H2
Great Western Rd. G81 8 A2
Great Western Rd. G15 13 E1
Great Western Rd. G12 24 A2
Great Western Rd. G13 14 A2
Great Western Rd. G60 7 A1
Great Western Ter. G12 23 G1
Great Western Ter La.
   G12 23 G1
Green Mt. G22 16 C4
Green Rd. PA2 42 C2
Green St. G40 37 G2
Green St. G81 8 C5
Greenbank Av. G46 57 F2
Greenbank Dri. PA2 43 G6
Greenbank St. G73 49 H1
Greendyke St. G1 37 E1
Greenend Pl. G32 27 H6
Greenfarm Rd. G77 56 A5
Greenfield Av. G32 27 G6
Greenfield Pl. G32 27 H6
Greenfield Rd. G73 50 A1
Greenfield St. G51 22 D5
Greenford St. G73 50 A1
Greenholm Av. G76 58 A4
Greenholm Av. G71 53 G2
Greenholme Ct. G44 48 C3
Greenholme St. G44 48 C3
Greenknowe Rd. G43 47 F3
Greenlaw Av. PA1 32 A1
Greenlaw Cres. PA1 32 B1
Greenlaw Dri. G77 56 B6

Greenlaw Dri. PA1 32 B2
Greenlaw Rd. G77 56 B6
Greenlaw Rd. G14 13 E4
Greenlea St. G13 14 C4
Greenlees Gdns. G72 51 F6
Greenlees Park. G72 51 F5
Greenlees Rd. G72 51 E6
Greenloan Av. G51 22 C5
Greenock Av. G44 48 D4
Greenock Rd. PA3 31 F3
Greenock Rd. PA4 12 A5
Greenrig. G71 53 H3
Greenrig St. G33 26 D2
Greenrig St. G71 53 H3
Greenshields Rd. G69 41 E2
Greenside Cres. G33 26 D2
Greenside Rd. G81 8 D1
Greenside St. G33 26 D2
Greentree Dri. G69 40 C4
Greenview St. G43 47 G1
Greenways Av. PA2 43 E3
Greenways Ct. PA2 42 D3
Greenwood Av. G72 52 B3
Greenwood Dri. G61 11 G5
Greenwood Quad. G81 12 D1
Greenwood Rd. G76 57 H4
Greer Quad. G81 8 D5
Grenville Dri. G72 51 E4
Gretna St. G40 38 B3
Greyfriars Rd. G51 53 F1
Greyfriars St. G32 27 F6
Greystone Av. G73 50 B3
Greywood St. G13 14 D4
Grier Path. G31 38 D2
Grierson St. G33 26 C5
Griffel Gdns. G32 40 A3
Griffel Rd. G32 40 A3
Griffen Av. PA1 30 B5
Grogarry Rd. G15 10 B4
Grosvenor Cres. G12 23 H1
Grosvenor La. G12 23 H1
Grosvenor Ter. G12 23 H1
Groveburn Av. G46 47 E5
Grovepark Ct. G20 24 C2
Grovepark Gdns. G20 24 C2
Grovepark Pl. G20 24 C2
Grovepark St. G20 24 C2
Grudie St. G34 28 D4
Gryffe Cres. PA2 42 C3
Gryffe St. G44 48 C2
Guildford St. G33 27 H3
Gullane St. G11 23 F3
Guthrie St. G20 15 G4

Haberlea Av. G53 46 A6
Haberlea Gdns. G53 46 A6
Haggs La. G41 35 G5
Haggs Rd. G41 35 G5
Haggswood Av. G41 35 F5
Haghill Rd. G31 26 B6
Haig Dri. G69 40 C3
Haig St. G21 25 H1
Hailes Av. G32 40 B3
Haining Rd. PA4 20 D2
Hairmyres St. G42 36 D5
Hairst St. PA4 20 D1
Halbeath Av. G15 9 H5
Halbert St. G41 36 A6
*Haldane La,
   Haldane St. G14 22 B2
Haldane St. G14 22 B2
Halgreen Av. G15 9 G6
Hall St. G11 23 F3
Hall St. G81 12 B2
Hallbrae St. G33 26 D2
Halley Dri. G13 13 E4
Halley Pl. G13 13 F4
Halley Sq. G13 13 F4
Halley St. G13 13 F4
Hallforest St. G33 27 G3
Hallhill Cres. G33 40 B1
Hallhill Rd. G32 39 G2
Halliburton Cres. G34 28 C5
Halliburton Ter. G34 28 D5
Hallidale Cres. PA4 21 F3
Hallrule Dri. G52 34 A1
Hallside Av. G72 52 B3
Hallside Blvd. G72 52 C6
Hallside Cres. G72 52 B4
Hallside Dri. G72 52 B3
Hallside Pl. G5 37 E3
Hallside Rd. G72 52 B5
Hallydown Dri. G13 14 B6
Halton Gdns. G69 40 C3
Hamilton Av. G41 35 F4
Hamilton Cres. G61 11 E1
Hamilton Cres. PA4 12 D6
Hamilton Cres. G72 51 H5
Hamilton Dri. G72 51 F4

Hamilton Drl. PA8 7 A5
Hamilton Dri. G46 57 H1
Hamilton Dri. G12 24 A1
Hamilton Park Av. G12 24 A2
Hamilton Rd. G32 40 A5
Hamilton Rd. G73 50 B1
Hamilton Rd. G72 51 F4
Hamilton St. PA3 31 H5
Hamilton St. G42 37 E5
Hamilton St. G81 12 D3
Hamilton Ter. G81 12 D4
Hamiltonhill Cres. G22 24 D1
Hamiltonhill Rd. G22 24 D1
Hangingshaw Pl. G42 49 E1
Hannay St. PA1 31 F6
Hanover Ct. PA1 32 B2
Hanover St. G1 5 E4
Hanson St. G31 25 H5
Hapland Av. G53 34 A5
Hapland Rd. G53 34 A5
Harbour La. PA3 31 H5
Harbour Rd. PA3 31 H4
Harbury Pl. G14 13 F4
Harcourt Dri. G31 26 A5
Hardgate Dri. G51 22 A5
Hardgate Gdns. G51 22 B5
Hardgate Path. G51 22 B5
Hardgate Pl. G51 22 A5
Hardgate Rd. G51 22 A5
Hardie Av. G73 50 B1
Hardridge Pl. G52 34 C5
Hardridge Rd. G52 34 C5
Harefield Dri. G14 13 H6
Harelaw Av. G78 55 G2
Harelaw Av. G44 48 A5
Harelaw Av. G78 54 B6
Harelaw Cres. PA2 43 F5
Harhill St. G51 23 E5
Harland St. G14 22 A1
Harlaw Gdns. G64 61 F3
Harley St. G51 35 G1
Harmetray St. G22 17 E4
Harmony Pl. G51 23 E5
Harmony Row. G51 23 E6
Harmony Sq. G51 23 E5
Harmsworth St. G11 22 D3
Harport St. G46 46 C4
Harriet Pl. G43 47 F2
Harriet St. G73 49 H1
Harris Cres. G60 7 C3
Harris Dri. G60 7 C3
Harris Gdns. G60 7 C3
Harris Rd. G60 7 C3
Harris Rd. G23 15 H1
Harrow Ct. G15 9 H5
Harrow Pl. G15 9 H5
Hart St. G31 38 D1
Hart St. G81 9 F2
Hartfield Cres. G78 54 C4
Hartfield Ter. PA2 32 A5
Hartlaw Cres. G52 33 G1
Hartree Av. G13 13 F2
Hartstone Pl. G53 46 A2
Hartstone Rd. G53 45 H2
Hartstone Ter. G53 46 A2
Harvey St. G4 25 E3
Harvie Av. G77 56 B5
Harvie St. G51 35 H1
Harwood St. G32 26 D5
Hastie St. G3 23 H4
Hatfield Dri. G12 14 D5
Hathaway Dri. G46 57 F1
Hathaway La. G20 16 A6
Hathaway St. G20 16 A6
Hathersage Av. G69 41 E2
Hathersage Dri. G69 40 D2
Hathersage Gdns. G69 41 E2
Hatton Gdns. G52 33 G3
Haugh Rd. G3 23 H4
Haughburn Pl. G53 45 H2
Haughburn Rd. G53 45 H2
Havelock La. G11 23 G2
Havelock St. G11 23 G2
Hawick Av. PA2 43 E4
Hawick St. G13 13 E4
Hawkhead Av. PA2 32 C5
Hawkhead Rd. PA1 32 C2
Hawthorn Av. G64 18 A2
Hawthorn Av. G61 11 F2
Hawthorn Dri. G78 55 G3
Hawthorn Gdns. G76 58 A5
Hawthorn Quad. G22 17 E5
Hawthorn Rd. G76 58 A5
Hawthorn St. G81 8 C4
Hawthorn St. G22 16 D6
Hawthorn Walk. G64 18 C3
Hawthorn Walk. G72 50 D3
Hawthornden Gdns. G23 16 A1
Hayburn Cres. G11 23 E2
Hayburn Gate. G11 23 F2
Hayburn La. G11 23 F1
Hayburn Pl. G11 23 F3
Hayburn St. G11 23 F3
Haylinn St. G14 22 C2
Haymarket St. G32 27 E6
Hayston Cres. G22 16 D5
Hayston St. G22 16 D6
Haywood St. G22 16 D4
Hazel Av. G44 11 F1
Hazel Dene. G64 18 B2
Hazelden Rd. G77 60 B4
Hazeldene Gdns. G44 48 A5
Hazellea Dri. G46 47 H5
Hazelwood Av. PA2 42 B5
Hazelwood Av. G77 60 C1
Hazelwood Gdns. G73 50 B5
Hazelwood Rd. G41 35 G2
Hazlitt Gdns. G20 16 C5
Hazlitt Pl. G20 16 C5
Hazlitt St. G20 16 C5
Heath Av. G64 18 A3
Heathcot Av. G15 9 G6
Heathcot Pl. G15 9 G6
Heather Av. G61 10 D1
Heather Av. G78 44 B4
Heather Av. G81 8 C1
Heatherbrae. G64 61 A4
Heatheryknowe Rd. G34 29 G5
Heathfield Dri. G62 6 E1
Heathfield St. G33 27 H5
Heathside Rd. G46 47 H5
Heathwood Dri. G46 47 E6
Hecla Av. G15 9 H5
Hecla Pl. G15 9 H6
Hecla Sq. G15 9 H6
Hector Rd. G41 47 H1
Helen St. G51 23 E6
Helensburgh Dri. G13 14 C5
Helenslea. G72 52 B5
Helenvale Ct. G31 38 C2
Helenvale St. G31 38 C3
Helmsdale Av. G72 53 E6
Helmsdale Dri. G72 42 C3
Hemlock St. G13 14 D4
Henderland Dri. G61 11 E6
Henderland Rd. G61 14 C1
Henderson Av. G72 52 B3
Henderson St. G20 24 B2
Henderson St. PA1 31 F5
Henderson St. G81 13 E3
Henrietta St. G14 22 A2
Henry St. G78 55 F1
Hepburn Rd. G52 21 H5
Herald Av. G13 14 B2
Herbert St. G20 24 B2
Herbertson St. G5 36 D2
Hercules Way. PA44 21 E3
Heriot Av. PA2 42 C5
Heriot Cres. G64 61 C2
Heriot Way. PA2 42 C4
Heritage Ct. G77 56 C5
Herma St. G23 16 A3
Hermiston Pl. G32 39 H1
Hermiston Rd. G32 27 G6
Hermiston St. G32 39 H1
Hermitage Av. G13 14 B4
Herndon Ct. G77 57 E5
Heron Ct. G81 8 D3
Heron St. G40 37 H2
Heron Way. PA4 20 D4
Herries Rd. G41 35 G5
Herriet St. G41 36 B4
Herschell St. G13 14 D5
Hertford Av. G12 15 F4
Hexham Gdns. G41 35 G5
Heys St. G78 55 G1
Hickman St. G42 36 D5
Hickman Ter. G42 36 D4
Hickory St. G22 17 F6
High Beeches. G76 59 F3
High Calside. PA2 43 G1
High Craighall St. G4 24 D3
High Flender Rd. G76 57 G5
High Rd. PA2 43 F1
High St. G1 5 F5
High St. G78 54 B5
High St. PA1 31 G6
High St. PA4 21 E1
High St. G73 49 H1
Highburgh Dri. G73 50 B3
Highburgh Rd. G12 23 G2
Highcroft Av. G44 49 F4
Highfield Av. PA2 43 F5
Highfield Cres. PA2 43 F5
Highfield Dri. G73 50 C5
Highfield Dri. G76 57 G4
Highfield Dri. G12 15 F4
Highfield Pl. G12 15 F4
Highland La. G72 23 F5
Hilary Av. G73 50 D3
Hilary Dri. G69 40 C2
Hilda Cres. G33 26 D1
Hill Av. G77 60 B1
Hill Cres. G76 58 A5
Hill St. G3 4 B2
Hillcrest. G76 59 F3
Hillcrest Av. G32 39 G6
Hillcrest Av. G81 8 D2
Hillcrest Av. PA2 43 E6
Hillcrest Av. G44 48 A4
Hillcrest Dri. G77 57 E6
Hillcrest Rd. G61 11 F5
Hillcrest Rd. G32 39 H6
Hillcrest St. G62 6 E2
Hillcroft Ter. G64 17 G3
Hillend Cres. G76 57 G5
Hillend Cres. G81 8 C2
Hillend Rd. G73 50 B4
Hillend Rd. G76 57 G5
Hillend Rd. G22 16 B4
Hillfoot Av. G61 11 F3
Hillfoot Av. G73 50 A1
Hillfoot Dri. G61 11 F3
Hillfoot Gdns. G71 53 H1
Hillfoot St. G31 25 H6
Hillhead Av. G73 50 A4
Hillhead Pl. G73 50 A5
Hillhead Rd. G21 18 C3
Hillhead St. G12 23 H3
Hillhead St. G62 6 E2
Hillhouse St. G21 17 H6
Hillington Cres. G52 34 A2
Hillington Gdns. G52 34 A2
Hillington Quad. G52 33 G2
Hillington Rd. G52 21 G4
Hillington Rd Sth. G52 33 G1
Hillington Ter. G52 33 G2
Hillkirk Pl. G21 25 G1
Hillkirk St. G21 17 G6
Hillneuk Av. G61 11 F3
Hillneuk Dri. G61 11 G3
Hillpark Av. PA2 43 G3
Hillpark Dri. G43 47 F3
Hillsborough Rd. G69 40 C2
Hillside Av. G61 11 F3
Hillside Av. G76 57 H4
Hillside Ct. G46 46 D5
Hillside Cres. G78 54 B5
Hillside Dri. G78 55 E1
Hillside Dri. G61 11 F3
Hillside Dri. G64 61 C3
Hillside Gro. G64 18 B3
Hillside Gro. G78 54 D1
Hillside Park. G81 8 D2
Hillside Quad. G43 47 F3
Hillside Rd. G78 54 D1
Hillside Rd. PA2 32 A5
Hillside Rd. G78 54 A5
Hillside Rd. G43 47 F3
Hillswick Cres. G22 16 D2
Hillview Cres. G71 41 H6
Hillview Dri. G72 57 H4
Hillview Gdns. G64 18 C3
Hillview Pl. G77 60 B1
Hillview Rd. PA5 42 A3
Hillview St. G32 39 E2
Hilton Gdns. G13 14 D3
Hilton Park. G64 61 B1
Hilton Rd. G64 61 B2
Hilton Rd. G62 6 C2
Hilton Ter. G64 61 B1
Hilton Ter. G72 50 D6
Hilton Ter. G13 14 D3
Hinshaw St. G20 24 B1
Hinshelwood Dri. G51 35 E1
Hobart Cres. G81 8 A3
Hobart St. G22 24 D1
Hobden St. G21 26 A2
Hoddam Av. G45 49 H6
Hoddam Ter. G45 49 H6
Hogan Ct. G81 8 B2
Hogarth Av. G32 26 C5
Hogarth Cres. G32 26 D5
Hogarth Dri. G32 26 D5
Hogarth Gdns. G32 26 C6
Hogganfield St. G33 26 D2
Holborn Av. PA3 30 D4
Holeburn La. G43 47 G3
Holeburn Rd. G43 47 G3
Holehouse Brae. G78 54 A4
Holehouse Dri. G13 13 G4
Holehouse Ter. G78 54 A5
Holland St. G2 4 B3
Hollinwell Rd. G23 15 H2
Hollowglen Rd. G32 39 G1
Hollows Av. PA2 42 C5
Hollows Cres. PA2 42 C5
Holly Dri. G21 25 H2
Holly Bank Pl. G72 51 G5
Holly St. G81 8 D4
Hollybank St. G21 25 H4
Hollybrook Pl. G42 36 D5
Hollybrook St. G42 36 D5
Hollybush Av. PA2 43 E6
Hollybush Rd. G52 33 F2
Hollymount. G61 11 F6
Holm Av. G71 53 H2
Holm St. G2 4 B4
Holmbank Av. G41 48 A1
Holmbyre Ct. G45 58 D2
Holmbyre Rd. G45 58 D1
Holmbyre Ter. G45 59 E1
Holmes Av. PA4 20 D3
Holmfauld Rd. G51 22 C4
Holmfauldhead Dri. G51 22 C5
Holmfauldhead Pl. G51 22 C4
Holmhead Cres. G44 48 C3
Holmhead Pl. G44 48 C3
Holmhead Rd. G44 48 C4
Holmhill Av. G72 51 F5
Holmhills Dri. G72 51 F5
Holmhills Gdns. G72 51 E5
Holmhills Gro. G72 51 F5
Holmhills Pl. G72 51 E5
Holmhills Rd. G72 51 E5
Holmhills Ter. G72 51 E5
Holmlea Rd. G44 48 C2
Holms Cres. PA8 7 A6
Holmwood Av. G71 53 H2
Holmwood Dri. G44 48 C5
Holmwood Gdns. G71 53 H2
Holyrood Cres. G20 24 B2
Holywell St. G31 38 B2
Honeybog Rd. G52 21 F6
Hood St. G81 9 F6
Hope St. G2 4 C5
Hopefield Av. G12 15 G5
Hopehill Gdns. G20 24 C2
Hopehill Rd. G20 24 C2
Hopeman. PA8 7 B5
Hopeman Av. G46 46 C4
Hopeman Dri. G46 46 C4
Hopeman Rd. G46 46 C5
Hopeman St. G46 46 C5
Hopetoun Pl. G23 16 A1
Horfield Dri. G44 48 D2
Hornbeam Dri. G81 8 C4
Horndean Ct. G64 61 C1
Horndean Cres. G33 28 A4
Horne St. G22 17 F5
Hornshill St. G21 25 H1
Horsburgh St. G33 28 A3
Horseshoe La. G61 11 E4
Horseshoe Rd. G61 11 E4
Horslethill Rd. G12 23 G1
Hotspur St. G20 16 A6
Houldsworth La. G3 24 A5
Houldsworth St. G3 24 A5
Househillmuir Cres. G53 46 A2
Househillmuir La. G53 46 A2
Househillmuir Pl. G53 46 A2
Househillmuir Rd. G53 45 G3
Househillwood Cres. G53 45 H2
Househillwood Rd. G53 45 G3
Housel Av. G13 13 H4
Houston Pl. G5 36 B1
Houston St. G5 36 B1
Houston St. PA4 12 D6
Howard St. G1 4 D5
Howard St. PA1 32 B2
Howat St. G51 23 E4
Howe St. PA1 42 C1
Howford Rd. G52 33 H3
Howgate Av. G15 9 H5
Howieshill Av. G72 51 G4
Howieshill Rd. G72 51 G4
Howth Dri. G13 14 D3
Howth Ter. G13 14 D3
Hoylake Pl. G23 16 A2
Hugh Murray Gro. G72 51 H4
Hughenden Dri. G12 15 F6
Hughenden Gdns. G12 23 F1
Hughenden La. G12 15 F6
Hughenden Rd. G12 15 F6
Hugo St. G20 16 B5
Humbie Ct. G77 60 D3
Humbie Gate. G77 60 D3
Humbie Gro. G77 60 D2
Humbie Lawns. G77 60 D3
Humbie Rd. G77 60 D2
Hume Dri. G71 53 G2
Hume St. G81 12 C2
Hunter Pl. G62 6 C3
Hunter Rd. G73 38 B5
Hunter Rd. G73 6 B2
Hunter St. G4 5 H5
Hunter St. PA1 31 G5
Hunterfield Dri. G72 50 D4
Hunterhill Av. PA2 32 A4
Hunterhill Rd. PA2 32 A4
Huntershill Rd. G64 17 H3
Huntershill St. G64 17 G4
Huntershill Way. G64 17 H3
Hunthill Pl. G76 58 B6
Huntingdon Rd. G21 25 F2
Huntingtower Rd. G69 40 C3
Huntly Av. G46 57 H1
Huntly Ct. G64 18 A3
Huntly Dri. G61 11 E2
Huntly Dri. G72 51 G5
Huntly Gdns. G12 23 G1
Huntly Gate. G46 47 G6
Huntly Rd. G12 23 G1
Huntly Rd. G52 21 F5
Huntly Ter. PA2 32 A5
Hurlet Cotts. G53 45 F3
Hurlet Rd. PA2 44 D1
Hurley Hawkin. G64 18 C2
Hurlford Av. G13 13 F4
Hutcheson Rd. G46 57 E1
Hutcheson St. G1 5 E5
Hutchinson Pl. G72 52 B5
Hutchison Ct. G46 57 F2
Hutchison Dri. G61 11 G6
Hutton. G12 15 E5
Hutton Dri. G51 22 C5
Huxley St. G20 16 B5
Hydepark St. G3 24 B6
Hyndal Av. G53 34 A6
Hyndland Av. G11 23 F2
Hyndland Rd. G12 23 F1
Hyndland St. G11 23 G3
Hyndlee Dri. G52 34 B2
Hyslop Pl. G81 8 C5

Iain Dri. G61 10 C2
Iain Rd. G61 10 C3
Ian Smith Ct. G81 12 D2
Ibrox St. G51 35 G1
Ibrox Ter. G51 35 F1
Ibroxholm Av. G51 35 F1
Ibroxholm Oval. G51 35 F1
*Ibroxholm Pl, Ibroxholm Av. G51 35 F1
Iddells Ct. G64 18 A3
Iddesleigh Av. G62 6 D2
Ilay Av. G61 14 D2
Ilay Ct. G61 15 E3
Ilay Rd. G61 15 E2
Inchbrae Rd. G52 34 A3
Inchcruin Pl. G15 9 G5
Inchfad Dri. G15 9 G5
Inchfad Pl. G15 9 G5
Inchinnan Rd. PA3 31 H4
Inchinnan Rd. PA4 20 C1
Inchkeith Pl. G32 27 G6
Inchlaggan Pl. G15 9 G5
Inchlee St. G14 22 C2
Inchmoan Pl. G15 9 G4
Inchoch St. G33 28 B3
Incholm La. G14 22 C3
Inchrory Pl. G15 9 G4
Incle St. PA1 32 A2
India St. G2 4 A3
INDUSTRIAL & RETAIL:
Abbey Mill Business Centre. PA1 32 A3
Abercorn Ind Est. PA3 31 H4
Albion Works Ind Est. G13 13 F4
Annick St Ind Est. G32 39 H2
Anniesland Ind Est. G13 14 C3
Atlas Ind Est. G21 25 H1
Auldhouse Retail Pk. G43 47 G2
Baljaffray Shopping Centre. G61 10 C1
Balmore Ind Est. G22 16 D3
Blythswood Retail Pk. PA4 12 C6
Braehead Shopping Centre. PA4 21 G2
Bridgewater Ind Pk. PA8 7 C6
Cairnbrook Ind Est. G34 29 E4
Cambuslang Investment Park. G32 51 F1
Carntyne Ind Est. G32 38 D1
Chapel St Ind Est. G20 16 A5
Cloberfield Ind Est. G62 6 D1

Kingfisher Gdns. G13 13 G3
Kinghorn Dri. G44 48 D2
Kinghorn La. G44 49 E2
Kinglas Rd. G61 10 C6
Kings Bri. G5 37 F2
Kings Cres. PA5 42 A2
Kings Cres. G72 51 G3
Kings Dri. G40 37 F3
Kings Dri. G77 60 E2
Kings Gdns. G77 60 E2
Kings Inch Dri. PA4 21 G2
Kings Inch Pl. PA4 21 G2
Kings Inch Rd. PA4 13 E6
Kings Park Av. G44 48 D3
Kings Park Rd. G44 48 D2
Kings Pl. G22 16 D4
Kingsacre Av. G44 49 E2
Kingsbarns Dri. G44 48 D2
Kingsborough Gdns. G12 23 F1
Kingsborough Gate. G12 23 F2
Kingsborough La. G12 23 F1
Kingsborough La East. G12 23 F1
Kingsbrae Av. G44 49 E2
Kingsbridge Cres. G44 49 F2
Kingsbridge Dri. G44 49 E3
Kingsburgh Dri. PA1 32 C1
Kingsburn Dri. G73 50 A3
Kingsburn Gro. G73 49 H3
Kingscliffe Av. G44 49 E2
Kingscourt Av. G44 49 E2
Kingsdale Av. G44 48 D2
Kingsdyke Av. G44 49 E2
Kingsford Av. G44 48 A5
Kingsford Ct. G77 56 A5
Kingsheath Av. G73 49 F3
Kingshill Dri. G44 49 E3
Kingshouse Av. G44 49 E2
Kingshurst Av. G44 49 E2
Kingsknowe Dri. G73 49 G3
Kingsland Dri. G52 34 A1
Kingsland La. G52 34 B1
Kingslynn Dri. G44 49 E3
Kingston Av. G78 54 B6
Kingston Pl. G81 7 D4
Kingston Rd. G78 54 B6
Kingston St. G5 36 C1
Kingsway. G14 13 H6
Kingsway Ct. G14 13 H6
Kingswood Dri. G44 49 E3
Kingussie Dri. G44 49 E3
Kiniver Dri. G15 13 H1
Kinloch Av. G72 51 G5
Kinloch Rd. PA4 20 B4
Kinloch Rd. G77 56 B5
Kinloch St. G40 38 B2
Kinmount Av. G44 48 D2
Kinnaird Av. G77 57 E6
Kinnaird Cres. G61 11 G4
Kinnaird Pl. G64 18 B3
Kinnear Rd. G40 38 A3
Kinnell Av. G52 34 B4
Kinnell Cres. G52 34 A4
Kinnel Pl. G52 34 B4
Kinning St. G5 36 B2
Kinnoul Gdns. G61 10 D1
Kinnoul La. G12 32 G2
Kinpurnie Rd. PA1 32 D1
Kinross Av. G52 33 H3
Kinsail Dri. G52 21 F6
Kinstone Av. G14 13 G5
Kintessack Pl. G64 61 F3
Kintillo Dri. G13 14 A5
Kintore Rd. G43 48 B3
Kintra St. G51 23 F6
Kintyre Cres. G77 56 A5
Kintyre St. G21 25 H4
Kippen Dri. G76 58 C6
Kippen St. G22 17 E5
Kippford St. G32 39 H3
Kirk Cres. G60 7 A1
Kirk Glebe. G78 54 C4
Kirk La. G43 47 G2
Kirk Pl. G61 11 E3
Kirk Pl. G71 53 H3
Kirk Rd. G61 11 E3
Kirk Rd. G76 59 F4
Kirk St. G62 6 C2
Kirkaig Av. PA4 21 F3
Kirkbean Av. G73 50 A5
Kirkburn Av. G72 51 F5
Kirkcaldy Rd. G41 35 H5
Kirkconnel Av. G68 13 F4
Kirkconnel Dri. G73 49 G4
Kirkdale Dri. G52 34 C3
Kirkdene Av. G77 57 F6
Kirkdene Bank. G77 57 F6
Kirkdene Cres. G77 57 F6
Kirkdene Gro. G77 60 F1
Kirkdene Pl. G77 57 F6
Kirkhill Av. G72 51 F6
Kirkhill Cres. G78 54 C4
Kirkhill Dri. G20 15 H5
Kirkhill Gate. G77 60 F1
Kirkhill Gdns. G72 51 F5
Kirkhill Gro. G72 51 F6
Kirkhill Pl. G20 15 H5
Kirkhill Rd. G71 53 H1
Kirkhill Rd. G77 60 F1
Kirkhill Ter. G72 51 F5
Kirkhope Dri. G15 13 H1
Kirkinner Rd. G32 40 A3
Kirkintilloch Rd. G64 61 B4
Kirkland St. G20 24 B2
Kirklandneuk Rd. PA4 20 B1
Kirklands Pl. G77 60 B3
Kirklands Rd. G77 60 B3
Kirkle Dri. G77 57 F6
Kirklea Av. PA3 30 D5
Kirklee Circus. G12 23 G1
Kirklee Gdns. G12 15 G6
Kirklee Gdns La. G12 15 G6
Kirklee Gate. G12 15 H6
Kirklee Pl. G12 15 H6
Kirklee Quad. G12 15 G6
Kirklee Rd. G12 15 G6
Kirklee Ter. G12 23 G1
Kirkliston St. G32 27 E6
Kirkmichael Av. G11 23 E2
Kirkmichael Gdns. G11 23 E2
Kirkmuir Dri. G73 50 A6
Kirknewton St. G32 39 G1
Kirkoswald Dri. G81 9 E5
Kirkoswald Rd. G43 47 G3
Kirkpatrick St. G31 38 A2
Kirkriggs Av. G73 50 A4
Kirkriggs Gdns. G73 50 A4
Kirkriggs Way. G73 50 A4
Kirkstall Gdns. G64 61 D1
Kirkstyle Cres. G78 54 B5
Kirkstyle La. G78 54 B5
Kirkton. PA8 7 B5
Kirkton. G60 7 B2
Kirkton Av. G78 55 E2
Kirkton Av. G13 13 G4
Kirkton Cres. G13 13 G5
Kirkton Rd. G72 51 G4
Kirkton Rd. G78 54 B5
Kirkton Side. G78 55 E3
Kirktonfield Rd. G78 54 C4
Kirkvale Ct. G77 57 F6
Kirkvale Cres. G77 57 F6
Kirkvale Dri. G77 57 E6
Kirkview Cres. G77 60 C2
Kirkview Gdns. G71 53 H1
Kirkwall Av. G72 53 E6
Kirkwell Rd. G44 48 D3
Kirkwood Av. G81 13 E1
Kirkwood Quad. G81 13 E1
Kirkwood St. G51 35 G2
Kirkwood St. G73 50 A1
Kirn St. G20 15 G3
Kirriemuir Av. G52 34 B3
Kirriemuir Gdns. G64 61 E3
Kirriemuir Pl. G52 34 B3
Kirriemuir Rd. G64 61 E3
Kirtle Dri. PA4 21 E3
Kishorn Pl. G33 27 H3
Kittochside Rd. G76 59 F4
Knapdale St. G22 16 C4
Knights Gate. G71 53 G3
Knightsbridge St. G13 14 B4
Knightscliffe Av. G13 14 C3
Knightswood Ct. G13 14 B4
Knightswood Rd. G13 14 B2
Knock Way. PA3 20 B5
Knockhall St. G33 28 A3
Knockhill Dri. G44 48 D2
Knockhill Rd. PA4 20 B3
Knockside Av. PA2 43 F5
Knollpark Dri. G76 57 G4
Knowe St. G62 6 D3
Knowehead Dri. G71 53 H3
Knowehead Gdns. G41 36 A3
Knowehead Gdns. G71 53 H3
Knowehead Ter. G41 36 A3
Knowes Av. G77 56 D6
Knowes Rd. G77 56 D6
Knowetap St. G20 16 A3
Knox Pl. G77 60 A1
Knox St. PA1 31 E6
Kyle Ct. G72 51 F3
Kyle Dri. G46 48 A6
Kyle Sq. G73 49 H4
Kyle St. G4 5 E2
Kyleakin Rd. G46 46 C5
Kyleakin Ter. G46 45 B6
Kylepark Av. G71 53 G2
Kylepark Cres. G71 53 G2
Kylepark Dri. G71 53 G2
Kylerhea Rd. G46 46 B6

La Belle Allee. G3 24 A4
La Belle Pl. G3 24 A4
La Crosse Ter. G12 24 A2
Laburnum Rd. G41 35 G2
Lacy St. PA1 32 B2
Lade Ter. G52 33 G3
Ladeside Clo. G77 56 A5
Ladhope Pl. G13 13 E2
Lady Anne St. G14 13 F5
Lady Isle Cres. G71 53 G3
Lady Jane Gate. G71 53 G5
Lady La. PA1 31 G6
Ladybank Dri. G52 34 C3
Ladyburn St. PA1 32 A3
Ladyhill Dri. G69 40 D3
Ladykirk Cres. PA2 32 A4
Ladykirk Dri. G52 34 A1
Ladyloan Av. G15 9 G4
Ladyloan Ct. G15 9 H4
Ladyloan Gdns. G15 9 H4
Ladyloan Pl. G15 9 G4
Ladymuir Cres. G53 34 A5
Ladywell St. G4 5 H4
Ladywood. G62 6 E2
Laggan Rd. G64 61 D4
Laggan Rd. G77 56 B4
Laggan Rd. G43 48 A4
Laggan Ter. PA4 20 B1
Laidlaw St. G5 36 C1
Laigh Park View. PA3 31 G3
Laigh Rd. G77 57 F5
Lainshaw Dri. G45 58 C1
Laird Pl. G40 37 G3
Lairds Gate. G71 53 G4
Lairg Dri. G72 53 F6
Lamb St. G22 16 D5
Lamberton Dri. G52 34 A1
Lambhill Quad. G41 35 H2
Lambhill St. G41 36 A2
Lambie Cres. G77 56 A6
Lamington Rd. G52 33 H2
Lamlash Cres. G33 27 F4
Lamlash Pl. G33 27 G4
Lamlash Sq. G33 27 H4
Lammermoor Av. G52 34 B3
Lammermuir Ct. PA2 43 G4
Lammermuir Dri. PA2 43 G4
Lammermuir Gdns. G61 10 C1
Lamont Rd. G21 18 A5
Lanark St. G1 37 F1
Lancaster Cres. G12 15 G6
Lancaster Cres La. G12 15 G6
Lancaster Rd. G64 61 D1
Lancefield Quay. G3 24 A6
Lancefield St. G3 24 B6
Landemer Dri. G73 49 H3
Landressy St. G40 37 G3
Lane Gdns. G12 23 F2
Lanfine Rd. PA1 32 C2
Lang Av. PA4 20 D3
Lang St. PA1 32 B3
Langa St. G20 16 A3
Langbank St. G5 36 D2
Langbar Cres. G33 28 B5
Langbar Path. G33 28 A5
Langcraigs Ct. PA2 43 F5
Langcraigs Dri. PA2 43 F6
Langcraigs Ter. PA2 43 F6
Langcroft Dri. G72 51 H4
Langcroft Pl. G51 22 B5
Langcroft Rd. G51 22 B6
Langcroft Ter. G51 22 B6
Langdale Av. G33 26 D2
Langdale St. G33 26 D2
Langfaulds Cres. G81 9 F2
Langford Dri. G53 45 H5
Langford Pl. G53 45 H6
Langhaul Rd. G53 33 F6
Langholm St. G14 13 G5
Langlands Av. G51 22 C5
Langlands Ct. G51 22 D5
Langlands Dri. G51 22 A5
Langlands Rd. G51 22 C5
Langlea Av. G72 50 D4
Langlea Ct. G72 50 D4
Langlea Dri. G72 50 D4
Langlea Gdns. G72 50 D4
Langlea Gro. G72 50 D4
Langlea Rd. G72 50 D4
Langlea Way. G72 50 D4
Langlees Av. G77 57 F6
Langley Av. G13 13 H3
Langmuirhead Rd. G33 19 E3
Langness Rd. G33 27 G5
Langrig Rd. G21 18 A6
Langshot St. G51 35 H1
Langside Av. G41 36 A6
Langside Dri. G43 48 A4
Langside Gdns. G42 48 C2
Langside La. G42 36 C5
Langside Pl. G41 48 B1
Langside Rd. G42 36 C6
Langside St. G81 9 G2
Langstile Pl. G52 33 F1
Langstile Rd. G52 33 F1
Langton Cres. G78 55 G3
Langton Cres. G53 34 A6
Langton Gdns. G69 40 C3
Langton Gate. G77 56 A6
Langton Pl. G77 56 A6
Langton Rd. G53 34 B6
Langtree Av. G46 57 E2
Lanrig Rd. G77 60 B2
Lansbury Gdns. PA3 31 F3
Lansdowne Cres. G20 24 B2
Lansdowne Cres La. G20 24 B2
Lanton Dri. G52 34 A1
Lanton Rd. G43 48 A4
Lappin St. G81 13 E2
Larbert St. G4 4 D2
Larch Av. G64 18 B2
Larch Rd. G41 35 F2
Larchfield Av. G77 60 C1
Larchfield Av. G14 13 H6
Larchfield Ct. G77 60 C1
Larchfield Dri. G73 50 B5
Larchfield Pl. G14 13 H6
Larchfield Rd. G61 14 D2
Larchgrove Av. G32 27 H6
Larchgrove Pl. G32 27 H6
Larchgrove Rd. G32 27 H6
Larchwood Ter. G78 55 H3
Largie Rd. G43 48 B4
Largo Pl. G51 22 D5
Larkfield St. G42 36 D4
Larkin Gdns. PA3 31 G3
Lasswade St. G14 13 E4
Latherton Dri. G20 15 H5
Latimer Gdns. G52 33 G3
Latimer Path. G52 33 G3
Lauder Dri. G73 50 C2
Lauder St. G5 36 C3
Lauderdale Dri. G77 60 B2
Lauderdale Gdns. G12 23 F2
Lauderdale La. G12 23 F1
Laurel Av. G81 8 A4
Laurel Park Gdns. G13 14 B5
Laurel Pl. G11 23 E1
Laurel St. G11 23 E2
Laurel Walk. G73 50 C5
Laurel Way. G78 44 B6
Laurelbank Rd. G32 51 H1
Lauren Way. PA2 42 D3
Laurence Ct. G15 9 G5
Laurence Dri. G15 9 G5
Laurence Dri. G61 10 D3
Laurence Gdns. G15 9 G5
Laurieston Rd. G5 37 E2
Laurieston Way. G73 50 A5
Laverockhall St. G21 25 G2
Law St. G40 38 A2
Lawers Dri. G61 10 C2
Lawers Rd. G43 47 F4
Lawers Rd. PA4 20 C4
Lawfield Av. G77 57 F6
Lawhill Av. G45 49 E5
Lawmoor Av. G5 37 E4
Lawmoor Pl. G5 37 E4
Lawmoor Rd. G5 37 E4
Lawmoor St. G5 37 E3
Lawmuir Cres. G81 9 G1
Lawn St. PA1 31 H6
Lawrence Av. G46 57 G2
Lawrence St. G11 23 G2
Lawrie St. G11 23 F3
Laxford Av. G44 48 C4
Lea Av. G78 54 B5
Leabank Av. PA2 43 H4
Leadburn Rd. G21 26 B1
Leadburn St. G32 27 E5
Leader St. G33 26 C3
Leander Cres. PA4 21 F3
Learmont Pl. G62 6 C2
Leckie St. G43 47 G1
Ledaig Pl. G31 26 C6
Ledaig St. G31 26 C5
Ledard Rd. G42 48 B1
Ledcameroch Cres. G61 11 E4
Ledcameroch Park. G61 10 D4
Ledcameroch Rd. G61 10 D4
Ledgowan Pl. G20 15 G3
Ledi Dri. G61 10 B1
Ledi Rd. G43 47 G4
Ledmore Dri. G15 9 H4
Lednock. G52 33 H2
Lednock Rd. G52 19 H6
Lee Av. G33 27 E3
Lee Cres. G64 61 B4
Lee Wood Dri. G44 58 B1
Leebank Dri. G44 58 B2
Leefield Dri. G44 58 B1
Leehill Rd. G21 17 G3
Leeside Rd. G21 17 G4
Leggaiston Rd. G53 46 B6
Leglan Wood Cres. G33 18 D5
Leglan Wood Dri. G33 18 D5
Leglan Wood Gdns. G33 18 D4
Leglan Wood Pl. G33 18 D5
Leglan Wood Rd. G33 18 D5
Leicester Av. G12 15 F6
Leighton St. G20 16 A4
Leitchland Rd. PA2 42 A4
Leith St. G33 26 C5
Leithland Av. G53 33 H6
Leithland Rd. G53 33 H5
Lembert Dri. G76 57 H3
Lendel Pl. G51 35 G1
Lendale La. G64 61 C1
Lenihall Dri. G64 59 F1
Lenihall Ter. G45 49 G1
Lennox Av. G62 6 D3
Lennox Av. G14 22 B1
Lennox Ct. G61 11 E1
Lennox Cres. G64 17 G3
Lennox Dri. G61 11 F2
Lennox Gdns. G14 22 B1
Lennox La E. G14 22 B1
*Lennox La W, Gleneagles La N. G14 22 B1
Lennox Rd. G81 9 E2
Lennox Ter. PA3 20 B5
Lentran St. G34 29 F5
Leny St. G20 16 B6
Lenzie Pl. G21 17 G5
Lenzie St. G21 17 G6
Lenzie Ter. G21 17 G5
Lenzie Way. G21 17 G5
Leslie Av. G77 56 C4
Leslie Rd. G41 36 A4
Leslie St. G41 36 B4
Lesmuir Dri. G14 13 G5
Lesmuir Pl. G14 13 G5
Leterfearn Gdns. G23 16 A1
Letham Ct. G43 47 H4
Letham Dri. G64 18 C2
Letham Dri. G43 47 H4
Lethamhill Cres. G33 27 E4
Lethamhill Pl. G33 26 D4
Lethamhill Rd. G33 26 D4
Letherby Dri. G44 48 D2
Lethington Av. G41 48 A1
Lethington Pl. G41 48 B1
Lethington Rd. G46 57 E4
Letterfearn Dri. G23 15 H1
Letterfearn Rd. G23 15 H1
Letterickhills Cres. G72 52 B6
Lettoch St. G51 23 E6
Leven Ct. G78 44 C4
Leven Dri. G61 11 F5
Leven Sq. PA4 20 B1
Leven St. G41 36 B4
Leven Way. PA2 42 B4
Levendale Rd. G53 33 F5
Levern Cres. G78 55 F2
Levern Gdns. G78 55 E1
Levern Rd. G78 45 E4
Levernside Av. G53 55 E2
Levernside Cres. G53 34 A6
Levernside Rd. G53 34 A6
Lewis Av. PA4 20 D4
Lewis Cres. G60 7 C3
Lewis Dri. G60 7 C3
Lewis Gdns. G61 10 B2
Lewis Gdns. G60 7 C3
Lewis Gro. G60 7 C3
Lewis Pl. G60 7 C3
Lewiston Rd. G23 15 H2
Lexwell Av. PA5 42 A2
Leyden Ct. G20 16 A6
Leyden Gdns. G20 16 A6
Leyden St. G20 16 A6
Liberton St. G33 26 C5
Libo Av. G53 34 B6
Liddell St. G32 39 H6
Liddesdale Av. PA2 42 B5
Liddesdale Pass. G22 17 E3
Liddesdale Rd. G22 16 D3
Liddesdale Sq. G22 17 F3
Liddesdale Ter. G22 17 F3
Liddoch Way. G73 49 H1
Liff Gdns. G64 18 C2
Liff Pl. G34 29 F4
Lightburn Pl. G32 27 G6
Lightburn Rd. G32 26 C6

Lightburn Rd. G72 52 A5
Lilac Av. G81 8 A3
Lilac Gdns. G64 18 A2
Lilac Wynd. G52 52 C5
Lillyhank Av. G72 51 H5
Lillybank Gdns. G12 23 H2
Lillybank Gdns La. G12 23 H2
Lillyburn Pl. G15 9 G4
Lily St. G49 38 A4
*Lime La, Earlbank
   La Sth. G14 22 B2
Lime St. G14 22 B2
Limecraigs Av. PA2 43 F6
Limecraigs Cres. PA2 43 F6
Limecraigs Rd. PA2 43 E6
Limekilns G81 9 F2
Limeside Av. G73 50 B2
Limeside Gdns. G73 50 C2
Limetree Cres. PA2 60 C1
Limetree Dri. G81 8 C4
Limeview Av. PA2 43 E6
Limeview Cres. PA2 43 E6
Limeview Rd. PA2 43 E6
Limeview Way. PA2 43 E6
Linacre Dri. G32 40 A2
Linburn Rd. G52 21 F6
Lincoln Av. G13 14 A4
Lincuan Av. G46 57 G2
Linden Dri. G81 8 D3
Linden Pl. G13 14 D3
Linden St. G13 14 D4
Lindores Av. G73 50 B2
Lindores St. G42 48 D1
Lindrick Dri. G23 15 H2
Lindsay Dri. G12 15 F4
Lindsay Pl. G12 15 F5
Linfern Rd. G12 23 G1
Links Rd. G32 40 A4
Linkwood Av. G15 9 H5
Linkwood Dri. G15 10 A5
Linkwood Gdns. G15 10 B5
Linkwood Pl. G15 9 H5
Linlithgow Gdns. G32 40 A2
Linn Cres. PA2 43 F5
Linn Dri. G44 48 B5
Linn Valley Vw. G45 49 F6
Linnet Pl. G13 13 G3
Linnhe Av. G44 48 C4
Linnhe Av. G64 61 D4
Linnhe Dri. G78 44 C4
Linnhead Dri. G53 45 H3
Linnhead Pl. G14 22 A1
Linnpark Av. G44 48 B6
Linnpark Ct. G44 48 B6
Linside Av. PA1 32 B3
Linthaugh Rd. G53 34 A4
Linthaugh Ter. G53 34 B6
Linthouse Bldgs. G51 22 C4
Linthouse Rd. G51 22 C4
Lintlaw Dri. G52 34 A1
Lintmill Ter. G78 54 A5
Linton St. G33 26 D5
Linwell Cres. PA2 43 F5
Linwood Av. G76 58 B4
Linwood Rd. PA1 30 A5
Lismore Av. PA2 20 D4
Lismore Ct. G12 15 F6
Lismore Dri. PA2 43 G5
Lismore Pl. G77 56 A5
Lister Gdns. G76 58 C6
Lister Rd. G52 21 G6
Lister St. G4 5 F2
Lithgow Cres. PA2 32 A5
Little Dover Hill. G31 5 G6
Little St. G3 24 B5
Littleholm Pl. G81 8 A4
Littlemill Cres. G53 45 H1
Littlemill Dri. G53 45 H1
Littleton Dri. G23 15 G2
Littleton St. G23 15 G2
Livingstone Av. G52 21 G5
Livingstone St. G81 12 C1
Lloyd Av. G32 39 F4
Lloyd St. G31 25 H5
Lloyd St. G73 38 B6
Loanbank Pl. G51 23 E6
Loanbank Quad. G51 23 E6
Loancroft Av. G69 41 F3
Loancroft Gate. G71 53 H4
Loancroft Pl. G69 41 E3
Loanfoot Av. G78 54 B6
Loanfoot Av. G13 13 G3
Loanhead Av. G52 27 E6
Loanhead Av. PA4 20 D1
Lobnitz Av. PA4 20 D2
Loch Achray St. G32 39 H3
Loch Broom Dri. G77 42 D3
Loch Inver Gro. G72 51 H4
Loch Katrine St. G32 39 H3
Loch Laidon St. G32 40 A3

Loch Rd. G62 6 E2
Loch Voil St. G32 40 A3
Lochaber Dri. G73 50 C5
Lochaber Rd. G61 11 G6
Lochaline Av. PA2 42 D2
Lochaline Dri. G44 48 C4
Lochalsh Dri. PA2 42 D3
Lochar Cres. G53 34 B5
Lochard Dri. PA2 42 D3
Lochay St. G32 39 H3
Lochbridge Rd. G34 28 D5
Lochbroom Dri. PA2 56 D1
Lochburn Cres. G20 16 A4
Lochburn Passage. G20 16 A4
Lochburn Rd. G20 16 A4
Lochburn St. G20 16 A4
Lochdochart Path. G34 29 F5
Lochdochart Rd. G34 29 F5
Lochearn Cres. PA2 42 D3
Lochearnhead Rd. G33 19 G6
Lochend Dri. G61 10 D5
Lochend Dri. G61 10 D5
Lochend Rd. G61 11 E5
Lochend Rd. G34 29 E4
Lochfauld Rd. G23 16 C1
Lochfield Cres. PA2 32 A6
Lochfield Dri. PA2 32 A6
Lochfield Gdns. G34 29 F4
Lochfield Rd. PA2 32 A6
Lochgilp St. G20 15 G3
Lochgoin Av. G15 9 G4
Lochgreen St. G33 26 D2
Lochiel La. G73 50 D5
Lochilbo Av. G13 13 G4
Lochinver Cres. PA2 42 D2
Lochinver Dri. G44 48 C4
Lochlea Av. G81 9 F5
Lochlea Rd. G76 58 A6
Lochlea Rd. G43 47 H3
Lochlea Rd. G73 49 H4
Lochleven La. G42 48 C2
Lochlibo Cres. G78 54 D3
Lochlibo Rd. G78 54 A4
Lochlibo Ter. G78 55 E3
Lochmaben Rd. G52 33 G3
Lochmaddy Av. G44 48 C4
Lochnagar Dri. G61 10 B1
Lochore Av. PA3 20 A6
Lochside. G61 11 E5
Lochside St. G41 36 A6
Lochview Cres. G33 27 E1
Lochview Dri. G33 27 E1
Lochview Gdns. G33 27 E2
Lochview Pl. G33 27 E1
Lochview Rd. G61 11 E5
Lochwood Gdns. G34 29 G5
Lochwood St. G33 26 D2
Lochy Av. PA4 21 F3
Lochy Gdns. G64 61 D3
Lockerbie Av. G43 48 B3
Lockhart Av. G72 52 A3
Lockhart Dri. G72 52 A3
Lockhart St. G21 26 B2
Locksley Av. G13 14 A2
Locksley Rd. PA2 42 C4
Locksley Way. PA2 42 C4
Logan Av. G77 56 B5
Logan Dri. PA3 31 F4
Logan St. G5 37 F4
Loganswell Dri. G46 56 C1
Loganswell Gdns. G46 56 C1
Loganswell Pl. G46 56 C1
Loganswell Rd. G46 56 C1
Lomax St. G33 26 C5
Lomond Av. PA4 20 C4
Lomond Cres. PA2 43 G4
Lomond Ct. G78 55 F2
Lomond Dr. G64 61 B2
Lomond Dri. G77 56 B4
Lomond Dri. G78 44 C5
Lomond Gdns. PA5 42 A2
Lomond Rd. G61 14 D1
Lomond Rd. G64 16 D5
Lomondside Av. G76 57 G3
London Rd. G32 40 A5
London Rd. G40 38 A2
London Rd. G1 37 F1
London St. PA4 13 E5
Lonend. PA1 32 A3
Long Row. G69 41 F1
Longay Pl. G22 17 E3
Longay St. G22 17 E3
Longcroft Dri. PA4 20 D1
Longden St. G81 13 E3
Longford St. G33 26 D4
Longlee. G69 41 E2
Longstone Pl. G33 27 G4
Longstone Rd. G33 27 F4
Lonmay Rd. G33 28 A5

Lonsdale Av. G46 47 G6
Lora Dri. G52 34 C2
Loretto Pl. G33 27 F4
Loretto St. G33 27 E5
Lorne Av. G52 61 F3
Lorne Cres. G64 61 F3
Lorne Rd. G52 21 F5
Lorne St. G51 35 H1
Lorne Ter. G72 51 E6
Lorraine Gdns. G12 23 G1
Lorraine Rd. G12 23 G1
Loskin Dri. G22 16 D3
Lossie Cres. PA4 21 F3
Lossie St. G33 26 C4
Lothian Cres. PA2 43 G4
Lothian Dri. G76 57 H3
Lothian Gdns. G20 24 A1
Lothian St. G52 21 E5
Louden Hill Way. G33 18 D5
Loudon Rd. G33 19 G6
Loudon Ter. G61 10 D1
Lounsdale Av. PA2 43 E2
Lounsdale Cres. PA2 43 E2
Lounsdale Dri. PA2 43 E2
Lounsdale Gro. PA2 43 E2
Lounsdale Ho. PA2 43 E2
Lounsdale Pl. G14 13 H6
Lounsdale Rd. PA2 43 E2
Lounsdale Way. PA2 43 E2
Lourdes Av. G52 34 B3
Lourdes Ct. G52 34 B3
Lovat Av. G61 11 E1
Lovat Pl. G73 50 D5
Love St. PA3 31 H4
Low Broadlie Rd. G78 54 B4
Low Cres. G81 13 E3
Low Flender Rd. G76 57 H6
Low Pd. PA2 43 F1
Lower Bourtree Dri.
   G73 50 B5
Lower Mill Rd. G76 58 B5
Lower Millgate. G71 53 H3
Lowndes St. G78 55 F2
Lowther Av. G61 10 C1
Loyal Gdns. G61 10 B1
Loyne Dri. PA4 21 F3
Luath St. G51 23 E4
Lubaig Gdns. G61 10 C1
Lubas Av. G42 49 F2
Lubas Pl. G42 49 F1
Lubnaig Rd. G43 48 A3
Luckies Fauld. G78 54 B5
Lucy Brae. G71 53 G3
Luffness Gdns. G32 39 G5
Lugar Dri. G52 34 C3
Lugar Pl. G73 49 G4
Luing Rd. G52 34 C2
Luma Gdns. G51 22 A5
Lumloch St. G21 17 H6
Lumsden St. G3 23 H4
Lunan Dri. G64 18 C2
Lunan Pl. G51 22 D6
Luncarty Pl. G32 39 G3
Luncarty St. G32 39 G3
Lunderston Dri. G53 45 G2
Lundie Gdns. G64 61 F4
Lundie St. G32 38 D4
Luss Rd. G51 22 D6
Lusset Glen. G60 7 C3
Lusset Rd. G60 7 C2
Lusshill Ter. G71 41 E4
Lybster Cres. G73 50 D6
Lyle Pl. PA2 32 A5
Lyle St. G62 6 C2
Lylesland Ct. PA2 43 H2
Lymburn St. G3 23 H4
Lyndale Pl. G20 15 H3
Lyndale Rd. G20 15 H3
Lyndhurst Gdns. G20 24 B1
Lyne Croft. G64 61 C1
Lyne Dri. G23 16 A2
Lynedoch Cres. G3 24 B4
Lynedoch Pl. G3 24 B4
Lynedoch St. G3 24 B4
Lynedoch Ter. G3 24 B4
Lynn Dri. G62 6 F2
Lynton Av. G46 57 E2
Lyon Rd. PA2 42 C3
Lyoncross Av. G78 44 D6
Lyoncross Cres. G78 44 D6
Lyoncross Rd. G53 33 H4
Lytham Dri. G23 16 A2

McClue Av. PA4 20 C1
McClue Rd. PA4 20 C1
McCracken Av. PA4 20 C2
McFarlane St. G81 13 E3
McCreery St. G81 13 E3
McCulloch St. G41 36 B3
MacDonald Cres. G81 12 D3
McDonald Pl. G78 54 C4
McDougall St. G43 47 G1
MacDuff. PA8 7 B6
MacDuff Pl. G31 38 C3
MacDuff St. G31 38 C3
McEwan St. G31 38 C2
Macfarlane Cres. G72 51 H4
McFarlane Rd. G61 11 F6
McFarlane St. G4 5 G6
McFarlane St. PA3 31 F4
McGhee St. G81 9 E5
McGowan St. PA3 31 G4
McGregor Ct. G72 51 H4
McGregor St. G51 22 D6
McGregor St. G81 12 D3
McGrigor Rd. G62 6 C1
McInlay St. G5 36 C3
McIntosh Ct. G31 25 G6
McIntosh St. G31 25 G6
McIntyre Pl. PA2 43 G2
MacIntyre St. G3 4 A4
MacIntyre Ter. G72 51 F3
McIver St. G72 52 B3
McKay Pl. G77 60 A1
McKean St. PA3 31 F4
McKechnie St. G51 23 E4
McKeith St. G40 37 G3
McKenzie Av. G81 9 E5
McKenzie St. PA3 31 E5
McKerrell St. PA1 32 A2
McKinley Pl. G77 60 B1
McLaren Cres. G20 16 A4
McLaren Gdns. G20 16 A4
McLean Pl. PA3 31 G3
McLean Sq. G51 23 H6
Maclean St. G41 35 H1
*Maclean St,
   Wood Quad. G81 13 E2
Macellan St. G41 35 H2
McLennan St. G42 48 C1
MacLeod St. G4 5 G4
Macleod Way. G72 51 H4
McNair St. G32 39 G2
McNeil Av. G81 13 E1
McNeil Gdns. G5 37 F3
McNeil St. G5 37 F3
McPhail St. G40 37 G2
McPhater St. G4 4 D2
Mace Rd. G13 14 A2
Machrie Dri. G45 49 H5
Machrie Dri. G77 56 C5
Machrie Rd. G45 49 G5
Machrie St. G45 49 G5
Mackies Mill Rd. PA2 52 A4
Madison Av. G44 48 D3
Madras Pl. G40 54 C5
Madras St. G40 37 G4
Mafeking St. G51 35 F1
Mafeking Ter. G78 54 A5
Magdalen Way. PA2 42 B5
Magnolia Dri. G72 52 C6
Magnus Cres. G44 48 D5
Maida St. G43 47 F2
Maidens Av. G77 57 E6
Maidland Rd. G53 46 B1
Mailing Av. G64 61 D3
Main Rd. PA4 43 F1
Main Rd. PA5 42 A2
Main St. G69 41 E2
Main St. G78 55 F2
Main St. G76 58 B5
Main St. G72 51 H3
Main St. G46 46 D5
Main St. G40 37 G4
Main St. G71 54 B5
Main St. G73 50 A1
Main St. G71 53 H3
Main St. G31 25 B5
Mainhill Av. G69 41 F1
Mainhill Dri. G69 41 F2
Mainhill Pl. G69 41 F1
Mainhill Rd. G69 41 G2
Mains Av. G46 57 F2
Mair St. G51 36 A1
Maitland Pl. PA4 20 C3
Maitland St. G4 4 D1
Malin Pl. G33 27 F5
Mallaig Pl. G51 22 C6
Mallard Rd. G81 8 D3
Malloch St. G20 16 A6
Maltbarns St. G20 24 C1
Malvern Way. PA3 31 G3
Mambeg Dri. G51 22 C5
Mamore Pl. G43 47 G3
Mamore St. G43 47 G3

Manchester Dri. G12 15 E5
Mannering Rd. PA2 42 B4
Mannering Rd. G41 35 G6
Mannering Way. PA2 42 B4
Mannofield. G61 10 D4
Manor Gate. G77 60 D2
Manor Pk Rd. PA2 43 E4
Manor Rd. PA2 42 C3
Manor Rd. G14 22 D1
Manor Rd. G15 13 G2
Manor Way. G73 50 B5
Manresa Pl. G20 24 C3
Manse Av. G61 11 F3
Manse Brae. G44 48 D3
Manse Ct. G78 55 G1
Manse Gdns. G32 40 A3
Manse Rd. G61 11 E3
Manse Rd. G61 59 F4
Manse Rd. G34 41 G1
Manse Rd. G78 54 B4
Manse Rd. G32 40 A3
Manse St. PA4 21 E1
Mansefield Av. G72 51 F5
Mansefield Cres. G60 7 B2
Mansefield Cres. G76 57 H5
Mansefield Rd. G76 58 A5
Mansel St. G21 17 H6
Mansewood Rd. G43 47 F3
Mansfield Rd. G52 21 F5
Mansfield St. G11 23 G5
Mansion Ct. G72 51 F3
Mansion St. G72 51 F3
Mansion St. G22 16 D6
Mansionhouse Av. G32 51 H1
Mansionhouse Dri. G32 39 H1
Mansionhouse Gdns.
   G41 48 A1
Mansionhouse Gro. G32 40 B3
Mansionhouse Rd. G41 48 A2
Mansionhouse Rd. G32 40 B3
Mansionhouse Rd. PA1 32 B1
Maple Av. G77 60 C1
Maple Cres. G72 52 C6
Maple Dri. G81 8 C3
Maple Dri. G78 55 H1
Maple Rd. G41 35 F2
Mar Dri. G61 11 F1
Mar Gdns. G73 50 C5
March St. G41 36 B5
Marchbank Gdns. PA1 32 D3
Marchfield Av. PA3 31 G3
Marchglen Pl. G51 22 B5
Marchmont Gdns. G64 61 B2
Maree Dri. G52 34 C3
Maree Gdns. G64 61 D3
Maree Rd. PA2 42 D3
Marfield St. G32 26 D6
Marina Ct. G81 8 C6
Marine Cres. G51 36 A1
Marine Gdns. G51 36 B1
Mariscat Rd. G41 36 A5
Marjory Dri. PA3 20 B6
Marjory Rd. PA4 20 B4
Markdow Av. G53 33 G6
Marlach Pl. G53 33 G6
Marlborough Av. G11 22 D2
Marlborough La G11 22 D2
Marlborough La Nth.
   G11 22 D1
Marlow St. G41 36 A2
Marlow Ter. G41 36 A2
Marmion Rd. PA2 42 B5
Marmion St. G20 16 A6
Marne St. G31 26 A5
Marnock Ter. PA2 32 B4
Marquis Gate. G71 53 G4
Marshalls La. PA1 31 H6
Mart St. G1 37 E1
Martha St. G1 5 E4
Martin Cres. G69 41 E2
Martin St. G40 37 H4
Martyrs Pl. G64 17 H3
Marwick St. G31 26 B5
Mary St. PA2 43 H3
Mary St. G4 24 D3
Mary Young Pl. G76 58 B5
Maryhill Rd,
Maryhill Rd,
   Nth Kelvinside. G20 24 B1
Maryland Dri. G52 34 C2
Maryland Gdns. G52 34 C2
Maryston Pl. G33 26 C3
Maryston St. G33 26 C2
Maryville Av. G46 57 G1
Maryville Gdns. G46 57 F1
Maryville La. G71 53 G1
Maryville View. G71 41 G6
Marywood Sq. G41 36 B5

Matherton Av. G77 57 F6
Mathieson Rd. G73 38 B6
Mathieson St. PA1 32 C2
Matilda Rd. G41 36 A3
Mauchline St. G5 36 C2
Maudslie St. G40 38 A2
Maukinfauld Ct. G32 38 D3
Maukinfauld Gdns. G32 38 D3
Maukinfauld Rd. G32 38 D4
Maule Dri. G11 23 E3
Mavis Bank. G64 17 H2
Mavis Bank Gdns. G51 24 A6
Mavis Valley Rd. G64 61 A1
Mavisbank Ter. PA1 32 A4
Maxton Av. G78 55 E1
Maxton Gro. G78 55 E1
Maxton Ter. G72 51 E6
Maxwell Av. G69 40 D2
Maxwell Av. G61 11 E6
Maxwell Av. G41 36 A3
Maxwell Dri. G69 40 C2
Maxwell Dri. G41 35 G3
Maxwell Dri. PA8 7 A5
Maxwell Gdns. G41 35 H3
Maxwell Gro. G41 35 H3
Maxwell La. G41 36 A3
Maxwell Oval. G41 36 B3
Maxwell Pl. G41 36 C3
Maxwell Rd. G20 14 C1
Maxwell Rd. G41 36 B3
Maxwell St. G69 41 E2
Maxwell St. G81 8 B4
Maxwell St. G1 4 D5
Maxwell St. PA3 31 H5
Maxwellton Rd. G33 26 C3
Maxwellton Rd. PA1 43 E1
Maxwellton St. PA1 31 F6
May Ter. G42 47 G6
Maybank La. G42 36 C5
Maybank St. G42 36 C5
Mayberry Cres. G32 40 A2
Mayberry Gdns. G32 40 A2
Mayberry Gro. G32 40 A2
Maybole Cres. G77 60 E1
Maybole Gro. G77 60 E1
Maybole St. G53 45 G3
Mayfield Av. G76 58 A4
Mayfield St. G20 16 B5
Meadow La. PA4 13 E6
Meadow Rd. G11 23 E3
Meadow Way. G77 56 B5
Meadow Well St. G32 39 G2
Meadowbank. G71 53 G3
Meadowbank La. G71 53 G3
Meadowbank Pl. G77 56 B6
Meadowburn. G64 61 C1
Meadowburn Av. G77 56 B6
Meadowhill. G77 56 B6
Meadowpark St. G31 26 A5
Meadowside Av. PA5 42 A2
Meadowside St. PA4 12 D5
Meadowside St. G11 23 E4
Mealkirk St. G81 9 F1
Mearns Rd. G77 60 A4
Mearns Rd. G76 57 G4
Mearns Way. G64 61 F3
Mearnscroft Gdns. G77 60 D2
Mearnscroft Rd. G77 60 D2
Mearnskirk. G77 60 C3
Mearnskirk Rd. G77 60 B3
Medlar Ct. G72 52 C6
Medwin St. G72 52 B4
Medwyn St. G14 22 C2
Meek Pl. G72 51 G4
Meetinghouse La. PA1 31 H6
*Megan Gate,
Megan St. G40 37 G3
Megan St. G40 37 G3
Meikle Av. PA4 20 D2
Meikle Rd. G53 46 B1
Meiklerig Cres. G53 34 A5
Meikleriggs Ct. PA2 43 E2
Meikleriggs Dri. PA2 42 D3
Meiklewood Rd. G51 34 B1
Melbourne Av. G81 8 A3
Melbourne Ct. G46 47 H6
Melbourne St. G31 5 H6
Meldon Pl. G51 22 C5
Meldrum Gdns. G41 35 H5
Meldrum St. G81 13 E2
Melford Av. G46 57 G1
Melford Way. PA3 20 B5
Melfort Av. G81 9 E6
Melfort Av. G41 35 F3
Melfort Ct. G41 9 E6
Mellerstain Dri. G14 13 F5
Melness Pl. G51 22 C5
Melrose Av. PA2 42 D4
Melrose Av. G73 50 A2
Melrose Gdns. G20 24 B1
Melvaig Pl. G20 15 H5
Melvick Pl. G51 22 C5
Melville Ct. G1 5 E5
Melville Gdns. G64 61 C3
Melville St. G41 36 B4
Memel St. G21 17 F6
Memus Av. G52 34 A3
Mennock Dri. G64 61 C1
Menock Rd. G44 48 D3
Menteith Av. G64 61 D4
Menteith Gdns. G61 10 C1
Menzies Dri. G21 18 A5
Menzies Pl. G21 18 A5
Menzies Rd. G21 18 A5
Merchant La. G1 5 E6
Merchiston St. G32 27 E6
Merkland St. G11 23 F3
Merksworth Way. PA3 31 G3
Merlin Way. PA3 20 C5
Merlinford Av. PA4 21 F2
Merlinford Cres. PA4 21 F2
Merlinford Dri. PA4 21 F2
Merlinford Way. PA4 21 F2
Merrick Gdns. G61 10 C1
Merrick Gdns. G51 35 F1
Merrick Way. G73 50 A6
Merryburn Av. G46 47 H4
Merrycrest Av. G46 47 G4
Merrycroft Av. G46 47 H4
Merryland Pl. G51 23 F6
Merryland St. G51 23 F6
Merrylee Cres. G46 47 G4
Merrylee Park Av. G46 47 G5
Merrylee Rd. G43 47 H3
Merryton Av. G15 10 B5
Merryton Av. G46 47 G5
Merryton Pl. G15 10 B5
Merryvale Av. G46 47 G4
Merryvale Pk. G46 47 G4
Merton Dri. G52 33 G1
Meryon Gdns. G32 40 A4
Meryon Rd. G32 40 A4
Methil St. G14 22 B2
Methuen Rd. PA3 20 A4
Methven Av. G61 11 H4
Methven Rd. G46 57 E5
Methven St. G81 8 B4
Methven St. G31 38 D3
Mews La. PA3 20 A6
Micklehouse Oval. G69 41 E1
Micklehouse Pl. G69 41 E1
Micklehouse Rd. G69 41 E1
Micklehouse Wynd. G69 40 D1
Mid Croft. G64 61 A2
Mid Wharf St. G21 25 E3
Midcroft Av. G44 49 F4
Middle Park. PA2 43 G3
Middlesex Gdns. G41 36 A1
Middlesex St. G41 36 A2
Middleton Cres. PA3 31 E4
Middleton Dri. G62 6 F2
Middleton Rd. PA3 31 E4
Middleton St. G51 35 G1
Middleward St. G81 9 F1
Midfaulds Av. PA4 21 E3
Midland St. G1 4 C5
Midlem Dri. G52 34 A2
Midlem Oval. G52 34 A2
Midlock St. G51 35 G1
Midlothian Dri. G41 35 H6
Midton St. G21 25 G2
Migvie Pl. G20 15 G5
Milan St. G41 36 C3
Milburn Way. PA4 21 E1
Milford St. G33 27 F5
Mill Ct. G73 49 H1
Mill Cres. G40 37 G3
Mill Rd. G72 52 A4
Mill Rd. G81 13 E4
Mill St. G40 37 G3
Mill St. PA1 31 H6
Mill St. G73 50 A2
Millar St. PA1 32 A2
Millar Ter. G73 38 B6
Millarbank St. G21 25 G1
Millarston Av. PA1 42 D1
Millarston Dri. PA1 42 D1
Millbeg Pl. G33 40 B1
Millbrae Ct. G42 48 B2
Millbrae Cres. G42 48 A2
Millbrae Cres. G81 13 E4
Millbrae Gdns. G42 48 C1
Millbrae Rd. G42 48 A2
Millbrix Av. G14 13 G5
Millburn Av. G73 49 H3
Millburn Av. G81 13 E3
Millburn Dri. PA4 21 E1
Millburn Rd. PA4 21 E1
Millburn St. G21 25 H4
Millcroft Rd. G73 37 G5
Milldam Rd. G81 9 E1
Milleg Cres. G69 40 C1
Millennium Ct. G34 29 E5
Millennium Gdns. G34 29 E5
Miller St. G69 41 E3
Miller St. G81 12 B2
Miller St. G1 5 E5
Millerfield Pl. G40 38 B4
Millerfield Rd. G40 38 A4
Millersneuk Cres. G33 19 F6
Millerston St. G31 38 A1
Millholm Rd. G44 48 C5
Millhouse Cres. G20 15 F3
Millhouse Dri. G20 15 F3
Millport Av. G44 49 E2
Millroad Dri. G40 37 G1
Millroad St. G40 37 G1
Millstream Ct. PA1 32 A3
Millview. G78 55 G1
Millview Mdws. G78 54 A5
Millview Pl. G53 45 H5
Millview Ter. G78 54 A5
Millwood St. G41 48 A1
Milnbank St. G31 25 H5
Milncroft Pl. G33 27 F4
Milncroft Rd. G33 27 F4
Milner La. G13 14 C6
Milner Rd. G13 14 D6
Milngavie Rd. G61 11 G1
Milnpark Gdns. G41 35 H2
Milnpark St. G41 36 A1
Milovaig St. G23 15 H1
Milrig Rd. G73 49 H2
Milton Av. G72 51 E3
Milton Douglas Rd. G81 8 D3
Milton Dri. G64 17 G3
Milton Gdns. G71 53 H1
Milton Mains Rd. G81 8 D3
Milton St. G4 4 D2
Miltonbank Dri. G64 17 G4
Miltonbank Pl. G64 17 G4
Miltonbank Rd. G64 17 G4
Milverton Av. G61 10 C3
Milverton Rd. G46 57 E2
Minerva St. G3 24 A5
Minerva Way. G3 24 A5
Mingarry St. G20 16 A6
Mingulay Cres. G22 17 F3
Mingulay Pl. G22 17 F3
Mingulay St. G22 17 E3
Minmoir Rd. G53 45 G2
Minnard Rd. G41 36 A5
Minstrel Rd. G13 14 B2
Minto Av. G73 50 C5
Minto Cres. G52 34 D2
Minto St. G52 34 D2
Mireton St. G22 16 D6
Mirren Dri. G81 8 C1
Mirrlees Dri. G12 15 G6
Mitchell Av. PA4 20 C3
Mitchell Av. G72 52 B3
Mitchell Dri. G73 50 A3
Mitchell Hill Rd. G45 59 G1
Mitchell La. G1 4 D4
Mitchell St. G1 4 D5
Mitre Ct. G11 22 D1
Mitre La. G11 22 C1
Mitre La N. G11 22 C1
Mitre Rd. G11 22 C1
Moat Av. G13 14 B3
Mochrum Rd. G43 48 A3
Moffat St. G5 37 F3
Mogarth Av. PA2 42 D4
Moidart Av. PA4 20 C1
Moidart Ct. G78 44 C4
Moidart Cres. G52 34 D2
Moidart Gdns. G77 56 C5
Moidart Pl. G52 34 D2
Moidart Rd. G52 34 D2
Moir St. G1 5 F6
Molendinar St. G1 5 F6
Molendinar Ter. G78 54 A5
Mollinsburn St. G21 25 G1
Monach Rd. G33 27 H5
Monar Dri. G22 24 D1
Monar Pl. G22 24 D1
Monar St. G22 24 D1
Monart Pl. G20 16 B6
Moncrieff St. PA3 31 H5
Moncur St. G40 5 G6
Moness Dri. G52 34 C2
Monifieth Av. G52 34 B4
Monikie Gdns. G64 61 F4
Monkcastle Dri. G72 51 F3
Monksbridge Av. G13 14 B2
Monkscroft Av. G11 23 E2
Monkscroft Ct. G11 23 E2
Monkscroft Gdns. G11 23 E2
Monkton Dri. G15 14 A1
Monkton Gdns. G77 60 E1
Monmouth Av. G12 15 E5
Monreith Rd. G43 48 A3
Monreith Rd East. G44 48 C3
Montague La. G12 15 F6
Montague St. G4 24 B3
Monteith Dri. G76 58 B3
Monteith Gdns. G76 58 B3
Monteith Pl. G40 37 F1
Monteith Row. G40 37 F1
Monteith Row La. G40 37 F1
Montford Av. G44 49 E2
Montgomery Av. PA3 20 C5
Montgomery Dri. G46 57 G2
Montgomery Rd. PA3 20 B5
Montgomery St. G72 51 B4
Montraive St. G73 38 B6
Montrave St. G52 34 B2
Montreith Av. G61 10 D6
Montrose Av. G32 39 G6
Montrose Av. G52 21 F4
Montrose Dri. G61 11 E1
Montrose Gdns. G62 6 E1
Montrose Rd. PA2 42 C5
Montrose St. G81 9 E6
Montrose St. G1 5 F4
Montrose Ter. G64 18 B3
Montrose Way. PA2 42 C5
Monument Dri. G33 18 D5
Monymusk Gdns. G64 61 F3
Monymusk Pl. G15 9 G3
Moodiesburn St. G33 26 D3
Moor Rd. G62 6 E2
Moorburn Av. G46 47 F6
Moorcroft Rd. G77 60 B2
Moore Dri. G61 11 F5
Moorehouse Av. PA2 43 E3
Moorfoot. G64 61 E3
Moorfoot Av. PA2 43 G4
Moorfoot Av. G46 47 E6
Moorfoot Path. PA2 43 G4
Moorfoot St. G32 26 D6
Moorfoot Way. G61 6 A4
Moorhill Cres. G77 60 B2
Moorhill Rd. G77 60 A1
Moorhouse Av. G13 13 F4
Moorhouse St. G78 55 G2
Moorpark Av. G52 33 G1
Moorpark Dri. G52 33 G1
Moorpark Sq. PA4 20 C2
Moraine Av. G15 13 H2
Moraine Circus. G15 13 H2
Moraine Dri. G15 13 H1
Moraine Dri. G76 57 G3
Moraine Pl. G15 13 H1
Morar Av. G81 9 E4
Morar Ct. G81 9 E4
Morar Cres. G64 61 B3
Morar Cres. G81 8 D4
Morar Dri. G61 11 G6
Morar Dri. PA2 42 D2
Morar Dri. G81 8 D4
Morar Dri. G73 50 B6
Morar Pl. G81 9 E4
Morar Pl. G77 56 B4
Morar Pl. PA4 20 C1
Morar Rd. G81 8 D4
Morar Rd. G52 34 D2
Morar Ter. G73 50 C5
Moray Dri. G76 58 B4
Moray Gdns. G71 53 H1
Moray Gdns. G76 58 B3
Moray Gate. G71 53 H4
Moray Pl. G64 61 E4
Moray Pl. G41 36 A5
Mordaunt St. G40 38 A4
Moredun Cres. G32 27 H6
Moredun Dri. PA2 43 E3
Moredun Rd. PA2 43 E3
Moredun St. G32 27 H6
Morefield Rd. G51 22 C6
Morgan Mews. G42 36 D4
Morina Gdns. G53 46 A6
Morion Rd. G13 14 B3
Morley St. G42 48 C2
Morningside St. G33 26 C5
Morrin Path. G21 25 F1
Morrin St. G21 25 F1
Morris Pl. G40 37 F2
Morrison Ct. G13 13 G5
Morrison Quad. G81 13 E1
Morrison St. G81 8 C2
Morrison St. G5 36 C1
Morriston Cres. PA4 21 F3
Morriston Park Dri. G72 51 F3
Morriston St. G72 51 F3
Morton Gdns. G41 35 G5
Morven Av. PA2 43 G4
Morven Av. G64 61 E4
Morven Dri. G76 57 G3
Morven Rd. G61 11 E2
Morven Rd. G72 51 E6
Morven St. G52 34 D2
Mosesfield St. G21 17 G5
Mosque Av. G1 37 E1
Moss Dri. G78 44 B4
Moss Heights Av. G52 34 B2
Moss La. G52 34 C4
Moss Park La. G52 34 C4
Moss St. PA1 31 H5
Moss-Side Rd. G41 36 A6
Mossbank Av. G33 27 E1
Mossbank Dri. G33 27 E1
Mosscastle Rd. G33 27 H2
Mossend La. G33 28 A5
Mossend St. G33 28 A5
Mossgiel Av. G73 49 H4
Mossgiel Cres. G76 58 B6
Mossgiel Dri. G81 9 E5
Mossgiel Gdns. G71 53 H1
Mossgiel Pl. G73 49 H4
Mossgiel Rd. G43 47 H3
Mosshead Rd. G61 11 F2
Mossland Rd. G52 21 E4
Mosslands Rd. PA3 31 G3
Mossneuk Dri. PA2 43 F5
Mosspark Av. G62 6 D1
Mosspark Av. G52 34 D4
Mosspark Blvd. G52 34 C3
Mosspark Dri. G52 34 A3
Mosspark Oval. G52 34 D4
Mosspark Rd. G62 6 E1
Mosspark Sq. G52 34 C4
Mossvale Cres. G33 27 H2
Mossvale La. PA3 31 G4
Mossvale Path. G33 27 H2
Mossvale Rd,
Craigend. G33 27 G1
Mossvale Rd,
Garthamloch. G33 28 B3
Mossvale Sq. G33 27 G2
Mossvale Sq. PA3 31 G4
Mossvale St. PA3 31 G4
Mossvale Walk. G33 27 H2
Mossvale Way. G33 27 H2
Mossview Quad. G52 34 B2
Mosswell Rd. G62 6 F2
Mote Hill Rd. PA3 20 B6
Moulin Circus. G52 33 G3
Moulin Pl. G52 33 H3
Moulin Rd. G52 33 H3
Moulin Ter. G52 33 H3
Mount Annan Dri. G44 48 D2
Mount Lockhart. G71 41 E5
Mount Lockhart Gdns.
G71 41 E5
Mount Lockhart Pl. G71 41 E5
Mount Pleasant Dri. G60 7 B2
Mount St. G20 24 B2
Mount Stuart St. G41 48 A1
Mount Vernon Av. G32 40 B4
Mountain Blue St. G31 38 A2
Mountblow Rd. G81 8 A2
Mountgarrie Rd. G51 22 C6
Moyne Rd. G53 33 G5
Mugdock Rd. G62 6 E2
Muir St. G64 61 C4
Muir St. PA4 20 D1
Muir Ter. PA3 20 A5
Muirbank Av. G73 49 G1
Muirbank Gdns. G73 49 G2
Muirbrae Rd. G73 50 A5
Muirbrae Way. G73 50 A5
Muirburn Av. G44 48 A5
Muirdrum Av. G52 34 B4
Muirdykes Av. G52 33 G1
Muirdykes Cres. PA3 31 E4
Muirdykes Rd. PA3 31 E4
Muirdykes Rd. G52 33 G1
Muiredge Ter. G69 41 E2
Muirend Av. G44 48 B4
Muirend Rd. G44 48 A5
Muirfield Ct. G44 48 B5
Muirfield Cres. G23 16 A2
Muirhead Ct. G69 41 E3
Muirhead Gdns. G69 41 F3
Muirhead Gro. G69 41 F3
Muirhead Rd. G69 41 E3
Muirhead Way. G64 61 F4
Muirhill Av. G44 48 A4
Muirhill Cres. G13 13 G4
Muirhouse Park. G61 6 A4
Muirhouse St. G42 36 C4
Muirkirk Dri. G13 14 D3
Muirlees Cres. G62 6 B2
Muirpark Av. PA4 20 C3
Muirpark Dri. G64 17 H2
Muirpark St. G11 23 F3
Muirshiel Av. G53 46 A3
Muirshiel Cres. G53 46 A3
Muirside Av. G32 40 B4

Park Ter. G46 47 G6
Park Ter. G3 24 A3
Park Ter La. G3 24 A3
Park View. PA2 43 G3
Parkbrae Gdns. G20 16 C5
Parkbrae Pl. G20 16 C5
Parkgrove Av. G46 47 H5
Parkgrove Ct. G46 47 H5
Parkgrove Ter. G3 24 A4
Parkgrove Ter La. G3 24 A4
Parkhall Rd. G81 8 B4
Parkhall Ter. G81 8 C3
Parkhill Dri. G73 50 A2
Parkhill Rd. G43 47 G1
Parkhouse Path. G53 45 H5
Parkhouse Rd. G53 45 F5
Parklands Rd. G44 48 B6
Parklee Dri. G76 59 F4
Parkneuk Rd. G43 47 F4
Parkside Gdns. G20 16 C5
Parkside Pl. G20 16 C5
Parnie St. G1 5 E6
Parsonage Row. G1 5 F5
Parsonage Sq. G4 5 F5
Partickbridge St. G11 23 G3
Partickhill Av. G11 23 F2
Partickhill Ct. G11 23 F2
Partickhill La. G11 23 F2
Partickhill Rd. G11 23 F2
Paterson St. G5 36 C1
Pathhead Gdns. G33 19 E4
Pathhead Rd. G76 59 F4
Patna St. G40 38 A3
Paton St. G31 26 A6
Patrick St. PA2 32 A4
Patterton Dri. G78 55 H2
Pattison St. G81 8 A5
Payne St. G4 25 E3
Peacock Av. PA2 42 C2
Peacock Dri. PA2 42 C2
Pearce St. G51 23 E4
Pearson Dri. PA4 21 E2
Peat Rd. G53 45 G3
Peathill St. G21 25 E2
Pedmyre La. G76 59 E4
Peebles Dri. G73 50 C2
Peel Glen Gdns. G15 10 A4
Peel Glen Rd. G15 10 A2
Peel La. G11 23 F2
Peel St. G11 23 F2
Peel Vw. G81 9 F5
Pegasus Av. PA1 30 B6
Pembroke St. G3 24 B5
Pencaitland Dri. G32 39 G4
Pencaitland Gro. G32 39 G4
Pendale Rise. G45 49 F6
Pendeen Cres. G33 40 B1
Pendeen Pl. G33 40 C1
Pendeen Rd. G33 40 B2
Pendicle Cres. G61 10 D5
Pendicle Rd. G61 10 D5
Penicuik St. G32 26 C6
Penilee Rd. PA1 21 E4
Penilee Ter. G52 33 E1
Peninver Dri. G51 22 C4
Penman Av. G73 49 G1
Pennan. PA8 7 B6
Pennan Pl. G14 13 G5
Penneld Rd. G52 33 F2
Penrith Av. G46 47 G6
Penrith Dri. G12 15 E4
Penryn Gdns. G32 40 A4
Penston Rd. G33 28 A5
Pentland Ct. G78 55 F3
Pentland Cres. PA2 43 G4
Pentland Dri. G78 55 F3
Pentland Dri. G64 61 F3
Pentland Dr. PA4 20 B4
Pentland Pl. G61 10 B2
Pentland Rd. G43 47 G4
Pentry Way. G78 55 F1
Percy Dri. G46 57 G2
Percy Rd. PA4 20 B4
Percy St. G51 35 G1
Perth Cres. G81 8 A3
Perth St. G3 4 A4
Petershill Ct. G21 26 B1
Petershill Dri. G21 26 B1
Petershill Pl. G21 26 B1
Petershill Rd. G21 25 G2
Peterson Dri. G13 13 F3
Peterson Gdns. G13 13 F3
Pettigrew St. G32 39 F2
Peveril Av. G73 50 B4
Peveril Av. G41 35 H6
Pharonhill St. G31 38 D2
Phoenix Pl. PA5 42 A2
Piccadilly St. G3 4 A5
Picketlaw Dri. G76 59 E4
Picketlaw Farm Rd. G76 59 E4
Piddell St. G81 9 E5
Piershill St. G32 27 E5
Pikeman Rd. G13 14 A4
Pilmuir Av. G44 48 B4
Pilrig St. G32 26 D6
Pilton Rd. G61 10 B5
Pine Av. G72 52 C5
Pine Pl. G5 37 E2
Pine Rd. G81 8 A4
Pine St. PA2 32 B5
Pinelands. G64 61 C1
Pinewood Sq. G15 10 B5
Pinkerton Av. G73 49 G1
Pinkerton La. G52 21 E4
Pinkston Dri. G21 25 F3
Pinkston Rd. G21 25 E2
Pinmore Path. G53 45 F3
Pinmore Pl. G53 45 F3
Pinmore St. G53 45 F3
Pinwherry Dri. G33 19 E4
Pitcairn St. G31 38 D3
Pitcaple Dri. G43 47 F3
Pitlochry Dri. G52 34 A2
Pitmedden Rd. G64 61 F3
Pitmilly Rd. G15 10 C4
Pitreavie Pl. G33 27 H3
Pitt St. G2 4 B4
Pladda Rd. PA4 20 D3
Plaintrees Ct. PA2 43 H3
Planetree Rd. G81 8 C4
Plant St. G31 26 B6
Plantation Pk Gdns. G51 35 H2
Plantation Sq. G51 36 A1
Playfair St. G40 37 H4
Plean St. G14 13 G6
Pleasance La. G43 47 G2
Pleasance St. G43 47 G1
Pollock Rd. G61 11 G5
Pollock Rd. G77 60 A1
Pollok Dri. G64 61 A3
Pollokshaws Rd. G41 47 F2
Pollokshields Sq. G41 36 A4
Polmadie Av. G5 37 F5
Polmadie Rd. G42 37 E5
Polmadie St. G42 37 E5
Polnoon Av. G13 13 H5
Polquhap Ct. G53 45 G1
Polquhap Gdns. G53 45 G1
Polquhap Pl. G53 45 G1
Polquhap Rd. G53 45 G1
Polsons Cres. PA2 43 G2
Polwarth La. G12 23 F1
Polwarth St. G12 23 F1
Poplar Av. G11 22 D1
Poplar Av. G77 60 C2
Poplar Dri. G81 8 C3
Poplar Way. G72 52 C5
Poplin St. G40 37 G4
Porchester St. G33 28 A3
Port Dundas Pl. G4 4 D2
Port Dundas Rd. G4 4 D1
Port Lethan. PA8 7 B6
Port St. G3 24 B5
Portal Rd. G13 14 A3
Porter St. G51 35 G2
Porterfield Rd. PA4 20 B2
Porters Well. G71 53 H3
Portessie. PA8 7 B6
Portman St. G41 36 A2
Portmarnock Dri. G23 15 H2
Portpatrick Rd. G60 7 A1
Portsoy. PA8 7 B6
Portsoy Av. G13 13 F3
Portsoy Pl. G13 13 F3
Portugal St. G5 36 D2
Possill Rd. G4 24 D2
Potter Clo. G32 38 D4
Potter Gro. G32 38 D4
Potter Pl. G32 38 D4
Potter St. G32 38 D4
Potterhill Av. PA2 43 G4
Potterhill Rd. G53 33 H4
Powburn Cres. G71 53 G2
Powfoot St. G31 38 C2
Powrie St. G33 27 H2
Preston Path. G42 36 D4
Preston Pl. G42 36 D4
Preston St. G42 36 D4
Prestonfield. G62 6 C3
Prestwick Pl. G77 60 F1
Prestwick St. G53 45 G3
Priesthill Av. G53 46 A3
Priesthill Cres. G53 46 A3
Priesthill Rd. G53 46 A3
Primrose Ct. G14 22 B2
Primrose St. G14 22 B2
Prince Albert Rd. G12 23 F1
Prince Edward St. G42 36 C5
Prince of Wales Gdns. G20 15 G2
Princes Gdns. G12 23 F2
Princes Gate. G71 53 G5
Princes Gate. G73 49 H1
Princes Pl. G12 23 G2
Princes Sq. G78 55 G1
Princes St. G73 49 H1
Princes Ter. G12 23 G2
Princess Cres. PA1 32 B1
Printers Land. G76 58 C5
Priory Av. PA3 20 B5
Priory Dri. G71 53 G2
Priory Pl. G13 14 C3
Priory Rd. G13 14 B3
Prosen St. G32 39 E4
Prospect Av. G72 51 E3
Prospect Av. G71 53 H2
Prospect Rd. G43 47 G1
Prospecthill Circus. G42 37 F6
Prospecthill Cres. G42 49 F1
Prospecthill Dri. G42 48 D1
Prospecthill Pl. G42 49 G1
Prospecthill Rd. G42 48 C1
Provand Hall Cres. G69 40 D3
Provan Rd. G33 26 C4
Provanhill Rd. G34 28 C3
Provanhill St. G21 25 G4
Provanmill Rd. G33 26 D2
Provost Driver Ct. PA4 21 E3
Purdon St. G11 23 F3

Quadrant Rd. G43 48 A3
Quarry Av. G72 52 B6
Quarry Pl. G72 50 D3
Quarry Rd. G78 44 B5
Quarry Rd. PA2 32 A6
Quarrybrae Av. G76 57 G4
Quarrybrae St. G31 38 D2
Quarryknowe. G73 49 G2
Quarryknowe St. G81 9 G2
Quarryknowe St. G31 38 D2
Quarrywood Av. G21 18 C6
Quarrywood Rd. G21 26 C1
Quay Rd. G73 37 H6
Quay Rd Nth. G73 37 H6
Queen Elizabeth Av. G52 21 E6
Queen Margaret Dri. G20 23 H1
Queen Mary Av. G81 9 F6
Queen Mary Av. G42 36 C6
Queen Mary St. G40 37 H3
Queen Sq. G41 36 B5
Queen St. G1 4 D5
Queen St. PA1 31 F6
Queen St. PA4 21 E1
Queen Victoria Dri. G14 14 A6
Queen Victoria Gate. G13 14 A5
Queens Av. G72 51 G3
Queens Ct. G62 6 E4
Queens Cres. G4 24 B3
Queens Dri. G42 36 B5
Queens Dri La. G42 36 C6
Queens Gdns. G12 23 G2
Queens Gate. G76 58 A3
Queens Gate La. G12 23 G2
Queens Park Av. G42 36 D6
Queens Pl. G12 23 G2
Queensberry Av. G61 11 E1
Queensberry Av. G76 57 H4
Queensborough Gdns. G12 23 E1
Queensby Av. G69 41 E1
Queensby Dri. G69 41 E1
Queensby Pl. G69 41 E1
Queensby Rd. G69 41 E1
Queensferry St. G5 37 G5
Queensland Ct. G52 34 B1
Queensland Dri. G52 34 A1
Queensland Gdns. G52 34 B1
*Queensland La East, Queensland Dri. G52 34 B1
*Queensland La West, Queensland Dri. G52 34 B1
Queenslie St. G33 26 D2
Quendale Dri. G32 39 E4
Quentin St. G41 36 A6
Quinton Gdns. G69 40 D2

Raasay Dri. PA2 43 G5
Raasay Pl. G22 17 E3
Raasay St. G22 17 E2
Radnor St. G3 23 H4
Radnor St. G81 8 D5
Radnor St. G81 8 C5
Raeberry St. G20 24 B2
Raeside Av. G77 60 B2
Raeswood Dri. G53 45 G1
Raeswood Gdns. G53 45 G1
Raeswood Pl. G53 45 G1
Raeswood Rd. G53 45 G1
Rafford St. G51 23 E6
Raglan St. G4 24 C3
Raith Av. G45 49 E5
Raithburn Av. G45 49 E5
Raithburn Rd. G45 49 E5
Ralston Av. G52 33 F3
Ralston Ct. G52 33 F3
Ralston Dri. G52 33 F3
Ralston Pl. G52 33 F3
Ralston Rd. G78 55 F2
Ralston Rd. G61 11 E3
Ralston St. PA1 32 B3
Ram St. G32 39 E1
Rampart Av. G13 13 H3
Ramsay Ct. G77 60 C2
Ramsay St. G81 8 B5
Ranald Gdns. G73 50 C5
Randolph Av. G76 58 B2
Randolph Dri. G76 58 B2
Randolph Gdns. G76 58 B2
Randolph La. G11 22 D1
Randolph Rd. G11 22 D1
Ranfurly Rd. G52 33 G2
Rankin Dri. G77 56 A5
Rannoch Av. G64 61 D3
Rannoch Av. G77 56 B4
Rannoch Dri. G61 11 G6
Rannoch Dri. PA4 20 D1
Rannoch Gdns. G64 61 E3
Rannoch Pl. PA2 32 B4
Rannoch Rd. G71 41 G6
Rannoch St. G44 48 C3
Raploch Av. G14 13 H6
Raploch Cres. G81 9 F1
Rashieburn. PA8 7 B6
Rashieglen. PA8 7 B6
Rashiehill. PA8 7 B6
Rashielee Av. PA8 7 B6
Rashielee Rd. PA8 7 B6
Rashiewood. PA8 7 B6
Rathlin St. G51 23 E4
Ratho Dri. PA8 17 G6
Rattray. PA8 7 B5
Rattray St. G32 38 D4
Ravel Row. G31 38 C2
Ravelston Rd. G61 14 D1
Ravelston St. G32 26 D6
Raven Ct. G64 17 H3
Ravenscliffe Dri. G46 47 F5
Ravenscraig Av. PA2 43 F3
Ravenscraig Dri. G53 46 A3
Ravenscraig Ter. G53 46 A3
Ravenshall Rd. G41 35 G6
Ravenstone Dri. G46 47 G4
Ravenswood Av. PA2 42 B5
Ravenswood Dri. G41 35 H6
Ravenswood Rd. G69 41 F2
Rayne Pl. G15 10 B5
Red Moss Rd. G81 8 B2
Red Rd. G21 26 B1
Red Rd Ct. G21 26 B1
Redan St. G40 37 H2
Redburn Av. G46 57 F3
Redcastle Sq. G33 28 A3
Redford St. G33 26 C5
Redgate Pl. G14 13 H6
Redhurst Cres. PA2 43 E5
Redhurst La. PA2 43 E5
Redhurst Way. PA2 43 F5
Redlands Rd. G12 15 G6
Redlands Ter. G12 15 G6
Redlawood Pl. G72 52 D3
Redlawood Rd. G72 52 D3
Redmoss St. G22 16 D6
Rednock St. G21 25 E1
Redpath Dri. G52 34 A1
Redwood Cres. G72 52 C5
Redwood Dri. G21 25 H1
Reelick Av. G13 13 F2
Reelick Quad. G13 13 F2
Regent Moray St. G3 23 H4
Regent Pl. G81 8 B5
Regent St. G81 8 B5
Regent St. PA1 32 B1
Regents Gate. G71 53 G5
Regents Park Sq. G41 36 B5
Regwood St. G41 47 H1
Reid Av. G61 11 G3
Reid St. G40 37 H4
Reid St. G73 50 A1
Reidvale St. G31 25 H6
Renfield La. G2 4 C4
Renfield St. PA4 13 E6
Renfield St. G2 4 D4
Renfrew Ct. G2 4 D2
Renfrew La. G2 4 D3
Renfrew Rd. G51 20 A6
Renfrew Rd. PA3 32 A2
Renfrew Rd. PA4 21 G3
Renfrew Rd. G51 22 B4
Renfrew St. G2 4 A2
Renshaw Dri. G52 33 H1
Renshaw Rd. PA5 42 A3
Renton St. G4 4 D1
Reston Dri. G52 33 H1
Reuther Av. G73 50 A1
Revoch Dri. G13 13 G3
Rhannan Rd. G44 48 C3
Rhannan Ter. G44 48 C4
Rhindhouse Pl. G69 41 F2
Rhindhouse Rd. G69 41 G2
Rhindmuir Av. G69 41 F1
Rhindmuir Ct. G69 41 F1
Rhindmuir Cres. G69 41 F1
Rhindmuir Dri. G69 41 F1
Rhindmuir Gdns. G69 41 F1
Rhindmuir Gro. G69 41 F1
Rhindmuir Path. G69 41 F1
Rhindmuir Pl. G69 41 F1
Rhindmuir Rd. G69 41 F1
Rhindmuir View. G69 41 G1
Rhindmuir Wynd. G69 41 F1
Rhinsdale Cres. G69 41 F2
Rhymer St. G21 25 G4
Rhymie Rd. G32 40 A4
Rhynie Dri. G51 35 F1
Riccarton St. G42 36 D5
Riccartsbar Av. PA2 43 F2
Richmond Av. G76 58 A4
Richmond Ct. G73 50 C1
Richmond Dri. G64 61 D1
Richmond Dri. G72 51 E4
Richmond Dri. G73 50 C2
Richmond Gro. G73 50 C2
Richmond Pl. G73 50 C1
Richmond Rd. G73 50 C1
Richmond St. G1 5 F4
Richmond St. G81 12 C2
Riddon Av. G13 13 E3
Riddon Pl. G13 13 F3
Riddrie Cres. G33 26 D4
Riddrie Knowes. G33 26 D4
Riddrie Vale Ct. G33 26 D4
Riddrie Vale St. G33 26 D4
Rigby St. G32 26 D6
Rigg Pl. G33 28 B5
Riggside Rd. G33 27 H2
Riglands Way. PA4 20 C1
Riglaw Pl. G13 13 H4
Rigmuir Rd. G51 22 B6
Rimsdale St. G40 37 H2
Ringford St. G21 25 G1
Ripon Dri. G12 15 E4
Risk St. G81 8 B4
Ritchie Pl. G77 60 A1
Ritchie St. G5 36 C3
*River Cart Walk, Marshall La. PA1 31 H6
River Ct. G76 58 B5
River Rd. G32 51 H1
Riverbank St. G43 47 G2
Riverford Rd. G43 47 G1
Riverford Rd. G73 38 B6
Riverside. G62 6 E3
Riverside Ct. G44 48 B6
Riverside Gdns. G76 58 B5
Riverside Pk. G44 48 C6
Riverside Pl. G72 52 B3
Riverside Rd. G43 48 A2
Riverside Ter. G76 58 B5
Riversoake Rd. G13 13 G6
Riverview Dri. G5 4 A6
Riverview Gdns. G5 4 B6
Riverview Pl. G5 4 B6
Roaden Av. PA2 42 C5
Roaden Rd. PA2 42 C5
Robert Burns Av. G81 9 E5
Robert Dri. G51 23 E5
Robert St. G51 23 E5
Robert Templeton Dri. G72 51 H4
Roberton Av. G41 35 G5
Roberts St. G81 8 B5
Robertson Av. PA4 20 C2
Robertson Clo. PA4 20 C2
Robertson Cres. G78 54 B5
Robertson Dri. PA4 20 C2
Robertson La. G2 4 C5
Robertson St. G78 55 E1
Robertson St. G2 4 C5
Robroyston Av. G33 26 D1
Robroyston Dri. G33 18 D6
Robroyston Rd. G33 18 D4
Robslee Cres. G46 47 E6
Robslee Dri. G46 47 F5
Robslee Rd. G46 47 E6
Robson Gro. G42 36 D4
Rockall Dri. G44 48 D5

Rockbank St. G40 38 A2
Rockburn Dri. G76 57 G3
Rockfield Pl. G221 18 C5
Rockfield Rd. G21 18 B5
Rockliffe St. G40 37 H4
Rockmount Av,. G78 55 G3
Rockmount Av. G46 47 E5
Rockwell Av. PA2 43 F5
Roddinghead Rd. G46 57 E5
Rodger Av. G77 56 A6
Rodger Dri. G73 50 A3
Rodger Pl. G73 50 A3
Rodil Av. G44 48 D5
Rodney St. G20 24 D2
Roebank Dri. G78 55 G3
Roebank St. G31 26 A5
Roffey Park Rd. PA1 32 D2
Rogart St. G40 37 H2
Rogerfield Rd. G34 29 F6
Rokeby La. G12 24 A2
Roland Cres. G77 60 D2
Roman Av. G61 11 F3
Roman Av. G15 13 G2
Roman Ct. G61 11 E4
Roman Cres. G60 7 A1
Roman Gdns. G61 11 F3
Roman Rd. G61 11 E4
Roman Rd. G81 8 D2
Romanhill Rd. G81 8 D1
Romney Av. G44 48 D4
Rona St. G21 26 A3
Rona Ter. G72 51 E6
Ronaldsay Dri. G64 61 F3
Ronaldsay Pass. G22 17 E4
Ronaldsay St. G22 17 E3
Ronay St. G22 17 E3
Rooksdell Av. PA2 43 F3
Ropework La. G1 4 D6
Rose St. G3 4 C2
Rosebank Dri. G72 51 H5
Rosebank Gdns. G71 40 D5
Rosebank Pl. G71 40 D5
Roseberry St. G5 37 F4
Rosedale. G64 18 A2
Rosedale. G64 61 D4
Rosedale Av. PA2 42 B6
Rosedale Dri. G69 40 D3
Rosedale Gdns. G20 15 G2
Rosefield Gdns. G71 53 H2
Roseknowe Rd. G42 37 F6
Roselea Dri. G31 25 H6
Roselea Dri. G62 6 F2
Roselea Gdns. G13 14 D3
Rosemount Av. G77 60 B3
Rosemount Mdws. G71 53 H6
Rosemount St. G21 25 H4
Roseness Pl. G33 27 F5
Rosevale Rd. G11 11 E4
Rosewood Av. PA2 43 E3
Rosewood St. G13 14 C3
Rosneath St. G51 23 E5
Ross Av. PA4 20 B4
Ross Hall Pl. PA4 21 E2
Ross Pl. G73 50 D5
Ross St. PA1 32 A4
Ross St. G31 5 G6
Rossendale Ct. G43 47 G1
Rossendale Rd. G43 47 G1
Rosshall Av. PA1 32 C3
Rosshill Av. G52 33 F1
Rosshill Rd. G52 33 F2
Rossie Cres. G64 61 E4
Rosslea Dri. G46 57 G1
Rosslyn Av. G73 50 B2
Rosslyn Rd. G61 10 C2
Rosslyn Ter. G12 23 G1
Rostan Rd. G43 47 G4
Rosyth Rd. G5 37 F5
Rotherwick Dri. PA1 33 E3
Rotherwood Av. G13 14 A1
Rotherwood Av. PA2 42 C4
Rotherwood La. G13 14 B1
Rotherwood Pl. G13 14 C2
Rotherwood Way. PA2 42 C4
Rothes Dri. G23 15 G2
Rothes Pl. G23 15 G2
Rottenrow. G4 5 F4
Rottenrow East. G4 5 G4
Rouken Glen Rd. G46 56 D1
Roukenburn St. G46 46 D5
Roundhill Dri. PA5 42 B2
Roundknowe Rd. G71 41 E4
Rowallan Gdns. G11 23 E1
Rowallan La. G76 58 A4
Rowallan La. G11 23 E1
Rowallan La East. G11 23 E1
Rowallan Rd. G46 57 E1
Rowallan Ter. G33 19 G6
Rowan Av. PA4 12 D6
Rowan Ct. G81 12 C2
Rowan Ct. G72 52 C5
Rowan Dri. G61 11 F1
Rowan Dri. G81 8 C4
Rowan Gdns. G41 35 F2
Rowan Gate. PA2 43 H3
Rowan Park Dri. G78 44 B4
Rowan Pl. G72 51 H3
Rowan Rd. G41 35 F2
Rowan St. PA2 32 A5
Rowand Av. G46 47 G6
Rowandale Av. G69 40 D2
Rowanlea Av. PA2 42 B6
Rowanlea Dri. G46 47 H5
Rowantree Av. G73 50 A4
Rowantree Gdns. G73 50 A4
Rowchester St. G40 38 A1
Rowena Av. G13 14 C2
Roxburgh Dri. G61 11 E1
Roxburgh Rd. PA2 42 B5
Roxburgh St. G12 23 H2
Roy St. G21 25 E2
Royal Cres. G3 24 A4
Royal Exchange Sq. G1 4 D4
Royal Inch Cres. PA4 13 E6
Royal Ter. G3 24 A4
Royston Rd. G21 25 G4
Royston Sq. G21 25 G4
Roystonhill. G21 25 G4
Rozelle Av. G15 10 C5
Rubislaw Dri. G61 11 E5
Ruby St. G40 37 H3
Ruchazie Pl. G33 27 E4
Ruchazie Rd. G32 27 E5
Ruchill Pl. G20 16 B5
Ruchill St. G20 16 A5
Ruel St. G44 48 C2
Rufflees Av. G78 44 D5
Rugby Av. G13 13 H3
Rullion Pl. G33 27 E5
Rumford St. G40 37 G3
Rupert St. G4 24 B3
Ruskin La. G12 24 A2
Ruskin Sq. G64 61 C4
Ruskin Ter. G12 24 A2
Ruskin Ter. G73 38 B6
Russell Dri. G61 11 E3
Russell Pl. G76 58 C6
Russell Rd. G81 8 A2
Russell St. PA3 31 G4
Rutherford Ct. G81 8 D6
Rutherglen Bri. G5 37 G4
Rutherglen Rd. G5 37 F4
Ruthven Av. G46 57 G2
Ruthven La. G12 23 G2
Ruthven Pl. G64 18 B3
Ruthven St. G12 23 G2
Rutland Ct. G51 36 A1
Rutland Cres. G51 36 A1
Rutland Pl. G51 36 A1
Ryan Rd. G64 61 D3
Ryan Way. G73 50 B6
Ryat Dri. G77 56 A5
Ryat Grn. G77 56 A5
Rye Cres. G21 18 B5
Rye Rd. G21 18 B6
Ryebank Rd. G21 18 B6
Ryecroft Dri. G69 41 E2
Ryedale Pl. G15 10 B5
Ryefield Rd. G21 18 B6
Ryehill Gdns. G21 18 C6
Ryehill Pl. G21 18 C5
Ryehill Rd. G21 18 B5
Ryemount Rd. G21 18 B5
Ryeside Rd. G21 18 B6
Rylands Dri. G32 40 B3
Rylands Gdns. G32 40 B3
Rylees Cres. G52 21 E6
Rylees Pl. G52 21 E6
Rylees Rd. G52 21 F6
Rysland Av. G77 56 C6
Rysland Cres. G77 56 C6
Ryvra Rd. G13 14 B5

Sackville Av. G13 14 D5
Sackville La. G13 14 D5
Saddell Rd. G15 10 B4
St Abbs Dri. PA2 42 D4
St Andrews Av. G64 61 A3
St Andrews Cres. PA3 31 F2
St Andrews Cres. G41 36 A3
St Andrews Dri. G61 10 D1
St Andrews Dri. PA3 31 G2
St Andrews Dri. G41 35 G5
St Andrews Dri West. PA3 31 F2
St Andrews Rd. PA4 20 D2
St Andrews Rd. G41 36 B3
St Andrews Sq. G1 5 F6
St Andrews St. G1 5 F6
St Anns Dri. G46 57 G1
St Blanes Dri. G73 49 G2
St Boswells Cres. PA2 42 D4
St Brides Rd. G43 48 A2
St Catherines Rd. G46 57 G1
St Clair Av. G46 47 G6
St Clair St. G20 24 B2
St Cyrus Gdns. G64 61 E4
St Edmunds Gro. G62 6 D1
St Enoch Pl. G1 4 D5
St Enoch Sq. G1 4 D5
St Fillans Rd. G33 19 H5
St Georges Rd. G3 4 A1
St Germains. G61 11 E5
St Helena Cres. G81 9 E2
St James St. PA3 31 G5
St James Av. PA3 31 E4
St James Rd. G4 5 F3
St Johns Ct. G41 36 A3
St Johns Quad. G41 36 A3
St Johns Rd. G41 36 A4
St Josephs Ct. G31 25 G5
St Josephs Vw. G31 25 G5
St Kenneth St. G51 22 C5
St Kilda Dri. G14 22 C1
St Leonards Dri. G46 47 G6
St Margarets Pl. G1 5 E6
St Mark Gdns. G32 39 E2
St Mark St. G32 39 E2
St Marnock St. G40 37 H2
St Marys Cres. G78 55 G2
St Marys Gdns. G78 55 G1
St Marys Rd. G64 61 A3
St Michaels Ct. G31 38 C2
St Michaels La. G31 38 C2
St Mirren St. PA1 31 H6
St Monance St. G21 17 G6
St Mungo Av. G4 5 E3
St Mungo Pl. G4 5 F3
St Mungo St. G64 61 B4
St Ninian Ter. G5 37 E2
St Ninians Cres. PA2 32 A5
St Ninians Rd. PA2 32 A4
St Peters La. G2 4 B4
St Peters Path. G4 24 C4
St Peters St. G4 24 C4
St Rollox Brae. G21 25 G2
St Ronans Dri. G73 50 C3
St Ronans Dri. G41 35 G6
St Stephens Av. G73 50 C6
St Stephens Cres. G73 50 D6
St Syrus Rd. G64 61 E4
St Vigeans Av. G77 60 A2
St Vincent Cres. G3 24 A5
St Vincent Cres La. G3 24 A4
St Vincent La. G2 4 B4
St Vincent Pl. G1 4 D4
St Vincent St. G2 4 A3
St Vincent Ter. G3 4 A3
Salamanca St. G31 38 C2
Salasaig Ct. G33 27 F5
Salen St. G52 34 D2
Salisbury Pl. G81 8 A3
Salisbury St. G5 36 D2
Salkeld St. G5 36 C3
Salmona St. G22 24 C1
Salterland Rd. G78 45 E4
Saltmarket. G1 5 E6
Saltmarket Pl. G1 5 E6
Saltoun La. G12 23 H2
Saltoun St. G12 23 G2
Salvia St. G72 51 E3
Sanda St. G20 16 A6
Sandaig Rd. G33 40 B1
Sandbank Av. G20 15 H4
Sandbank Cres. G20 15 H4
Sandbank Dri. G20 15 H4
Sandbank St. G20 15 H3
Sandbank Ter. G20 15 H4
Sandend. PA8 7 B5
Sandend Rd. G53 45 G2
Sanderling Rd. PA3 31 G2
Sandfield Av. G62 6 E2
Sandfield St. G20 16 A6
Sandgate Av. G32 40 A4
Sandhaven Rd. G53 45 G2
Sandholes St. PA1 31 F6
Sandholm Pl. G14 13 G5
Sandholm Ter. G14 13 G5
Sandiefield St. G5 36 D2
Sandilands St. G32 39 G2
Sandmill St. G21 25 H4
Sandra Rd. G64 61 E3
Sandringham Av. G77 57 E5
Sandwood Path. G52 33 G1
Sandwood Rd. G52 33 G1
Sandy Rd. G11 23 E3
Sandy Rd. PA4 20 C4
Sandyfaulds Sq. G5 37 E3
Sandyfaulds St. G5 37 E3
Sandyford Pl La. G3 24 A4
Sandyford Rd. PA4 20 A4
Sandyford St. G3 23 G4
Sandyhills Cres. G32 39 G4
Sandyhills Dri. G32 39 G4
Sandyhills Gro. G32 39 H4
Sandyhills Pl. G32 39 G4
Sandyhills Rd. G32 39 G4
Sannox Gdns. G31 26 B4
Sanquhar Dri. G53 33 G6
Sanquhar Gdns. G53 45 G1
Sanquhar Pl. G53 45 G1
Sanquhar Rd. G53 33 G6
Saracen St. G22 16 D6
Sardinia La. G12 23 H2
Saturn Av. PA1 30 B5
Saucel St. PA2 43 H1
Saucelhill Ter. PA2 32 A4
Sauchiehall La. G2 4 B2
Sauchiehall St. G2 4 A2
Saughs Av. G33 19 E5
Saughs Dri. G33 19 E4
Saughs Gate. G33 19 E4
Saughs Pl. G33 19 E5
Saughs Rd. G33 18 D5
Saughton St. G32 26 D5
Saunders Ct. G78 55 F1
Savoy St. G40 37 G3
Sawmillfield St. G20 24 D3
Saxon Rd. G13 14 B4
Scadlock Rd. PA3 31 E5
Scalpay Pass. G22 17 E4
Scalpay Pl. G22 17 E3
Scalpay St. G22 17 E3
Scapa St. G23 16 A3
Scaraway Dri. G22 17 E2
Scaraway Pl. G22 17 E2
Scaraway St. G22 17 E2
Scaraway Ter. G22 17 F2
Scarba Dri. G43 47 F3
Scarrel Dri. G45 49 H5
Scarrel Gdns. G45 49 H5
Scarrel Rd. G45 49 H5
Scarrel Ter. G45 50 A5
Schaw Ct. G61 11 E2
Schaw Dri. G61 11 E2
Schaw Dri. G81 9 G2
Schaw Rd. PA3 32 B1
Scholars Way. G61 10 C1
School Av. G72 51 G4
School Rd. G77 60 B1
School Rd. PA1 33 E1
School Wynd. PA1 31 H6
Schoolfield La. G64 61 C4
Scioncroft Av. G73 50 B2
Scone Pl. G77 60 F1
Scone St. G21 25 E2
Sconser St. G23 15 H1
Scorton Gdns. G69 40 C3
Scotland St. G5 36 A2
Scotsburn Rd. G21 18 B6
Scotstoun St. G14 22 B2
Scott Dri. G61 10 C3
Scott Rd. G52 21 F4
Scott St. G69 41 E2
Scott St. G81 8 A5
Scott St. G3 4 B2
Scotts Rd. PA2 32 C3
Seafield Av. G61 11 F1
Seafield Dri. G73 50 C6
Seaforth Cres. G78 44 C4
Seaforth Rd. G81 12 C1
Seaforth Rd Nth. G52 21 G5
Seaforth Rd Sth. G52 21 G5
Seagrove St. G32 26 D6
Seamill Path. G53 45 F4
Seamill St. G53 45 F4
Seamore St. G20 24 B2
Seath Rd. G73 37 H6
Seath St. G42 36 D5
Seaward Pl. G41 36 B2
Seaward St. G41 36 A2
Second Av. G61 11 F5
Second Av. G71 41 G6
Second Av. G81 8 C5
Second Av. G33 19 G6
Second Av. PA4 20 D3
Second Av. G44 48 D2
Second Gdns. G41 35 E3
Second St. G71 41 H6
Seedhill. PA1 32 A3
Seedhill Rd. PA1 32 A3
Seggielea Rd. G13 14 C5
Seil Dri. G44 48 D4
Selborne Pl. G13 14 C6
Selborne Pl La. G13 14 C6
Selborne Rd. G13 14 C6
Selby Gdns. G32 40 B2
Selkirk Av. G52 34 A3
Selkirk Av. PA2 42 D4
Selkirk Dri. G73 50 C2
Sella Rd. G64 61 F2
Selvieland Rd. G52 33 F1
Sempill Av. PA8 7 A6
Seres Rd. G76 57 H3
Sergeant Law Rd. PA2 42 D6
Seton Ter. G31 25 H6
Settle Gdns. G69 40 C3
Seventh Av. G71 53 H1
Seyton Av. G46 57 G2
Shaftesbury St. G81 8 B6
Shaftesbury St. G3 4 A3
Shafton Pl. G13 14 C2
Shafton Rd. G13 14 C2
Shakespeare Av. G81 8 C4
Shakespeare St. G20 16 A6
Shamrock St. G4 4 C1
Shandwick St. G34 28 D4
Shanks Av. G78 55 G2
Shanks St. G20 16 A6
Shanks Way. G78 44 C4
Shannon St. G20 16 B5
Shapinsay St. G22 17 E3
Sharp St. G51 23 E4
Shaw Ct. PA8 7 A5
Shaw Rd. G62 6 D4
Shaw Rd. G77 60 C1
Shaw St. G51 23 E5
Shawbridge St. G43 47 F2
Shawfield Dri. G51 37 G4
Shawhill Cres. G77 60 C2
Shawhill Rd. G41 47 G1
Shawholm Cres. G43 47 F2
Shawlands Arc. G41 47 H1
Shawmoss Rd. G41 35 G6
Shawpark St. G20 16 A5
Shawwood Cres. G77 60 C2
Sheddens Pl. G32 39 E1
Sheepburn Rd. G71 53 G2
Sheil Ct. G78 44 C4
Sheila St. G33 26 D1
Sheildaig Dri. G73 50 A5
Sheldaig Rd. G22 16 D2
Shelley Dri. G81 8 C4
Shelley Rd. G12 14 D6
Sherbrooke Av. G41 35 G4
Sherbrooke Dri. G41 35 G3
Sherbrooke Gdns. G41 35 G3
Sherburn Gdns. G69 40 C3
Sherriff Park Av. G73 50 A2
Sherwood Av. PA1 32 B1
Sherwood Dri. G46 47 E6
Sherwood Pl. G15 10 B5
Shetland Dri. G44 48 D4
Shettleston Rd. G31 38 C1
Shiel Rd. G64 61 D4
Shielbridge Gdns. G23 16 A1
Shieldburn Rd. G51 22 B6
Shieldhall Gdns. G51 22 A5
Shieldhall Rd. G51 22 A5
Shields Rd. G41 36 A5
Shilford Av. G13 13 G4
Shillay St. G22 17 F3
Shilton Dri. G53 46 A3
Shinwell Av. G81 12 D1
Shiskine Dri. G20 15 G3
Shiskine St. G20 15 G3
Shore St. G40 37 H5
Shortridge St. G20 16 A6
Shortroods Av. PA3 31 G4
Shortroods Cres. PA3 31 G4
Shortroods Rd. PA3 31 G4
Shotts St. G33 28 A5
Shuna Pl. G20 16 A5
Shuna St. G20 16 A5
Shuttle St. G1 5 F5
Shuttle St. PA1 31 H6
Sidland Rd. G21 18 B5
Sidlaw Av. G78 55 F3
Sidlaw Rd. G61 10 C2
Sielga Pl. G34 28 D4
Siemens Pl. G21 26 A3
Siemens St. G21 26 A3
Silk St. PA1 31 H6
Silkin Av. G81 12 D1
Silverburn St. G33 26 D5
Silverdale St. G31 38 C3
Silverfir Ct. G5 37 F3
Silverfir Pl. G5 37 F3
Silverfir St. G5 37 F3
Silvergrove St. G5 37 G2
Simons Cres. PA4 13 E6
Simpson Ct. G71 8 C6
Simpson Gdns. G78 55 E2
Simpson St. G20 24 B2
Simshill Rd. G44 48 D5
Sinclair Av. G61 11 E2
Sinclair Dri. G42 48 B1
Sinclair Gdns. G64 18 A3
Sinclair St. G62 6 E2

Sinclair St. G81 13 E3
Singer Rd. G81 8 B5
Singer St. G81 8 D6
Sir Michael Pl. PA1 43 G1
Sixth Av. PA4 20 C3
Sixth St. G71 41 H6
Skaethorn Rd. G20 15 F4
Skaterigg Dri. G13 14 D5
Skaterigg Gdns. G13 14 D5
Skaterigg La. G13 14 C5
*Skelbo Pth, Skelbo Pl. G34 29 F3
Skelbo Pl. G34 29 F3
Skene Rd. G51 35 F2
Skerray Quad. G22 16 D2
Skerray St. G22 16 D2
Skerryvore Pl. G33 27 G5
Skerryvore Rd. G33 27 G5
Skibo La. G46 46 C6
Skipness Dri. G51 22 C5
Skirsa Ct. G23 16 C3
Skirsa Pl. G23 16 B3
Skirsa Sq. G23 16 B3
Skirsa St. G23 16 A3
Skirving St. G41 36 A6
Skye Av. PA4 20 D3
Skye Cres. PA2 43 G5
Skye Cres. G60 7 C3
Skye Dri. G60 7 C3
Skye Gdns. G61 10 B2
Skye Rd. G73 50 C6
Slatefield St. G31 38 A1
Slenavon.G73 50 D6
Sloy St. G22 17 E6
Smeaton Dri. G64 61 C1
Smeaton St. G20 16 B5
Smith Cres. G81 8 D3
Smith St. G14 22 C3
Smith Ter. G73 38 B6
Smithhills St. PA1 31 H5
Smithycroft. G33 26 D4
Snaefell Av. G73 50 C4
Snaefell Cres. G73 50 C4
Snowdon St. G5 37 F3
Snuffmill Rd. G44 48 C4
Society St. G31 38 B1
Soho St. G40 37 H1
Sollas Pl. G13 13 F2
Solway Rd. G64 61 F3
Solway St. G40 37 H4
Somerford Rd. G61 14 D1
Somerled Av. PA3 20 A4
Somerset Pl. G3 24 B4
Somerset Pl Mews. G3 24 B4
Somervell St. G72 51 E3
Somerville Dri. G42 48 D1
Sorby St. G31 38 C2
Sorn St. G40 38 A3
South Annandale St. G42 36 C5
South Av. G81 8 C6
South Av. PA4 20 D2
South Av. PA2 44 A1
South Bank St. G31 12 C3
South Bar Av. G13 13 G4
South Brae La. G13 14 D6
South Campbell St. PA2 43 H2
South Chester St. G32 39 F2
South Claremont La. G62 6 D3
South Crosshill Rd. G64 61 C3
South Douglas St. G81 12 C3
South Elgin Pl. G81 12 D3
South Elgin St. G81 12 D3
South Erskine Pk. G61 10 D3
South Frederick St. G1 5 E4
South Gate. G62 6 E3
South Glassford St. G62 6 F3
South Mains Rd. G62 6 C4
South Moraine La. G15 14 A1
South Park Av. G12 24 A3
South Park Av. G78 55 F1
South Park Dri. PA2 43 G3
South Portland St. G5 36 D1
South Rd. G76 58 C6
South Scott St. G69 41 E3
South St. G14 22 A1
South Vesalius St. G32 39 F2
South View. G81 8 B5
South Woodside Rd. G4 24 A2
Southampton Dri. G12 15 E5
Southbank St. G31 38 C2
Southbrae Dri. G13 14 A6
Southcroft Rd. G5 37 G6
Southcroft St. G51 23 F5
Southdeen Av. G15 10 B6
Southdeen Rd. G15 10 B6
Southend Rd. G81 9 E3
Southern Av. G73 50 B4
Southesk Av. G64 61 B2
Southesk Gdns. G64 61 B2
Southfield Av. PA2 43 G5
Southfield Cres. G53 46 A1
Southill Av. G73 50 B3
Southinch Av. G14 13 E4
Southlea Av. G46 47 E6
Southloch Gdns. G21 25 H2
Southloch St. G21 25 H2
Southmuir Pl. G20 15 H5
Southpark Ter. G12 24 A2
Southview Av. G64 17 H3
Southview Av. G76 58 B5
Southview Dri. G61 10 C3
Southview Ter. G64 17 G4
Southwold Rd. PA1 33 F2
Southwood Dri. G44 49 E3
Soutra Pl. G33 27 F4
Spean St. G44 48 C2
Speirs Rd. G61 11 G5
Speirsfield Gdns. PA2 43 G1
Speirshall Clo. G14 13 F5
Speirshall Ter. G14 13 F5
Spence St. G20 15 G2
Spencer Dri. PA2 42 B5
Spencer St. G81 8 D5
Spencer St. G13 14 D3
Spey Av. PA2 42 B4
Spey Dri. PA44 21 E3
Spey Rd. G61 10 C6
Spey St. G33 27 E4
Spiers Wharf. G4 24 D3
Spiersbridge Av. G46 46 C6
Spiersbridge Gro. G46 46 D5
Spiersbridge La. G46 46 C6
Spiersbridge Rd. G46 46 D6
Spiersbridge Ter. G46 46 C6
Spindlehowe Rd. G71 53 H3
Spinners Gdns. PA2 43 E1
Spinners La. G81 9 E1
Spittal Rd. G73 49 G4
Spoolers Rd. PA1 43 E1
Spout Mouth St. G1 5 F6
Springbank St. G20 24 B1
Springbank Rd. PA3 31 G3
Springbank Ter. PA3 31 G3
Springboig Av. G32 27 H6
Springboig Rd. G32 27 H6
Springburn Rd. G21 25 G3
Springburn Rd. G64 17 G5
Springburn Way. G21 25 G1
Springcroft Av. G69 41 E1
Springcroft Cres. G69 29 E6
Springcroft Dri. G69 40 D1
Springcroft Gdns. G69 29 E6
Springcroft Gro. G69 29 E6
Springcroft Rd. G69 29 E6
Springcroft Wynd. G69 29 E6
Springdale Dri. PA2 42 C3
Springfield Av. G64 17 H3
Springfield Av. PA1 32 C3
Springfield Ct. G1 4 D5
Springfield Cres. G64 61 C4
Springfield Dri. G78 55 H3
Springfield Gro. G78 55 G4
Springfield Pk Rd. G73 50 B3
Springfield Quad. G5 36 B1
Springfield Quay. G5 36 B1
Springfield Rd. G64 61 C4
Springfield Rd. G40 38 A4
Springfield Rd. G78 54 C5
Springfield Sq. G64 61 C4
Springhall Dri N. G69 28 D6
Springhall Dri S. G69 28 D6
Springhill Farm Gro. G69 28 D6
Springhill Farm Pl. G69 28 C6
Springhill Farm Rd. G69 28 C6
Springhill Farm Way. G69 28 C6
Springhill Gdns. G41 36 A6
Springhill Parkway. G69 28 D6
Springhill Rd. G78 55 F4
Springhill Rd. G69 40 C2
Springhill Rd. G76 58 B4
Springkell Av. G41 35 F4
Springkell Dri. G41 35 F4
Springkell Gdns. G41 35 H5
Springkell Gate. G41 35 G5
Springside Pl. G15 10 A4
Springvale Ter. G21 25 G1
*Sproul Pl, Graham St. G78 44 B6
Spruce Dri. G72 52 C5
Spruce St. G22 17 E5
Spynie Pl. G64 61 F3
Squire St. G14 22 C2
Stable Gro. PA1 43 E1
Stable Pl. G62 6 D1
Stable Rd. G62 6 D1
Staffa Av. PA4 20 D4
Staffa Dri. PA2 43 G5
Staffa Rd. G72 51 E6
Staffa St. G31 26 B5
Staffin Dri. G23 15 H1
Staffin St. G23 15 H1
Stafford St. G4 5 E1
Stag St. G51 23 F5
Stamford St. G40 38 A2
Stamperland Av. G76 58 B4
Stamperland Dri. G76 58 B4
Stamperland Gdns. G76 58 B2
Stamperland Hill. G76 58 A3
Stanalane St. G46 46 D5
Standburn Rd. G21 18 C4
Stanely Av. PA2 43 E4
Stanely Ct. PA2 43 E4
Stanely Cres. PA2 43 E4
Stanely Dri. PA2 43 F3
Stanely Rd. PA2 43 F4
Stanford St. G81 12 C2
Stanhope Dri. G73 50 C4
Stanley Dri. G64 61 D2
Stanley St. G41 36 A2
Stanmore Rd. G42 48 D1
Stark Av. G81 8 B2
Startpoint St. G33 27 F5
Station Brae. G78 54 A4
Station Cres. PA4 13 E6
Station Rd. G61 10 C5
Station Rd. G76 58 C6
Station Rd. G69 41 F3
Station Rd. G46 47 G6
Station Rd. G20 15 G3
Station Rd. G33 19 F6
Station Rd. G62 6 E3
Station Rd. G78 54 B5
Station Rd. G60 7 B2
Station Rd. PA1 42 D1
Station Rd. PA4 13 E6
Station Rd. G71 53 H3
Steel St. G1 5 F6
Stenton St. G32 26 D6
Stepford Path. G33 28 D6
Stepford Pl. G33 28 C6
Stepford Rd. G33 28 C6
Stephen Cres. G69 40 C2
Stephenson St. G40 37 G1
Stephenson St. G52 21 E4
Stepps Rd. G33 27 H4
Stevenson St. PA2 43 G1
Stevenson St. G81 8 B5
Stevenson St. G40 5 G6
Stevewright St. G73 38 B5
Stewart Av. G77 56 C5
Stewart Av. PA4 20 B4
Stewart Ct. G78 44 D5
Stewart Cres. G78 44 D5
Stewart Dri. G76 57 H3
Stewart Dri. G81 8 D3
Stewart Pl. G78 44 D5
Stewart Rd. PA2 43 H4
Stewart St. G81 8 B5
Stewart St. G78 44 D5
Stewart St. G4 4 C1
Stewart St. G62 6 E3
Stewarton Dri. G72 51 E4
Stewartville St. G11 23 F3
Stirling Av. G61 11 E6
Stirling Dri. G61 10 D2
Stirling Dri. G64 61 A2
Stirling Dri. G73 50 B4
Stirling Gdns. G64 61 A2
Stirling Rd. G4 5 G3
Stirling Way. PA4 20 D4
Stirlingfauld Pl. G5 36 D2
Stirrat St. PA3 31 E4
Stirrat St. G20 15 G4
Stobbs Dri. G78 44 C4
Stobbs Pl. G34 29 F4
Stobcross Rd. G3 23 G5
Stobcross St. G3 24 A5
Stobcross Wynd. G5 23 G5
Stobhill Rd. G21 17 G4
Stock Av. PA2 43 H2
Stock St. PA2 43 G2
Stockholm Cres. PA2 43 H2
Stockiemuir Av. G61 10 D1
Stockiemuir Rd. G61 10 D1
Stockiemuir Rd. G62 6 A2
Stockwell Pl. G1 5 E6
Stockwell St. G1 5 E6
Stoddard Sq. PA5 42 A2
Stonebank Gro. G45 49 F6
Stonedyke Gro. G15 10 B6
Stonefield Av. G12 15 F5
Stonefield Av. PA2 32 A6
Stonefield Cres. PA2 43 H4
Stonefield Cres. G76 57 G3
Stonefield Dri. PA2 32 A6
Stonefield Gdns. PA2 43 H3
Stonefield Grn. PA2 43 H3
Stonefield Gro. PA2 43 H4
Stonefield Park. PA2 43 H4
Stonelaw Dri. G73 50 B2
Stonelaw Rd. G73 50 A1
Stonelaw Twrs. G73 50 B3
Stoneside Dri. G43 47 E3
Stoneside Sq. G43 47 E3
Stoney Brae, Glenburn. PA2 43 H5
Stoney Brae, Paisley. PA2 31 G5
Stonyhurst St. G22 24 C1
Storie St. PA1 31 G6
Stormyland Way. G78 55 F2
Stornoway St. G22 17 E3
Stow Brae. PA1 43 H1
Stow St. PA1 43 H1
Stranka Av. PA2 43 E2
Stranraer Dri. G15 14 A1
Stratford St. G20 16 A6
Strathallow Pl. G73 50 C5
Strathay Pl. G20 15 H5
Strathblane Rd. G62 6 F2
Strathbran St. G31 38 C3
Strathcarron Cres. PA2 32 C6
Strathcarron Dri. PA2 32 C6
Strathcarron Pl. PA2 32 C6
Strathcarron Rd. PA2 32 B6
Strathcarron Way. PA2 32 C6
Strathcarrow Pl. G20 15 H5
Strathclyde Dri. G73 49 H2
Strathclyde Path. G71 53 G3
Strathclyde St. G40 38 A5
Strathcona Dri. G13 15 E4
Strathcona Gdns. G13 15 E4
Strathcona Pl. G73 50 D5
Strathcona St. G13 14 D4
Strathdee Av. G81 9 E3
Strathdee Rd. G44 58 A1
Strathdon Av. PA2 43 F2
Strathdon Av. G44 58 B1
Strathdon Dri. G44 58 B1
Strathearn Rd. G76 58 A5
Strathendrick Dri. G44 48 A4
Strathmore Av. PA1 33 E2
Strathmore Gdns. G73 50 D5
Strathmore Rd. G22 16 D3
Strathord St. G32 39 F3
Strathtay Av. G44 58 A1
Strathview Gro. G44 58 A1
Strathview Park. G44 58 A1
Strathyre Gdns. G61 11 H3
Strathyre St. G41 48 A1
Stratton Dri. G46 47 F6
Stratton St. G32 26 D5
Strauss Av. G81 13 F2
Stravaig Pth. PA2 42 D5
Stravaig Walk. PA2 42 D5
Stravanan Av. G45 59 F1
Stravanan Ct. G32 51 F2
Stravanan Rd. G45 59 F1
Stravanan St. G45 59 F1
Stravanan Ter. G45 59 F1
Streamfield Gdns. G33 18 D3
Streamfield Gate. G33 18 D3
Streamfield Lea. G33 18 D3
Streamfield Pl. G33 18 D3
Strenabey Av. G73 50 C4
Striven Gdns. G20 24 B2
Stroma St. G21 26 B3
Stromness St. G5 36 C2
Strone Rd. G33 27 G5
Stronend St. G22 16 D6
Stronsay Pl. G64 61 F3
Stronsay St. G21 26 B2
Stronvar Dri. G14 13 H6
Strowan Cres. G32 39 G3
Strowan St. G32 39 G3
Struan Av. G46 47 F5
Struan Gdns. G44 48 C4
Struan Rd. G44 48 C4
Struie St. G34 28 D5
Struma Dri. G76 57 G3
Stuart Av. G73 50 B4
Stuart Av. G60 7 C3
Stuart Dri. G64 17 G3
Stuart Rd. G76 59 F3
Stuart St. G60 7 C3
Succoth St. G13 14 D4
Sugworth Av. G69 41 E2
Sumburgh St. G33 27 E5
Summer St. G40 37 H2
Summerfield St. G40 38 A4
Summerhill Dri. G61 10 C5
Summerhill Gdns. G61 10 C5
Summerhill Pl. G61 10 B5
Summerhill Rd. G61 10 A4
Summerhill Rd. G76 58 B4
Summerlea Rd. G46 46 D5
Summerlee St. G33 27 H5
*Summertown Path, Summertown Rd. G51 23 F6
Summertown Rd. G51 23 F6
Sunart Av. PA4 20 B1
Sunart Gdns. G64 61 E4
Sunart Rd. G64 61 E4
Sunart Rd. G52 34 D2
Sunbury Av. G76 57 G4
Sundale Av. G76 57 H5
Sunningdale Av. G77 56 D6
Sunningdale Rd. G23 15 H2
Sunningdale Wynd. G71 53 H6
Sunnybank Dri. G76 57 H4
Sunnybank Gro. G76 57 H5
Sunnybank St. G40 38 A4
Sunnylaw Dri. PA2 43 E3
Sunnylaw St. G22 16 C6
Sunnyside. G81 13 G1
Sunnyside Dri. G76 57 H3
Sunnyside Dri. G15 13 G2
Sunnyside Pl. G78 55 F2
Sunnyside Rd. PA2 43 G3
Surrey St. G5 36 D2
Sussex St. G51 36 A1
Sutcliffe Ct. G13 14 C4
Sutcliffe Rd. G13 14 C4
Sutherland Av. G61 11 E1
Sutherland Av. G41 35 F4
Sutherland Dri. G46 57 H2
Sutherland La. G12 23 G2
Sutherland Rd. G81 12 C1
Sutherland St. PA1 31 G5
Sutherness Dri. G33 27 F5
Swallow Gdns. G13 13 G3
Swallow Rd. G81 9 F1
Swan St. G81 8 C5
Swan St. G4 5 E1
Swanston St. G40 37 H5
Sween Av. G44 48 C4
Swift Cres. G13 13 G3
Swindon St. G81 8 B5
Swinton Av. G69 41 F2
Swinton Cres. G69 41 F2
Swinton Dri. G52 34 A2
Swinton Gdns. G69 41 F2
Swinton Pth. G69 41 G1
Swinton Pl. G52 34 A2
Swinton Rd. G69 41 E2
Swinton View. G69 41 F2
Switchback Rd. G61 14 D1
Sword St. G31 25 H6
Swordale Pl. G34 28 D5
Sycamore Dri. G81 8 C4
Sycamore Way. G76 59 F4
Sycamore Way. G72 52 C5
Sydenham La. G12 23 G1
Sydney St. G81 8 A4
Sydney St. G31 5 H6
Syke St. G69 41 E2
Sylvan Pl. G76 58 C6
Sylvania Way. G81 12 C1
Sylvania Way Sth. G81 12 C2
Symington Dri. G81 8 D6
Syriam Pl. G21 17 H6
Syriam St. G21 17 H6

Tabard Pl. G13 14 A3
Tabard Rd. G13 14 A3
Tabernacle La. G72 51 F3
Tabernacle St. G72 51 F4
Tait Av. G78 44 D5
Talbot Ct. G13 13 H5
Talbot Dri. G13 13 H5
Talbot Pl. G13 13 H5
Talbot Ter. G71 53 H1
Talbot Ter. G13 13 H5
Talisman Rd. PA2 42 B5
Talisman Rd. G13 14 B4
Talla Rd. G52 33 G1
Tallant Rd. G15 10 B5
Tallant Ter. G15 10 C5
Tambowie Av. G62 6 C2
Tambowie Cres. G62 6 D2
Tambowie St. G13 14 C3
Tamshill St. G20 16 B5
Tanar Av. PA4 21 F3
Tanar Way. PA4 21 F3
Tanera Av. G44 49 E4
Tanfield Pl. G32 27 H6
Tanfield St. G32 27 H6
Tankerland Rd. G44 48 C3
Tanna Dri. G52 35 E4
Tannadice Av. G52 34 B3
Tannahill Rd. PA3 31 E4